RELIGIO ET ERUDITIO

Biblical & Theological Essays

---†---

VOLUME 3 2018–2019

Edited by Ray Van Neste and Jacob Shatzer
Union University School of Theology and Missions

Copyright © 2019 Union University

All rights reserved. No part of this publication may be reproduced, distributed or transmitted in any form or by any means, including photocopying, recording, or other electronic or mechanical methods, without the prior written permission of the author, except in the case of brief quotations embodied in critical reviews and certain other noncommercial uses permitted by copyright law. For permission requests, write to the author, addressed "Attention: Permissions Coordinator," at the address below.

Ray Van Neste
1050 Union University Drive
Jackson, TN 38305

Cover design: Song Kim
Interior design: Jeff Thompson

"The essays in this volume—all of them written by students majoring in Bible and theology—are a testament to the intellectual acumen of the students and the strength of the School of Theology and Missions at Union University. Even though these students are undergraduates completing their capstone Senior Seminar, they often write at levels far beyond their years. This collection of biblical and theological essays contains work that makes a contribution to the field of study, marshals and assesses various arguments well, and illuminates and informs the area of study. Some of these students no doubt have bright careers as scholars ahead of them. What is noteworthy and reassuring is that many of them are intending to enter Christian ministry. For all of this we in churches, colleges, and seminaries can be thankful, as these students make their intellectual gifts available to the academy and the church. I think that fellow students and scholars alike will enjoy the fruits of these students' labors, and I commend them and their professors for the work that they have done."

Stanley E. Porter, President, Dean, and Professor of New Testament, McMaster Divinity College, Hamilton, ON Canada

"The collection of these essays demonstrates the grammatical, exegetical, historical, and theological skill of the young authors who wrote them. I was amazed as I read to see the sophistication and depth of the work produced by college students. All who take the time to read will be challenged and stimulated by excellent scholarship."

Thomas Schreiner, James Buchanan Harrison Professor of New Testament Interpretation and Professor of Biblical Theology, Southern Baptist Theological Seminary

"It is a shame when high caliber work by undergrad students never has the opportunity to bless a wider audience. These volumes will surely encourage those who read them and are a testimony to the high caliber of the faculty and students at the Union University School of Theology and Missions."

**Andrew Abernethy, PhD
Associate Professor of Old Testament
Degree Coordinator—M.A. in Biblical Exegesis
Wheaton College**

"While many continue to lament the state of the humanities in higher education, here is an impressive collection of essays from students (!) that suggests all is not lost. The range and depth of these essays indicate the vibrant learning community of the School of Theology and Missions at Union University. The students and professors should be congratulated on their combined efforts that have culminated in these outstanding essays. As one who teaches in a graduate school, I'd take a classroom full of these students with a grateful heart and an eager mind."

**Mark Gignilliat, Professor of Divinity,
Beeson Divinity School**

"These volumes are a celebration of undergraduate academic achievement, but more than that, they are creative, serious, thought-provoking, and edifying essays which make a contribution to Christian intellectual discourse. Covering a wide variety of topics in Bible, theology, philosophy, and the arts, I found them to be engaging and informative."

**Eric Tully, Associate Professor of Old
Testament and Semitic Languages,
Trinity Evangelical Divinity School**

"Union's Religio et Eruditio covers a host of important biblical and theological topics. It exhibits some of the most advanced scholarship from undergraduate seniors that I have seen."

**Jacob M. Pratt, Assistant Professor of New Testament
and HermeneuticsDirector of PhD Studies,
Southeastern Baptist Theological Seminary**

"This book offers far more than an impressive selection of biblical and theological essays. Yes, the reader will certainly benefit from fresh academic research that is clear, accessible, and useful for the church. More than that, however, this book is an apologetic for sound theological education. Every page of every essay will remind the reader of the importance of training the next generation of Christian scholars."

**Adam P. Groza, Vice President for Enrollment and
Student Services, and Associate Professor of
Philosophy of Religion, Gateway Seminary**

CONTENTS

Series Introduction 7

**Dining With The Divine: A Biblical-Theological
Exploration of The Lord's Supper** 9

Wesley Chatham | Advisors: Dr. Ray Van Neste, Dr. Mark Dubis, Dr. George Guthrie

**God, His People, and Mission to the Nations:
A Biblical-Theological Exploration of the Theme
of Missions in the Old and New Testament** 53

Jonathan E. Pope | Advisors: Dr. Ray Van Neste, Dr. Mark Dubis, Dr. George Guthrie

**The Votary of the Blue Flower:
A Historical Reflection on Hope in
the Life and Thought of C.S. Lewis** 97

Seth Reid | Advisors: Dr. David Thomas, Dr. Keith Bates, Dr. Justin Barnard

Eating Is Meeting– Calvin and the Real Presence 145

Ryan Sinni | Advisors: Dr. Justin Barnard, Dr. Nathan Finn, Dr. Aaron O'Kelley

**In Search of Markan Intention: A Call
to Continue the Conversation About
the Longer Ending of Mark** 207

Brandon Harper | Advisors: Dr. Mark Dubis, Dr. Jacob Shatzer, Dr. Brad Green

The Centrality of Adoption for John Calvin 243

Josh Leamon | Advisors: Dr. Brad Green, Todd Augustine and Alex Huguenard

**An Evaluation of Divine Love in
Thomas Aquinas and Martin Luther** 265

Briley Ray | Advisors: Dr. Brad Green, Dr. Jacob Shatzer, Dr. Henry Allen

SERIES INTRODUCTION

At Union University, every student majoring in the School of Theology & Missions takes a capstone course called Senior Seminar. The course provides students the opportunity to take all of the research and writing skills that they have honed over several years and apply those to a large research project. We don't do this because we think every student will become a research scholar; rather, we do this because we believe the skills that students build for researching and writing well are skills that transfer to being thoughtful servants of God in any setting. To research well, to write well, is an excellent preparation for thinking well and—Lord willing—living and serving well.

Our School also enjoys a close relationship with Union's Honors Community under the direction of Scott Huelin. Students throughout the university have the opportunity to pursue "Discipline-Specific Honors," which allows them to work closely with faculty in their major to write a thesis. Mark Dubis guides the DSH program for the School of Theology & Missions. Students voluntarily increase their workload in four major courses—Senior Seminar being the final one—to do thesis research over the course of several semesters. In Senior Seminar, these students produce their honors thesis.

What you hold in your hand are some of the finest fruits of these labors over the years. We are in general proud of our students and their work, but these research essays rise to the top. We have gathered them here to honor the work of these students and their faculty mentors. Yet these volumes of essays do more than honor work done. They also commend to you, our readers, the scholarly value of the product. In short, our students do great work, and others should benefit from that work.

It is an honor for us to be even marginally associated with this fine work as editors of this volume. Now we would like to get out of the way and to give our fine students the stage.

DINING WITH THE DIVINE: A BIBLICAL-THEOLOGICAL EXPLORATION OF THE LORD'S SUPPER

Wesley Chatham

INTRODUCTION

The Lord's Supper is one of the most precious gifts God gave to his church. The ordinance[1] was intended to be practiced after Jesus' ascension in order to nourish and strengthen the people of God. They were invited to enter into a divine fellowship with the Lord over this meal as a commemoration of his death, a celebration of his resurrection, and an expectation of the eschatological feast that awaits them in heaven. However, the observance of the ordinance in contemporary Protestantism is often a far cry from the joyous celebration that God intended his children to experience. The current practice of the Lord's Supper, particularly in Southern Baptist life, has become a mere addition to the service rather than an integral part of congregational worship. In order to restore the sacrament to its proper place in the life of the congregation, one must grasp the true significance of the Lord's Supper and the way Christ is present within it. The claim of this thesis is that God establishes a precedent throughout the Bible that he desires intimate relationships with his people, which he often confirms or establishes by his presence over a sacred meal. The same is also true today, as the work of the Spirit causes Jesus Christ to be truly and spiritually present with his people as they come to the Lord's Table.

For the sake of this paper, it is necessary to define precisely what "spiritual presence" means. This view proposes that Christ is indeed truly present in the Lord's Supper, but not physically present. The majority of Protestantism has affirmed that to suggest Christ is physically present on earth during

---

[1] For the sake of this paper, the terms "ordinance," "sacrament," "Lord's Supper," and "Lord's Table" will be used interchangeably.

the Lord's Supper would surely be a contradiction because he is present in heaven. Nor does Christ transmit himself into the bread and wine and somehow cause them to become his body and blood as the believer partakes in the Supper.[2] Instead, the spiritual presence view asserts that Christ is spiritually present at the Table in a way that he is not present anywhere else. Although the Lord is indeed perpetually present with his people, the Lord's Supper is an occasion of a more intimate presence and union with his people. However, the fact that Christ is spiritually present does not mean that it is any less real than a Lutheran or Catholic view, as believers are able to truly encounter and experience communion with him.[3] The Lord's Supper is therefore a clear, tangible presentation of the gospel and an invitation for the church to experience a divine encounter with the risen Christ.

A tremendous amount of studies have been devoted to the doctrine of the Lord's Supper, which might lead one to ask what the purpose of another such study is. The uniqueness of this paper is that it traces God's presence within sacred meals throughout the biblical narrative and argues that the idea of Christ's spiritual presence in a meal does not merely occur ex nihilo in the New Testament; instead, it follows the pattern that God sets throughout Scripture. Each of these biblical examples illustrate that God was uniquely present among his people and that each meal is pointing to a deeper communion that believers would experience with the institution of the Lord's Supper. The Lord's presence and fellowship with his people within these meals should therefore serve as a basis for rightly understanding the Lord's Supper.

The paper will then examine the treatment of the Lord's Supper by the apostle Paul and argue that 1 Corinthians 10:14–22 supports Christ's spiritual presence at the Table. Through an exegetical analysis of the text, I will argue that in Paul's mind, the Lord's Supper is more than a remembrance of Christ's death. It is a participation in the body and blood of Christ and

---

[2] Wayne Grudem, *Systematic Theology: An Introduction to Biblical Doctrine* (Grand Rapids: Zondervan, 1994), 995.
[3] J. van Genderen and W. H. Velema, *Concise Reformed Dogmatics* (Phillipsburg, NJ: P&R Publishing, 2008), 811.

is meant to strengthen our union with him through his unique presence in the sacrament. Although the Supper does cause believers to look back to what Christ did for them, it should also cause them to sense Christ's spiritual presence as the church feeds on him together.

Finally, the question of what this understanding of the Lord's Supper should do for the church today must be considered. The paper will close with the practical and pastoral implications of Christ's spiritual presence at the Table and the importance of allowing this reality to shape our theology and practice. The Lord's Table should ultimately be a place where believers reaffirm their commitment to Christ and are comforted by his grace. They come to the Table fully cognizant of their own sin and receive the spiritual food that their souls crave from being in Christ's presence. This is brought about only by the Holy Spirit and is mediated through the elements. Therefore, every facet of this sacred ordinance must be considered carefully, as it was designed for the glory of God and the edification of his church. The Supper is also meant to bring unity among the body of Christ; therefore, we must consider whether our current communion services accurately convey the corporate element of the sacrament as they ought. The sacrament should be a frequent celebration of this bond that believers share as the church and the union they share with Christ himself. When rightly celebrated, the Lord's Supper will point believers to Christ and strengthen their relationship with him. The goal is that by examining this prominent biblical theme, readers would come away with a more complete understanding of the Lord's Supper. This understanding will ultimately transform the manner in which believers approach the Table and cause them to see that that the Lord himself is inviting them to come and dine with him.

BIBLICAL THEOLOGY OF SACRED MEALS

The practice of eating is often seen as one of the most mundane tasks that an individual engages in. Although a normal diet today traditionally involves eating three times each day, the meals that one consumes are often forgettable. In a culture that prioritizes efficiency, meals have rapidly become less memorable and anything but sacred. However, a shared meal is one of the foremost ways that friendship can be celebrated, deepened, and remembered. It is from this strain of thought that Old Testament ritualistic meals developed; the Israelites often practiced these feasts in order to reaffirm and celebrate their close association with Yahweh.[4] Therefore, the theme of meals and feasting is an important concept throughout Scripture and essential to understanding the Bible's message. Since God's design from the beginning of time has been to be in relationship with his people, one of the most fundamental ways that he achieves this is by revealing himself through a shared feast. When one thinks of sacred meals, the tendency might be to think solely in terms of the Lord's Supper. However, the practice of sacred meals is not exclusively a New Testament concept, but one that spans the entire canon of Scripture. From the provision of food that God gave man in the Garden of Eden to the marriage feast of the Lamb in Revelation, it is evident that the theme of sacred meals has an integral place throughout the biblical canon. Through each of these meals, God illustrates his perpetual desire to be in fellowship with his people and he expresses this desire in a distinct way by inviting them to enjoy sacred meals with him.

Old Testament Sacred Meals

The consumption of food is essential for sustaining human life, and yet it can often be taken from granted by many individuals. Nevertheless, it is crucial to note that from the beginning, God gives food to mankind not out of obligation, but out of grace. The passage describing the creation of man tells us that God gave him "every plant yielding seed that is on the face of all the earth, and every tree with seed in its fruit...for food" (Gen. 1:29 ESV). God's specific address to man, as

---

[4] Leslie McFall, "Sacred Meals," in *New Dictionary of Biblical Theology*, ed. T. Desmond Alexander and Brian S. Rosner (Downers Grove, IL: InterVarsity, 2000), 750.

well as the addition of giving him the fruits for food (rather than just the plants which he gave to the animals) emphasizes mankind's unique fellowship they share with the Lord. In many of the ancient Near East traditions, the sole function of humankind was simply to attend to the needs of the gods, including providing food for them.[5] However, the stark contrast of the Genesis narrative tells us that God is not served by human hands, but instead he is the one who chooses to serve his creation. In this text, God is the one who provides food for mankind and establishes them as vice-regents in his kingdom, to work and keep the sphere where he placed them. Furthermore, God not only placed Adam and Eve in the Garden of Eden and provided them with a means of nourishment, but he also granted them the gift of his presence. He walked with them in Eden, and in doing so, Yahweh displayed his desire for intimacy with man and the sanctity of dining in his presence. As Yahweh establishes his covenant with Adam, he does so in Adam's midst in the garden, and his provision of food is an unmistakable element of this covenant. This connection of food and God's presence is foundational to his relationship with humankind and this theme is only amplified as the biblical narrative unfolds.

As the story of Scripture progresses, ritual feasts and banquets become increasingly important both socially and spiritually to the people of Israel. One of the central feasts of Israel was Passover, which was a continuous seven-day period of remembrance that the Lord commanded as a commemoration of his deliverance of the Israelites out of slavery. Not only was Passover a critical event in the Israelites' history, but it would also become the central reaffirmation of their identity as the people of God. A key element of God's Passover instructions in Exodus 12 was for a lamb to be carefully chosen beforehand, one per household. If there were too few people in the household, then the lamb could be shared with another household (Ex. 12:3-4). All the people of Israel were commanded to participate, and God commanded that the entirety of the meat from the

---

[5] John Walton, ed., *Zondervan Illustrated Bible Commentary* (Grand Rapids: Zondervan, 2009), 1:21.

lamb must be consumed; thus, tremendous emphasis was placed on sharing a single animal. Verse 4 then stipulates that the lamb must be chosen "according to what each can eat." The meat must be equally dispersed and consumed completely in order to ensure that the full sacredness of the sacrifice was remembered. The significance of participating in the Passover meal among one's household is that it was designed to be a communal event from its conception, not a matter of private worship. This principle foreshadows the commemoration of the Messiah as the superior Passover lamb, who would be broken and shared in by all of mankind.[6] The Passover meal was meant to bring unity among the Israelites, just as the broken body of Christ would eventually bring unity among the body of believers in the New Testament.

The Passover meal that Israel shared would be sacred not as a one-time event but as a continual reminder of God's provision. Enns describes that through the Exodus, "God's people are being 'recreated'; they are starting over."[7] Through his deliverance of the Israelites, Yahweh graciously allowed his children a new beginning and promised them a hopeful future. Therefore, the importance of the Passover meal for the Israelites was not solely confined to the past; although it was based on God's providential action of delivering them from slavery, Israel's subsequent celebrations of Passover were inextricably tied to the future hope that they had been given as a result. This unquestionably foreshadows the institution of the Last Supper in the New Testament, when the Lord Jesus commands us to remember a deliverance from a bondage to something much more substantial than the Egyptians. It is evident then, that the Passover must be viewed as something more than simply a ritualistic Old Testament practice. It was a cause for remembrance and celebrations for later generations, as well as a testament to God's covenantal love for his people that would endure until the end of time. However, it is also crucial to note that subsequent generations of Israelites saw

---

[6] Douglas Stuart, *Exodus*, New American Commentary (Nashville: Broadman & Holman, 2006), 274.

[7] Peter Enns, *Exodus*, NIV Application Commentary (Grand Rapids: Zondervan, 2000), 247.

themselves as participating in the Exodus by means of the Passover.[8] The Israelites felt a unique connection to their ancestors whom Yahweh had delivered out of Egypt as well as to the person of Yahweh himself. The partaking of the cup in the Passover was seen not just as a remembrance of the Exodus but as a participation in it. The Mishnah, an early collection of rabbinic oral traditions, demands that Israelite men in each generation regard themselves as if they came out of Egypt. The father of the house recites God's redemptive acts using first person pronouns: "It is because of what the Lord did for me when I came forth out of Egypt."[9] For the Israelites, the observance of Passover established a special connection with a historical event that had ongoing effects for their lives. Thus, it was more than a memorial practice for the following generations, but a participatory act of worship that reaffirmed the fresh start that they had been given. The Israelites were spiritually encouraged and experienced a deeper connection to God through this sacred meal. The Passover never waned in its significance, because as it was repeatedly celebrated, those who did so saw it as transformative for their own lives as well.

Another central theme that emerges amongst the biblical meals is the divine invitation for God's people to dine in his presence. One of the most evident scriptural examples of this is Exodus 24:8-11, which confirms the covenant between Israel and Yahweh through both eating and bloodshed. Although this type of meal would have been common in other ancient Near East traditions, this is a unique and significant occurrence among the Israelites.[10] In verse 8, Moses throws blood on the people, which distinguishes this blood as "the blood of the covenant." The shedding of blood occupies a vital place in ritualistic meals, and in this case it must be considered in light of other sacred instances. For example, in both the Passover and the Lord's Supper, blood was a critical symbol in the covering of sins. Therefore, this blood in Exodus 24 is both

---

[8] Ibid., 260.
[9] Anthony Thiselton, *The First Epistle to the Corinthians: A Commentary on the Greek Text* (Grand Rapids: Eerdmans, 2000), 758.
[10] Craig Blomberg, *Contagious Holiness: Jesus' Meals with Sinners* (Downers Grove, IL: InterVarsity, 2005), 38.

emblematic of the covenant that the people have entered into and a precursor to the blood of the new covenant that Jesus will eventually shed on man's behalf. Verse 9 reveals that Moses, Aaron, Nadab, Abihu, and seventy elders of Israel went up to meet with God; the specificity of who is permitted to ascend the mountain reveals the sacredness of communing with God. The author then tells us that Moses and those with him saw what appeared to be "a pavement of sapphire stone under the Lord's feet" (Ex. 24:10). This was most likely lapis lazuli, a precious stone that was widely known in Mesopotamia and reserved for thrones and royal chambers.[11] Israel's elders had been invited into a sacred feast in the presence of royalty, the King of Kings. This meal that Israel's leaders had entered into was no ordinary meal, but a sacred feast with God himself, which was intended to evoke a sense of awe and wonder from its participants.

As they were beholding God, verse 11 tells us that the leaders of Israel "ate and drank." Although it is not mentioned what they consumed, it is evident that what the text has in view here is a covenantal meal. The practice of eating was common in solidifying covenant agreements between individuals in the ancient Near East, and that is most likely what is occurring here. Yet, the uniqueness of this instance is that the agreement is by no means equal; the covenant has been arranged and the meal prepared based on Yahweh's standards rather than Israel's. As this is a covenantal meal, the focus here is not fundamentally on what the leaders ate, but more importantly on why they ate and who they ate it with. A similar meal occurs in Exodus 18:12, when Jethro, Aaron, and the elders of Israel eat bread before God. However, the meal on Mount Sinai can be seen as a heightening of this text, as God is explicitly present on the mountain, and he chooses specifically who will come up to eat where he is. In choosing these individuals to eat with him on the mountain, God establishes them as his people under his covenant. He also chooses to do so over a meal, which is in alignment with other biblical examples. By allowing mankind to see a part of himself and granting them the privilege of eating with him, God

---

[11] John Walton, Victor Matthews, and Mark Chavalas, *The IVP Bible Background Commentary: Old Testament* (Downers Grove: InterVarsity, 2000), 105.

revealed another element of his character and also gave man a new means of communing with him. However, the theophany that occurs in Exodus 24 is by no means complete; instead, the text gives us simply a description of what lies beneath God's feet. In the same way that the elders of Israel only beheld God in part on Mount Sinai, as New Testament believers celebrate the sacrifice given on their behalf as they participate in the Lord's Supper, they are endowed with a glimpse or a mere shadow of the fullness of God's glory in the process. Like the seventy elders of Israel, the congregation of faithful believers behold the glory of God as they eat and drink in communion. The presence of God and the ratification of his covenant with Israel over a meal further reveals that God desires to commune with his children, but it simultaneously shows that he determines the manner in which this occurs.

The way that God initiates these sacred meals also often involves an element of sacrifice. The Passover was a time of remembrance through the sacrifice of a lamb, and likewise Moses' peace offerings on the altar preceded the ratification of the Sinai covenant. Another example of this occurs in Leviticus 7:11–18, where God provided the instructions for peace offerings made at the altar. Wenham notes that there are numerous similarities between Leviticus 7 and the New Testament, one of which is that "care and attention to detail" are aspects that cannot be avoided in worshipping God.[12] Yahweh invariably requires that he be worshipped in a specific way, and this is also the case here. As God prescribes specific details for the sacrificial meal, he does so in a way that reflects his holiness and graciousness in inviting man to his table. In several ways in this passage, God specifically denotes this as a special type of offering that includes a fellowship meal with him. First, the thanksgiving offering had to include several types of bread. As the people brought their offering to God, verse 14 says they were to "offer one loaf from each offering, as a gift to the Lord." In this way, the offering transcended being only a sacrifice, and eventually became a meal that was enjoyed between God and

---

[12] Gordon Wenham, *The Book of Leviticus, New International Commentary on the Old Testament* (Grand Rapids: Eerdmans, 1979), 128.

man. Those who offered these sacrifices to the Lord did so in celebration that they had fellowship with him. Collins points out that this fellowship is one that is based on forgiveness, achieved by the shedding of blood.[13] It follows then, that those who made these offerings were not simply practicing the ritual out of compulsion, but instead they felt a genuine connection to God by means of a participatory act. Another similarity between this text and other sacred meals is the stipulation that it must all be eaten on the day of the sacrifice. Verse 15 echoes the same command that God gave the Israelites in Exodus 12: that none of it should remain until morning. This provides a clear textual connection between the two meals, while also symbolizing that the sacrifice must be accepted and thus consumed, or else it would be wasted. This type of offering was also the only offering which the layperson could eat under Old Testament law, as well as one of the only times that the people of Israel were permitted to eat the meat of the sacrifice.[14] While it would be only speculation to argue why God distinguished the peace offering in particular, it is evident that he desired mankind to have intimate fellowship with him over this meal. Furthermore, this sacrifice was unique in that it was the only animal sacrifice that was not associated with the forgiveness of sins. It was instead intended to be an expression of gratitude that increased the intimacy one had with Yahweh. One is likewise not forgiven of sins by participating in the Lord's Supper, but it is meant to be a celebration in which the believer gives thanks to Christ for what he has done and is simultaneously comforted by the Lord's grace.

New Testament Sacred Meals

Throughout the New Testament, shared meals represented intimate κοινωνία with the meal's participants. Because ritualistic meals and banquets were an essential part of the New Testament culture, those with whom one shared meals were indicative of his or her social status. During his ministry, Jesus

---

[13] John Collins, "The Eucharist as Christian Sacrifice: How Patristic Authors Can Help Us Read the Bible," *Westminster Theological Journal* 66, no. 1 (Spring 2004), 4.
[14] Wenham, *Leviticus*, 123.

garnered an infamous reputation for sharing meals with sinners and those of the lowest social class. Therefore, in the eyes of the Pharisees, Jesus' eating with sinners was an acceptance of their lifestyles and a shameful practice.[15] These meals played a central role in his ministry, however, as a large portion of his teaching took place in such settings. As Jesus invited sinners to dine with him, he was doing much more than enjoying ordinary meals; he was setting a remarkable precedent for who was qualified to share in fellowship meals with God. Mark 2:13–17 and its parallels in the other Synoptic Gospels (Mt. 9:9–13, Lk. 5:2–32) present a key example of this truth. Jesus called Levi, a tax collector, to follow him in verse 14, and he immediately shared a meal with him at Levi's house. The Pharisees' disapproval in verse 16 suggests that this was a regular practice of Jesus. Blomberg points out that Jesus does not "require repentance in advance of having table fellowship with sinners." Instead, he extends them an invitation to repentance.[16] Rather than his purity being defiled by his contact with these individuals, Jesus' holiness has been extended to them. In the process, Jesus is shifting the paradigm of mealtime fellowship and reforming social norms about who was qualified to dine with God. In the same way that God confirmed the Israelites' identity as his people and invited them to eat a meal in his presence on Mount Sinai, Jesus' meals with sinners exemplified a gracious invitation for anyone to come and dine with him. This precedent would continue with the institution of the Lord's Supper, where anyone who repents and professes faith in Christ is invited to come to the Table. Their access is not based on their own holiness but on the holiness of Christ, who invites everyone who trusts in him to experience his presence in the Supper.

These meals not only exemplified God's desire to call "sinners to repentance" (Lk. 5:32), but also provided a glimpse of a future banquet that would take place. Jesus gave a parable of a dinner banquet in Luke 14:15–24, where the host invited many guests. Prior to the parable, a guest of Jesus makes a

---

[15] Craig Keener, *The IVP Bible Background Commentary: New Testament*, 2nd ed. (Downers Grove: InterVarsity, 2014), 134.

[16] Craig Blomberg, *Contagious Holiness: Jesus' Meals with Sinners* (Downers Grove: InterVarsity, 2005), 102.

short statement in verse 15 about those who "will eat" in the kingdom of God. From the outset, this passage is denoted as one with eschatological implications, with a focus on the culmination of God's Kingdom as a type of feast. In verse 18, however, those who were invited to the banquet begin to make excuses as to why they cannot attend. In this era, to dine at the table with those of great wealth was of the utmost privilege. As Nathan Macdonald notes, "To be admitted to the table would have been an important marker of social status and influence." Furthermore, banquets were sources of honor that was meant to be ascribed to the host.[17] In other words, to refuse such an invitation would have been insulting to the host of the feast. However, the people's refusal did not deter the fact that the party would occur, as the host then commands the servant to invite the "poor and crippled and blind and lame," and eventually extend the invitation to all people (Lk. 14:21, 23). The fact that this invitation was extended to the maimed is significant because they were previously not allowed to participate in Jewish worship.[18] Jesus' invitation of the masses in this parable exemplifies that people from any social class are welcome at his table; it also mirrors the plan of God for an even greater feast at the end of time; now, however, the means of attending this feast is not based on the sacrifices one makes or simply one's adherence to the Old Testament laws but solely on accepting the invitation of the banquet's host: Jesus himself. Throughout time, God has instituted many sacred meals for all people, all with the goal of pointing towards the ultimate banquet that will take place in the eschaton.

The progression of sacred meals throughout the canon is ultimately amplified in the New Testament with the institution of the Lord's Supper. The way that believers previously dined with God would now be replaced by a superior fellowship meal. By offering this meal, Jesus replaced the Passover, the most theologically significant meal for Jews, with the Lord's Supper. The similar occasions of these meals are significant, as in both

---

[17] Nathan Macdonald, *Not Bread Alone: The Uses of Food in the Old Testament* (New York: Oxford University Press, 2008) 157, 204.
[18] Darrell Bock, *Luke*, Baker Exegetical Commentary on the New Testament (Grand Rapids: Baker, 1996), 2:1266.

cases the meal occurred just before a major turning point in redemptive history. God prefaced the most fundamental event in Jewish history, the Exodus, with a sacred meal to celebrate his loving-kindness in delivering them from slavery. Likewise, Jesus instituted the Lord's Supper on the night of Passover, just before he suffered on the cross to deliver mankind from sin and death. Each meal is an occasion that causes future generations to prepare their hearts and remember what had been done on their behalf. Whereas Israel's firstborn had been saved in the Passover, God's firstborn would not be spared and become the means of salvation for all mankind. The Lord's Supper thus replaces Passover as the celebration of a greater sacrifice and a more intimate sacred meal. Although the disciples had gathered to remember the slain Passover lamb, Jesus reoriented their minds to a new sacrifice that would be given on their behalf.

Accounts of the Lord's Supper occur in all three Synoptic Gospels and have substantial present and eschatological implications. In all three synoptic accounts, Jesus tells his disciples that his blood "is the blood of the covenant" (Mt. 26:28, Mk. 14:24, Lk. 22:20). This is an evident allusion to Exodus 24:8 and Moses' declaration at the original covenant meal at Sinai. Just as God rescued Israel and gave them a new beginning with the covenant at Sinai, Jesus now promises his followers another new beginning and a more intimate relationship with him through this Eucharist meal. Matthew's account adds that Christ's blood is poured out "for the forgiveness of sins" (Mt. 26:28), which points to the fact that Christ himself has now become the ultimate sacrifice in order to establish a greater covenant.[19] The symbolic consumption of Jesus' body and blood have thus replaced the previous tradition of sacrificing and consuming the meat of animals. Christ has established himself as the superior sacrifice and functions as the "antitype of the Passover lamb."[20] In the same way that the Passover had a future orientation, the Lord's Supper also serves as a sign of things to come. Bock argues that Jesus' desire to eat

---

[19] R. T. France, *Matthew: An Introduction and Commentary*, Tyndale New Testament Commentaries. IVP/Accordance electronic ed. (Downers Grove: InterVarsity Press, 1985), 369.

[20] Charles Scobie, "Worship," in *The Ways of Our God: An Approach to Biblical Theology* (Grand Rapids: Eerdmans, 2003), 603.

this meal prior to his passion was because it was a "pledge to have another meal later."[21] Christ promises his disciples that they too will partake in this meal that will take place in the Kingdom of God (Mt. 26:29), which will only be consummated in this way in the future. Thus, the Lord's Supper simultaneously serves as the fulfillment of the Old Testament institution (the Passover) and the initial foretaste of the final covenantal meal that will take place in eternity. As with the other sacred meals, those who partake in the Lord's Supper must do so while simultaneously looking backward in reflection and looking forward in anticipation. The Lord's Supper thus serves to bind believers into closer fellowship to the risen Christ, the ultimate sacrifice for their sins. They also trust in the hope that his current spiritual presence pales in comparison to the final banquet that those who are in Christ will eventually enjoy.

The Lord's Supper instituted a new covenant by the blood of Christ and was given to the church to be a central aspect of its worship. However, the writings of the apostle Paul demonstrate that this was not always the case. In Corinthians 11, the Corinthians had neglected the true purposes of the Lord's Supper: to commune with Christ and to unify the church. Among the Corinthians, one's seat at meals was dependent on social status, which was causing competition among church members. McRae argues that this competition was even present in the Lord's Supper, with some members receiving more food and more honorable seats.[22] It is for this reason that Paul could write that "it is not the Lord's Supper that you eat" (v. 20). He draws from the words of Jesus in his teaching on the Supper, writing that he "passed on" what he received from the Lord (v. 23). Paul is responsible for sorting out the abuses of the Supper that were prominent among the Corinthians and he appeals to the words of Christ to demonstrate the weightiness of the sacrament.[23] One of the foremost things that the Lord's Supper is meant to do is to cultivate unity among the body of Christ. The

---

[21] Darrell Bock, *Luke,* Baker Exegetical Commentary on the New Testament (Grand Rapids: Baker, 1996), 2:1719.

[22] Rachel M McRae,"Eating with Honor: The Corinthian Lord's Supper in Light of Voluntary Association Meal Practices." *Journal of Biblical Literature* 130, no. 1 (2011): 166.

[23] Roy E. Ciampa and Brian S. Rosner, *The First Letter to the Corinthians* (Grand Rapids: Eerdmans, 2010), 548.

invitation to participate in the Supper is no longer confined to a select number of people as it was at Sinai, but it has now been extended to all people who profess faith in Christ. As believers partake in the Supper, they must inevitably be humbled and drawn into closer fellowship by their common need for Christ's sacrifice. What happens at the Lord's table, then, is the initiation of a community of believers who commonly celebrate the same sacrifice and experience the presence of the Lord together.

Verses 24 and 25 command that believers are to "do" (ποιεῖτε) the Lord's Supper, meaning that it is a participatory act of worship. Both imperatives are followed by the phrase εἰς τὴν ἐμὴν ἀνάμνησιν, meaning that the ordinance is to be done "in remembrance" of Christ. By saying that the sacrament is to be done "in remembrance," Paul is not referring to a mental recollection of facts. The act of remembrance does not merely evoke a memory but actualizes the effects of that memory.[24] When the church remembers the Lord's sacrifice during the Supper, they are thereby sharing in the benefits of that sacrifice. They are communing with the Lord in a real sense, allowing him to apply these spiritual benefits of strength and comfort to their lives. As believers observe the Supper "in remembrance" of Christ, they are also not remembering in a remorseful sense. Christ's followers are not to mourn over his death, as if we were still in the grave. Instead, they are called to joyfully celebrate that the Lord triumphed over death, applied the benefits of his death to everyone who believes in him, and dwells with them even as they participate in the ordinance. The Lord's Supper is not simply a memorial, where Christ is distant and unengaged. Instead, it is a genuine encounter with him, where believers proclaim his death and celebrate his spiritual presence with them. The communicants not only celebrate the sacrifice that has been made on their behalf but also profess his resurrection and rest in the hope that they have as a result. Paul then writes that believers "proclaim the Lord's death until he comes" (v. 26). The Lord's Supper is

---

[24] Ceslas Spicq, "μιμνῄσκομαι," in *Theological Lexicon of the New Testament*, ed. James D. Ernest, Accordance electronic ed. (Peabody: Hendrickson, 1994), 2:500.

a powerful proclamation of the gospel, where the elements point beyond themselves and point to the glories of Christ. The Lord's Supper will be observed until Christ comes and a superior meal replaces it, which is the messianic banquet. Therefore, the Lord's Supper is meant to be a proclamation of the Lord's death that unites believers to him more intimately, while also serving as a foretaste of the meal that awaits them in the future.

The various examples of sacred meals throughout Scripture eventually find a climax in a feast that has yet to occur: the marriage supper of the Lamb. Early Jews often thought of the afterlife as a banquet where the faithful would enjoy God and dine with him forever, which all of the biblical meals point toward.[25] This theme presents itself clearly throughout the Book of Revelation, beginning in Revelation 3:20, where God says that if anyone opens the door, he "will come in to him and eat with him, and he with me." This is portrayed not merely as a one-time occurrence, but a perpetual state of fellowship between both the believer and God. Communion with God is once again described here in terms of food, where the believer is enjoying a continual fellowship meal with God. Those who enter into this fellowship will be eternally satisfied, both physically and spiritually. God promises that they will neither hunger nor thirst anymore (Rev. 7:16), which points to this eternal banquet as the consummate mealtime fellowship. It also parallels Jesus' words in John 6:35, that anyone who believes in him will neither hunger nor thirst again; this does not simply mean the satisfaction of one's physical needs but the fulfillment of one's even greater spiritual need.[26] Finally, the culmination of the Bible's sacred meals occurs in Revelation 19:6–10, where John describes it as the "marriage supper of the Lamb." This feast will be the realization of Matthew 8:11, when Jesus prophesied that "many will come from east and west and recline at table with Abraham, Isaac, and Jacob in the kingdom of heaven." It will even be a superior banquet to the ones that Jesus spoke

---

[25] Craig Keener, *The IVP Bible Background Commentary: New Testament*, 2nd ed. (Downers Grove: InterVarsity, 2014), 218.

[26] Robert Mounce, *The Book of Revelation*, Rev. ed., New International Commentary on the New Testament (Grand Rapids: Eerdmans, 1997), 166.

of in Luke 14 and Matthew 22. The fact that John denotes this is a marriage banquet implies that an irrevocable union has been formed between the guests and the Lamb.[27] Even in the institution of the Lord's Supper, Jesus called his disciples to look expectantly toward this meal. The benefactors of this banquet are the κεκλημένοι, "those who have been invited" (Rev. 19:9). Those whom the Lamb has invited, meaning all faithful believers in Christ, can confidently expect the eternal joy of this banquet. God's presence at the meal will no longer be spiritual, but it will be his physical presence with his people. This banquet is one that continues for all eternity, in which God in all his glory dwells among his people. From the beginning, God's provision of food and his dwelling with man in table fellowship has been a foretaste of this coming feast. Therefore, as believers eat the bread and drink from the cup, they must rest in the fact that Christ is spiritually present with them now and long for the future banquet that awaits them in the Kingdom of God.

Given the Old Testament precedent and the fact that God describes our eternal state with him as a feast, it should come as no surprise that he is by no means absent from the sacred meal of the Lord's Supper today. All of the sacred meals throughout the canon are meant to convey Christ's spiritual presence and intimacy with his people, although each meal presents this truth in different ways. They are a tangible display of God's grace, which is evident in the Garden of Eden and in the fellowship obtained with God through the peace offering in Leviticus. They also confirm our identity as the people of God. God established the Israelites as his chosen people and displayed this by the Passover meal and the ratification of his covenant through the meal at Sinai. As we can also see through the example of Jesus' meals with sinners, they represent the heart of God for people from every nation and background to come and dine at his table. And ultimately, they point to the great feast that all Christians will enjoy in the new heaven and the new earth. The end of all things consummates

---

[27] George Beasley-Murray, "Revelation," in *New Bible Commentary: 21st Century Edition*, ed. D. A. Carson, G. J. Wenham, R. T. France, and J. T. Motyer, Accordance electronic ed. (Downers Grove: InterVarsity, 1997), 1449.

in this meal, with believers eating with one another while being face-to-face with our God. From the beginning in the Garden of Eden, it has long been God's design that we would eat with him, as every sacred meal has its fulfillment in this eschatological feast.

As believers begin to understand sacred meals in this light, the Lord's Supper should consequently be seen as one of the central ways that God has established for us to commune with him. As Blomberg states in his book, the church "cannot celebrate the Eucharist infrequently and as more of an afterthought to worship."[28] Instead, churches today must recover the central role that these meals play in worship and the fact that they are sacred and not spiritually dry or outdated. As believers partake in the Lord's Supper, it is essential that they recapture the genuine connection to the Lord that the Israelites felt in observing the Passover. When they participated in the Passover, later generations of Israelites saw themselves as participating in the Exodus, and believers who eat the Lord's Supper are likewise participating in the sacrifice of Christ's body and blood. Believers must recover the same wonder and excitement in communion that the Israelite elders had on Sinai. They are connected with Christ in an extraordinary way at his Table and his desire is for them to understand his imminence, thus drawing nearer to him and fully trusting in his promises as they partake of the elements. The precedent that has been set throughout Scripture should be a guiding principle for how we approach the Lord's Table today, with a reverence and awe at the privilege of dining with our Creator. Believers today must be reminded that just as the Lord appeared to his people in a unique way over a meal, he continues to do so today as believers gather for the Lord's Supper around his table. As we feast with God and in community with other believers, it should be a constant reminder of God's grace toward us and a precursor of the consummate meal that awaits us in heaven.

---

[28] Blomberg, *Contagious Holiness*, 179.

EXEGESIS OF 1 CORINTHIANS 10:14-22

Translation of 1 Corinthians 10:14-22

14 So then, my beloved, flee from idolatry. **15** I speak as to sensible people; judge for yourselves what I say. **16** The cup of blessing which we bless, is it not a participation in the blood of Christ? The bread which we break, is it not a participation in the body of Christ? **17** Because there is one bread, we who are many are one body, for we all partake from the one bread. **18** Look at Israel according to the flesh; are not the ones who eat the sacrifices participants in the altar? **19** What am I saying then? That food offered to idols is anything or that an idol is anything? **20** No, but the things they sacrifice, they sacrifice to demons and not to God. I do not want you to be participants with demons. **21** You cannot drink the cup of the Lord and the cup of demons; you cannot partake of the table of the Lord and the table of demons. **22** Or are we provoking the Lord to jealousy? We are not stronger than he, are we?

Introduction

Throughout the biblical canon, sacred meals establish a unique fellowship with the divine where God is spiritually present with his people. The central text for truly understanding how this occurs in in the Lord's Supper is 1 Corinthians 10:14-22. This passage is only one of two Pauline texts on the ordinance of the Lord's Supper, with this one serving as a complement to the lengthier discussion in 1 Corinthians 11. However, this passage has been largely overlooked in terms of what it means for our understanding of the Supper, as most scholars tend to focus solely on the passage in chapter 11. Nevertheless, this text provides many helpful insights into the theology and practice of the Lord's Supper that allow for a more complete understanding of how Paul understood this sacred practice and what this means for the church today.

Background and Context

The city of Corinth was a major city in the ancient world, well-known for its widespread idolatry and debauchery. The city was particularly known for its worship of Aphrodite, the goddess of love, among many other gods. The temptation to be led astray by worshipping other gods was thus a constant threat for Christians. First Corinthians was written by Paul to address many of the problems that he had heard were facing the church: disunity, immorality, idolatry, and issues in worship. Thus, 1 Corinthians as a whole is a profound example of Paul applying his theological convictions to the practical issues facing the church.[29] Paul is clearly seen exercising his apostolic authority throughout the letter by attempting to correct the Corinthians' behavior in accordance with the gospel. The dominant theme in 1 Corinthians 10 is idolatry, which motivates Paul to use the spiritual presence of Christ at the Lord's Supper as a basis to flee from it. Many of the Corinthians had begun to embrace a sacramentalism about the Lord's Supper that they believed made them immune from the dangers of idolatry. Because they had begun to eat God's sacramental food, they believed that they could attend idol feasts with no repercussions. In doing so, he draws an extended example from the nation of Israel. Paul is seeking to remove any notion that merely taking the Lord's Supper guarantees spiritual security for the Corinthians. Although all of the nation of Israel ate the same spiritual food and drink, this did not guarantee God's protection, as they were overthrown in the wilderness (vv. 3–5). By misunderstanding the Lord's spiritual food as automatic protection from idols, the Corinthians had missed the true purpose of the Lord's Supper as a spiritual encounter with Christ that is meant to nourish and encourage its recipients. Therefore, after setting up this example, Paul will go on to explain the true purpose of the Lord's Supper and how this precludes any temptation to idolatrous feasts.

---

[29] Scott J. Hafemann, "Corinthians, Letters to the," in *Dictionary of Paul and His Letters* (Grand Rapids: InterVarsity, 1993), 164.

Before moving into an exposition of the text, it is important to note some of the major issues that initially arise from this passage. The apostle uses the word κοινωνία ("participation") and its cognates several times throughout this passage to describe what truly occurs during this meal; thus, the text must be closely analyzed in order to grasp what Paul means by his use of this word. At the crux of the issue is whether Paul implies that the participant has spiritual fellowship with the Lord or simply with one's fellow participants as they eat in the Lord's honor. Another key question is how participation in these meals exclude one another and what lies at the heart of Paul's conclusion. Finally, one must answer what Paul's exhortation for the Corinthians to flee idolatry, which is rooted in the Lord's Supper, means for the way the church should understand this sacred meal today.

Many commentators argue that this passage does not provide a significant view of Paul's doctrine of the Lord's Supper and thus neglect the wider implications of this passage. Garland determines that "Paul is not setting forth teaching about the Lord's Supper" in this passage.[30] While this is not Paul's sole purpose in this passage, the manner in which Paul views the Lord's Supper is evident here and should not be overlooked. Likewise, Blomberg concludes that we should not draw any doctrinal conclusions from Paul's argument here.[31] However, within the flow of Paul's argument, this passage offers one of the most definitive glimpses into the apostle's theology and practice of this sacred ordinance. It clearly exemplifies that Paul views the Lord's Table as a union between the believer and the risen Christ and a unifying omponent of the church's worship. Through a verse-by-verse analysis of the text and interaction with relevant scholarly literature on the topic, this section will evaluate what the passage means for our contemporary understanding of the presence of Christ at the Lord's Supper and how believers should approach the Lord's Table in light of this truth.

---

[30] David Garland, *1 Corinthians* (Grand Rapids: Baker), 476.
[31] Craig Blomberg, *1 Corinthians* (Grand Rapids: Zondervan, 1994), 194.

Verse 14

Paul begins the passage with an exhortation to flee from idolatry, which serves as the central statement for all of chapters 8–10.[32] In light of his previous use of the example of the Israelites, Paul now draws the conclusion that the Corinthians must flee from idolatry, lest their fate be the same as the Israelites before them. He uses the example of the Lord's Supper as grounds for his exhortation, assuming that a true understanding of the Lord's Supper will cause the Corinthians to flee idolatry. Verse 14 begins with the conjunction διόπερ, which is a strong and infrequently used connective meaning "so then." It is used only here and in 8:13 in the New Testament, where Paul previously discussed food offered to idols. It serves to connect the proceeding statements with what Paul has previously said. The vocative phrase ἀγαπητοί μου shows that Paul loved the Corinthians, despite their unwillingness to heed his words. Many translations render this as "my dear friends" (NIV, CSB, NRSV, NET). Although there is no real difference in meaning, "my beloved" more fully captures the affection which Paul has for these saints and why he is appealing to them so strongly. Paul wants them to feel the gravity of his exhortation, and it is out love and genuine concern for them that he appeals to them in this way. At the heart of verse 14 is the strong imperative φεύγετε, which conveys actively escaping from this sin rather than a passively avoiding it.[33] The imperfective aspect of the imperative stresses that this is meant to be an action that is done ongoingly rather than a single time. Paul clearly sees imminent danger regarding any association with idols, which is why he commands them to continually flee. The Corinthians cannot continue to blatantly walk in idolatry and expect the Lord to rescue them; they must actively flee from it. Robertson and Plummer note that the apostle uses the preposition ἀπό rather than ἐκ, which means that the Paul was not calling the

---

[32] Ben Witherington, *Conflict and Community in Corinth: A Socio-Rhetorical Commentary on 1 and 2 Corinthians* (Grand Rapids: Eerdmans, 1995), 224.
[33] Thiselton, *The First Epistle to the Corinthians*, 754.

Corinthians out of idolatry but to flee from it.³⁴ Paul's strong exhortation provides the basis for his argument and a reminder for believers not to test God by the worship of idols.

Verse 15

Paul will eventually go on to ground his exhortation in an example from the Lord's Supper, which he believes the Corinthians will be able to understand. Thus, he begins by referring to them as φρονίμοις, or "sensible people." Some, such as Witherington, suggest that Paul is being facetious by referring to them in this way.³⁵ However, given the severity of the matter and that he has previously referred to them as "his beloved," it is doubtful that Paul has a sarcastic intent here. Keener notes that complimenting one's audience was a common technique in ancient writing in order to secure their favor, and this is undoubtedly what Paul has in mind here.³⁶ It would have been common for the Corinthian saints to boast in their knowledge of things, to which Paul responds that they should then be able to logically discern the truthfulness of what he says. The inclusion of ὑμεῖς is emphatic and stresses that the Corinthians can discern Paul's point for themselves. The verb φημι is a shift from λέγω earlier in the verse and refers to what Paul is preparing to say rather than what he has already said.³⁷ The verb is also more formal than λέγω, indicating that Paul is not preparing to make a mere suggestion but an argument based on his apostolic authority. He expects them to understand that when one truly grasps what occurs in the Lord's Supper, it will inevitably lead him or her to flee from idolatry.

---

³⁴ Archibald Robertson and Alfred Plummer, *A Critical and Exegetical Commentary on the First Epistle of St. Paul to the Corinthians* (Edinburgh: T. & T. Clark, 1967), 211.
³⁵ Witherington, *Conflict and Community in Corinth*, 224.
³⁶ Craig S. Keener, *The IVP Bible Background Commentary: New Testament* (Downers Grove: InterVarsity), 480.
³⁷ Gordon D. Fee, *First Epistle to the Corinthians* (Grand Rapids: Eerdmans, 2014), 513.

Verse 16

Verse 16 begins the thrust of Paul's support for his exhortation, setting forth a series of rhetorical questions to make his case. He begins by asking, "The cup of blessing which we bless, is it not a participation in Christ's blood?" The phrase τὸ ποτήριον τῆς εὐλογίας does not indicate that the cup itself was blessed but that a blessing was offered over the cup to God.[38] Thiselton affirms that Greek-speaking Jews would offer a blessing over this cup to God for all that he had provided.[39] In this context, the allusion to the Passover is clear. Most scholars affirm that the cup Paul is referring to here is the third cup of the Passover seder. Over this cup, a blessing was offered to God in gratitude for his deliverance of Israel through the Exodus.[40] The partaking of this cup in the Passover was seen not just as a remembrance of the Exodus but as a participation in it. Paul is clearly drawing on the idea that in the Passover ritual, successive generations of Jews viewed themselves as participating in the Exodus. As the Israelites physically celebrated the Exodus, they were in turn spiritually participating in their ancestors' deliverance and deepening their union with Yahweh.

The same sort of participation is apparent here, indicated by the word κοινωνία. As noted earlier, the meaning of this word has generated considerable debate. The central question is whether within the context of worship κοινωνία refers to a common enjoyment of a relationship with Christ himself or only with fellow believers.[41] Hainz argues for the latter interpretation, arguing that Paul's concern is "the various relationships between those who partake at the table of the Lord and those who partake at the altar."[42] However, Silva notes that throughout the Pauline corpus, κοινωνία never has a secular connotation, nor does it ever refer to the local congregation. Instead, it always refers to the relationship of faith to Christ. Thus, he argues that the word in this passage

---

[38] Robertson and Plummer, *First Epistle*, 211
[39] Thiselton, *First Epistle to the Corinthians*, 756.
[40] Ibid., 758.
[41] Fee, *First Epistle to the Corinthians*, 466.
[42] J. Hainz, "κοινωνία," in *The Exegetical Dictionary of the New Testament* (Grand Rapids: Eerdmans, 1991) 2:304.

refers to a spiritual union with Christ and incorporation into his death, resurrection, and glory.[43] Although participation in Christ happens through faith, it is experienced in "an enhanced form...in the sacrament."[44] Such a relationship can only come about through the work of the Holy Spirit that unites the believer's heart to Christ. By partaking of the elements, participants are drawn into a unique encounter with the Lord. Fitzmyer goes too far in saying that the believer who partakes of the cup literally partakes of Christ's blood.[45] The language of "participation" leads us away from that conclusion, as the cup is not the blood of Christ itself but rather a participation in it. This means a sharing in the benefits of his shed blood and being spiritually nourished, which does not come from an innate power within the cup itself but from Christ alone.

Similarly, Paul then asks, "The bread we break, is it not a participation in the body of Christ?" The phrase ἄρτον ὃν κλῶμεν would have been very familiar to Paul's readers, as it was a common way of referring to a shared meal.[46] Conzelmann sees τοῦ σώματος ("body") not as the correlate to blood, but rather as a reference to the church.[47] Fee supports this interpretation, as he views the cup as the vertical dimension of the meal, meaning the portion that unites the believer to Christ. The bread serves as the horizontal dimension of the meal, or the portion that binds believers' hearts together.[48] Although it sounds attractive, there is little from this text that supports this division between the elements of the Supper. Instead, Paul's focus is on the bread and the cup, which symbolize the body and blood of Christ. Both elements operate together in the Supper to draw believers into a special fellowship with the exalted Christ. Horrell thus misses the full scope of Paul's point by arguing that his focus is almost solely on each believer's

---

[43] Moises Silva, "κοινός," in *The New International Dictionary of New Testament Theology and Exegesis* (Grand Rapids: Zondervan, 2014) 2:711-712.

[44] F. Hauck, "κοινός," in *Theological Dictionary of New Testament Theology* (Grand Rapids: Eerdmans, 1965) 3:805.

[45] Joseph A. Fitzmyer, *First Corinthians: A New Translation with Introduction and Commentary* (New Haven: Yale University Press, 2008), 389.

[46] Ciampa and Rosner, *The First Letter to the Corinthians*, 475.

[47] Hans Conzelmann, *1 Corinthians: A Commentary on the First Epistle to the Corinthians* (Philadelphia: Fortress, 1975), 172.

[48] Fee, *First Epistle to the Corinthians*, 522.

relationship to one another rather than the believer's relationship to Christ in the Supper.⁴⁹ Although there is a horizontal element of the Lord's Supper which brings about κοινωνία amongst fellow believers, that is not the full extent of Paul's argument here. There is a genuine connection to Christ himself, which Calvin describes as Christ engrafting us into his body.⁵⁰ For Calvin and for Paul, there is a genuine connection to Christ that the believer is meant to experience through the elements. In Paul's view, the Christian who shares in the cup and bread of the Lord's Supper participates in an even greater redemption than the Exodus, one that was achieved "through the 'body and blood' of Christ."⁵¹ As they commune with Christ, Christians are reminded of his death that purchased their salvation and are restored with fresh hope from being in his presence.

Verse 17

Fellowship with the risen Christ naturally leads to fellowship with other believers, which Paul addresses in v. 17. As each believer is united to Christ at the Lord's Table, they are then naturally drawn into a deeper unity with their brothers and sisters. The ὅτι at the beginning of the verse is causal, indicating the reason there is one body. Conzelmann argues that the church becomes the body of Christ through the partaking of the bread in the Lord's Supper.⁵² But this presses Paul's point too much and is guilty of excessive sacramentalism. Rather, Paul's meaning is that the εἷς ἄρτος brings the Corinthians together into deeper communion with one another, which in turn will allow them to go deeper in their fellowship with Christ as a body of believers. The singular loaf from which all of the Corinthians partake is meant to serve as a reminder of their unity through Christ and avert them from worshipping any false gods.⁵³ However, the one loaf itself is not what unifies

---

[49] David G. Horrell, "The Lord's Supper at Corinth and in the Church Today," *Theology* 98, no. 783 (May 1995): 199.
[50] John Calvin, *Calvin's Commentaries,* trans. John King (Edinburgh: Calvin Translation Society, 1847).
[51] Thiselton, *First Epistle to the Corinthians,* 758.
[52] Conzelmann, *1 Corinthians,* 172.
[53] Blomberg, *1 Corinthians,* 193.

the body, but Christ himself, who is symbolized through the one loaf. The three instances of "one" in this verse indicate not simply believers' mutual unity, but also their relationship to Christ that sustains and strengthens this unity.[54] When celebrated rightly, the body of Christ thus becomes united to the Lord in a way that is distinctively achieved through their common sharing in the Lord's Supper. The Spirit is evidently at work in this event, drawing each participant's heart more towards Christ and toward his brothers and sisters. From Paul's treatment of the Lord's Supper in this passage, it is clear that the spiritual union of believers to Christ by no means negates the horizontal fellowship the church shares through the meal but rather strengthens it. When each member of the congregation understands that he or she is individually united to Christ in a unique way, this in turn increases the fellowship the believers share with one another. The text itself is a clear indication that Paul has both ideas in mind rather than one without the other. Just as the Spirit is the one who unites our hearts to Christ, he also joins believers' hearts together to bring about unity among them.[55] To participate in the Lord's Supper is to first and foremost commune with Christ and be drawn into a spiritual union with him, and secondly to be drawn into deeper unity with fellow believers.

Verse 18

Paul's principle of participation is valid not only in pagan meals and in the Lord's Supper but also in the Old Testament sacrifices of the Israelites, which he uses here as further support for his point. Paul uses the second imperative in the passage, βλέπετε (literally meaning "look at") to lead the Corinthians to consider the nation of Israel and learn from this example. The apostle clearly sees a parallel between these sacrifices and the Lord's Supper, and he uses them both to show the presence of God at these meals naturally indicates the same is true for the presence of demons at pagan meals. A consideration of how

---

[54] J. Smit, "'Do Not Be Idolaters' Paul's Rhetoric in First Corinthians 10:1 22," *Novum Testamentum* 39, no. 1 (1997): 45
[55] Garland, *1 Corinthians*, 477.

Paul saw a parallel between these sacrifices and the Lord's Supper is noteworthy here. In these sacrifices, Yahweh provided specific instructions for how they were to be conducted and exemplified tremendous graciousness in inviting man to his table. Certain sacrifices would be eaten partially by the person making the sacrifice and the rest would be burned on the altar and given to God (Lev. 7). Thus, the offering transcended being simply the sacrifice of an animal and became a sacred meal that was enjoyed between Yahweh and man. Those who offered these sacrifices to the Lord did so in celebration that they had fellowship with him. Fee rightly adds that this shared meal bound its participants together in "common worship of Yahweh."[56] Paul's point is that because the Lord was clearly present in the sacrifices the Israelites made at the altar, then he is likewise present in the Lord's Supper and in the meals offered to idols. Through their sacrifices, the Israelites were participating in the altar and in the worship of Yahweh. In the same way, Christians who participate in the Lord's Supper are united with the Lord in a unique way at the Table. As members of the New Covenant, believers today share in an even greater meal and greater connection with God through what Christ has done on our behalf.

Despite some commentators' arguments, there is no indication that the Israelites saw themselves as eating God's flesh by their consumption of the sacrifices. Paul clearly does not mean that the Israelites were physically eating the altar by their participation in the sacrifices, nor did they see the altar as a circumlocution for God. There is no evidence that θυσιαστηρίου (or its Hebrew equivalent) was ever used in this way.[57] Instead, they viewed Yahweh as near to them and present at the altar as they shared this meal. Paul argues that those who eat (οἱ ἐσθίοντες) the sacrifices are thereby participants (κοινωνοί) in the altar. A better understanding of how Paul was using the term κοινωνία in v. 16 can be drawn from his use of κοινωνοί in v. 18. To be a participant in the altar for the Old Testament Israelites meant to share in the

---

[56] Fee, *First Epistle to the Corinthians*, 519.
[57] J. Y. Campbell, "KOINΩNIA and its Cognates in the New Testament," *Journal of Biblical Literature* 51, no. 4 (December 1932): 378.

spiritual benefits of what was taking place at the altar. At the altar, guilt was being removed, forgiveness and peace were being offered, and the one eating the sacrifice became a participant in the event. There was a spiritual transaction taking place between God and man, and the believer thus became the beneficiary of what God was doing. When this understanding of κοινωνοὶ is applied to the use of κοινωνία in v. 16, it means that believers who participate in the Lord's Supper are sharing in the benefits of what Christ accomplished on the cross. They are reminded that their own sins have been forgiven and their own guilt has been removed, not by their own merits or works but based on what Jesus has done on their behalf. At the Table, the participants feed on Christ and are drawn nearer to him, just as the Israelites were drawn nearer to Yahweh at the altar. It is not simply a memorial of a past event, but an occasion in which they encounter the Savior and gain a spiritual benefit from his presence.

Verse 19

With verse 19, Paul begins to transition into drawing a conclusion based on what he has said in the preceding verses. He begins with the question: Τί οὖν φημι; by using a rhetorical question here, Paul is anticipating a potential objection the Corinthians could make to his argument. Thiselton rightly contends that Paul uses the verb φημι to clarify the scope of his argument and remove any hint of contradiction.[58] Some Corinthians had evidently begun to believe that their Christian faith had somehow given them the ability to eat idol meat without it affecting their Christian life. Because Paul has been arguing that the Lord is spiritually present at the Table and in the sacrifices of Israel, he must now clarify how this relates to his prohibition of their participation in idol feasts. The apostle clearly is not contradicting himself, as he has previously said that there is only one God and thus an idol has no real existence (8:4). In these idol feasts, Paul maintains that the εἰδωλόθυτόν ultimately remains a piece of meat and sacrificing

---

[58] Thiselton, *First Epistle to the Corinthians*, 733.

it to a false god does nothing to change that. Similarly, an εἴδωλόν remains merely a configuration of the material it is made out of.[59] Although these things have no real existence, Paul is not saying that idols or food offered to idols are nothing in the sense that they have no power. This would negate his argument that participating in these meals is incompatible with participating in the Lord's Supper. As he will go on to explain next, there is an underlying spiritual reality behind these idols that excludes believers' association with them.

Verse 20

The strong adversative conjunction ἀλλ᾽ indicates that the answer to Paul's previous statement is a resounding negative, which he will go on to make clear from Scripture. He quotes from Deuteronomy 32, reminding the Corinthians of the Israelites who rejected their God for demons. Hays makes the clear connection between this text and Deuteronomy 32; in both cases the concern is that "God's own people" are engaged in this "abhorrent practice."[60] Some commentators therefore suggest that the implied subject of θύουσιν is Israel, but Ciampa and Rosner's interpretation of it referring to pagans is more plausible.[61] Paul is offering an application of this text for his own day: while he does not affirm the real existence of pagan gods, he does affirm the existence of spiritual powers hostile to God.[62] While the idols themselves are simply inanimate objects, Paul sees these demons as using idols and food offered to them for their own advantage.

By knowingly partaking in these meals, Paul affirms that the Corinthians would become participants (κοινωνοὺς) in the sacrifices. As with v. 18, how Paul uses this participation language can broaden our understanding of κοινωνία in terms of the Lord's Supper. When the Corinthians participated in these meals, they were entering into an alliance with the demons. Whether they realize it or not, the Corinthians were forming a fellowship with the demons and becoming susceptible to their power. They were inviting the presence of these evil spirits into

---

[59] Fitzmyer, *First Corinthians*, 393.
[60] Richard B. Hays, *First Corinthians* (Louisville: John Knox, 1997), 169.
[61] Ciampa and Rosner, *First Letter to the Corinthians*, 479.
[62] Hays, *First Corinthians*, 169.

the meal and allowing them to exercise dominion over their lives. The Corinthians therefore cannot simply be casual attenders at these meals and remain innocent for it. Paul forbids them from attending, as such a meal not only establishes one as being in communion with pagans but with the demons that are being worshipped.[63] It is noteworthy that Paul says that by participating in these meals, the Corinthians do not become participants with pagans but with the demons themselves. If this same logic informs our understanding of the Lord's Supper, then it becomes clear that one has κοινωνία with Christ himself, not merely his or her fellow Christians. At the Lord's Table, there is a uniting of the believer and Jesus. Participation in the blood and body of Christ means entering into a deeper fellowship with him as opposed to demons. It means as believers experience him at the Table, they are to give him more dominion in their lives and become vulnerable to his desire for them. As they feed on Christ and drink from the cup of his blood, partakers experience a more intimate relationship with him.

Verse 21

Paul's teaching in these verses is not merely a suggestion or a personal opinion; it is authoritative. He transitions from language of desire with the verb θέλω to the language of impossibility with the verb δύνασθε in verse 21. The impossibility of one doing this is strictly moral, as Robertson and Plummer note.[64] This means that although it is logically possible for one to attend the Lord's Supper as well as an idol feast, it is not morally possible. Anyone who would enjoy the one must in turn renounce the other. To do so would be to incur God's wrath, which supports Fee's point that this verse functions as a warning and a prohibition.[65] Paul's rhetoric in this verse is clearly drawn from the language of the Lord's Supper, as he defines the prohibition in terms of both of the Supper's elements. As in verse 16, the first one mentioned is "the cup." As this identifies one with the death of Christ, it thereby

---

[63] Ciampa and Rosner, *First Letter to the Corinthians*, 482.
[64] Robertson and Plummer, *First Epistle*, 217.
[65] Fee, *First Epistle to the Corinthians*, 521.

constitutes covenant loyalty to God exclusively.[66] The converse, then, is also true: to drink from the cup of demons constitutes loyalty to them. Paul again reiterates his view of participating in the Supper with the phrase τραπέζης κυρίου μετέχειν.[67] The fact that this place is referred to as the "table of the Lord" means that one cannot neglect the fellowship that one has with the Lord, as Fee does.[68] Keener notes that Old Testament uses the phrase "table of the Lord" to indicate the place where offerings were made, which highlights the sacredness of this place.[69] For Paul, this place is now the table of the Lord's Supper. Although no sacrifice occurs at the Lord's Table as it did in the Old Testament, Paul now views this as a place where believers celebrate the definitive sacrifice that was made for them and are spiritually nourished through communion with the risen Christ. Table fellowship in the ancient world denoted intimate relations and thus the table of Lord and the table of demons are mutually exclusive. The manner in which Paul discusses these meals shows that he does not see them as casual occasions. In his commentary on the verse, Calvin writes that "in all sacred observances, there is a profession of fellowship," and we can only be "admitted by Christ to the sacred feast of his body and blood when we have first of all bid farewell to every thing sacrilegious."[70] One cannot passively participate in them and not expect to experience the consequences. To attend both meals would be the worship of two deities, which is utterly unacceptable to God. In order to be a partaker of the body and blood of Christ, one must consequently flee from partaking in idolatry. Taken together, both ποτήριον and τραπέζης in this verse illustrate that Paul's argument is grounded in the Lord's Supper and in the reality that those who share in them have a special unity with Christ.

---

[66] Thiselton, *First Epistle to the Corinthians*, 777.
[67] Campbell, "ΚΟΙΝΩΝΙΑ," 376; he notes the similarities between μετέχειν and κοινωνία.
[68] Fee, *First Epistle to the Corinthians*, 522.
[69] Keener, *IVP Background Commentary*, 481.
[70] Calvin, *Commentaries*.

Verse 22

After the strong language of verse 21, Paul closes with two final rhetorical questions. The assumption in Paul's mind is that by continuing to participate in both meals, the Corinthians are provoking the Lord to jealousy. The negative particle μὴ indicates that Paul is anticipating an emphatically negative response. Paul is emphatic that human beings are not stronger than God, but the question then becomes what does this have to do with idolatry? It does not, as some commentators have suggested, have to do with the "strong" in the church. If it did, Paul would have referred to them with a label related to their knowledge rather than their strength.[71] In his analysis of this verse, Rosner sees a mutual stress on the impotence of believers and the omnipotence of God. Believers are incapable of challenging God and getting away with it. In light of the Old Testament, it is clear that idolatry arouses God's jealously and inevitably incites his wrath. Thus, Paul is not simply saying do not disobey God because he is omnipotent but also do not tempt him, as provoking God to jealousy ultimately leads to his punitive wrath.[72] Paul's question thus serves as a powerful statement against being accommodating to other beliefs at the expense of the gospel. It shows that a Christian cannot attend a pagan meal with a friend and expect not to be held accountable. By continuing to assert themselves to be stronger than the Lord by participating in the idol feasts, the Corinthians will be subject to the Lord demonstrating his own strength by punishing them. However, when believers become aware of their own impotence, they are able to fully trust in the sufficiency of Christ and expect him to meet with them when they come to his Table. They then realize that he alone is the one who can sustain them and begin to submit to him as a result. A true understanding of the Lord's Supper will lead Christians to cling to Christ exclusively and to embrace all the spiritual benefits he has to offer them.

---

[71] Brian S. Rosner, "'Stronger Than He?' The Strength of 1 Corinthians 10:22b," *Tyndale Bulletin* 43, no. 1 (May 1992): 171.
[72] Ibid., 179.

Conclusion

Many of the Corinthians had begun to believe that the Lord's Supper provided them with a spiritual security and thus unrestricted freedom to participate in whatever pagan meals they wanted. In the process, they completely missed the true purpose of the Supper as a spiritual encounter with Christ. In 1 Corinthians 10:14-22, Paul is not arguing for the spiritual presence of Christ at the Lord's Supper. Instead, he is arguing from this conclusion. He expects the Corinthians to grasp that Christ is spiritually present and make the conclusion that demonic spirits are likewise present in the idolatrous feasts. As believers come to the Table, they are not simply remembering what Jesus has done in the past. They are also simultaneously participating in the benefits of his death and declaring him to be Lord of their lives. The Spirit thus communicates the benefits of Christ's death and resurrection to the believer who eats by faith. This passage has significant implications for how the Lord's Supper should be viewed and administered. First and foremost, this passage serves as a critical reminder that the Lord's Table must be reserved solely for those for those who are believers. One cannot truly share in the benefits that Paul outlines in this passage apart from faith in Christ. Offering the cup and bread to an unbeliever is not a healthy means of evangelism. Secondly, it should cause us to consider whether our current mode of doing communion emphasizes the κοινωνία that it ought among our brothers and sisters. The Table was never meant to be an individualistic event, but rather a corporate celebration and a key facet of our worship. And finally, understanding the spiritual presence of Christ at the Table should draw us to approach it with hope and expectation. Sharing the bread and cup with our fellow believers ought to be a practice that spiritually nourishes us and leads us to renew our covenant loyalty to Christ each time we engage in it. What truly occurs at the Lord's Table is far more significant than the physical act of eating and drinking that occurs in the believer's mouth. It is a spiritual encounter in which believers truly encounter the risen Savior. They reaffirm their commitment to Christ and are drawn closer to him. The Lord's Supper is precisely for those who are aware of their brokenness and need for Christ.

As believers come to the Table, they should find refreshment through the elements and a comforting reminder of Christ's provision for them.

PASTORAL AND PRACTICAL IMPLICATIONS

Throughout the biblical narrative, we have seen the various occasions of God preparing sacred meals for his people. He established these meals and appeared to the participants in order to give them a deeper fellowship with him. This is clearly the case with the Lord's Supper, as Paul affirms that believers participate in the body and blood of Christ and enter into a unique spiritual union with him. However, the Lord's Supper is not merely a theological concept that was intended to be processed in the mind. Instead, it is a divine sacrament that was designed to be enacted in the life of the local church. The preceding arguments are thus of little significance if they are not practically applied to the church's theology and practice of the Supper. Therefore, this section will explore the practical implications of this understanding of the Lord's Supper in the life of the church.

The first implication of Christ's spiritual presence is that it offers a spiritual benefit to the communicants. Just as God displayed his grace in providing for Adam and Eve in the Garden, he offers the church today the sacrament to display and extend that grace. The gift of the Lord's Supper is a promise that those who approach the Table will experience a sacred fellowship with their Savior. In this meal, believers are united to Christ in a deeper way, not through the elements themselves or through the minister but through the graciousness of God and the work of the Spirit.[73] Although believers and Christ are spatially distant from one another, it is the Spirit that unites them together.[74] Therefore, believers' participation in the body and blood of Christ does not necessitate that he be physically present in the elements because the Spirit works to join the

---

[73] Leanne Van Dyk, "The Reformed View," in *The Lord's Supper: Five Views*, ed. Gordon T. Smith (Downers Grove: IVP Academic, 2008), 79.

[74] John Calvin, *Calvin's Commentaries*, trans. John King, Accordance electronic ed. (Edinburgh: Calvin Translation Society, 1847).

believer and Christ. The elements remain bread and wine, but they are employed by God in the sacrament to spiritually feed his people. Just as normal food nourishes our physical bodies, so the bread and cup give nourishment and refreshment to our souls.[75] The present Christ uses them to strengthen and satisfy our hearts from his presence and to increase the participants' faith. They are consequently led to trust in him more fully because of feeding on him at the Table. Observance of the Lord's Supper not only increases believers' faith, but it also leads to a deeper and more intimate fellowship with the Lord himself. As we encounter the Lord spiritually at his Table, our commitment to him is renewed afresh each time. Van Dyk notes that Calvin is particularly helpful in this regard, as he reminds us that the Supper is the occasion in which our union with Christ is confirmed and sustained.[76] The Lord's Supper is thus meant to be a participatory act that reaffirms our covenant with Christ. While believers physically eat and drink the bread and wine, they are simultaneously spiritually feeding on Christ. Therefore, participating in the body and blood of Christ means not merely remembering his death but also receiving spiritual nourishment from him. The church is shaped and spiritually formed not merely by the practice of the ritual but because Christ himself is present at the meal.[77] The Supper is one of the means that the Lord uses to transform the church in a way that will be evident both in its worship and its witness in the world. Contrary to many modern churches' practice, the sacrament was never intended to be a remorseful or spiritually dry experience. The Lord has set before his people a bountiful spiritual feast and it ought to be approached in a spirit of wonder and expectation of a spiritual benefit for those who commune with Christ.

The second implication for the church's practice of the Supper is its frequency. How often ought the church partake of the Lord's Supper? Although there is no set pattern commanded in Scripture, the New Testament displays a pattern of consistent observance. For example, the previous analysis of 1 Corinthians 10 and 11 showed that it was a major problem in the church,

---

[75] Grudem, *Systematic Theology*, 990.
[76] Van Dyk, "The Reformed View," 76.
[77] Peter Leithart, "The Way Things Really Ought to Be: Eucharist, Eschatology, and Culture," *Westminster Theological Journal* 59 (1997): 175.

which implies that it was frequently celebrated.[78] The Supper likely would not have become such a problem if it was an infrequent practice. The practice of the church in the book of Acts also shows a pattern of consistent communion. In Acts 2:42, Luke writes that the church devoted themselves to the apostles' teaching, fellowship, the breaking of bread, and prayer. Marshall argues that the phrase "breaking of bread" (τῇ κλάσει τοῦ ἄρτου) is Luke's way of referring to the Lord's Supper.[79] The sacrament was clearly a central part of the church's worship and was frequently practiced. This becomes even more clear later when Luke writes in Acts 20:7 that the church was gathered together "to break bread" (κλάσαι ἄρτον). The infinitival phrase indicates that the purpose of their gathering was to participate in the Lord's Supper.[80] The ordinance was evidently an integral and frequent aspect of their worship designed to increase their communion with Christ and one another.

Each biblical example displays Christ's intention to meet with his people regularly at his Table. The most common argument against regular observance of the Lord's Supper is that it will lose its meaning over time. Van Neste contends that this cannot be the case, since this line of thinking is not applied to other means of grace, such as prayer, Bible reading, or preaching.[81] In the same way that these practices deepen believers' relationships with the Lord the more frequently they are practiced, the Lord's Supper does so as well. The purpose of the Lord's Supper is to be a proclamation of the gospel and a deepening of the union of the believer and Christ; such a practice could never become less meaningful if it is approached in the right spirit. Paul clearly understood Christians as entering into a sacramental union with Christ through participation in the Lord's Supper. This union is reaffirmed and strengthened as the believer continues to participate in the sacrament. The promise

---

[78] Ray Van Neste, "The Lord's Supper in the Context of the Local Church," in *The Lord's Supper: Remembering and Proclaiming Christ Until He Comes*, ed. Thomas R. Schreiner and Matthew R. Crawford (Nashville: B&H Academic, 2010), 371.

[79] I. Howard Marshall, *Acts: An Introduction and Commentary*, Tyndale New Testament Commentaries, IVP/Accordance electronic ed. (Downers Grove: InterVarsity, 1980), 89.

[80] Ibid., 344.

[81] Van Neste, "The Lord's Supper in the Context of the Local Church," 373.

of Christ's presence awaiting believers at the Table will lead them to joyfully look forward to the ordinance each week. The impetus for frequent celebration becomes clear when believers truly understand that Christ is not removed from the ordinance but is present with them as they share in it. In order to restore the Lord's Supper to its proper place in the life of the congregation, frequent participation is essential.

Furthermore, pastors must faithfully teach their people what truly occurs during this sacred ordinance and why it is worthy of frequent celebration. A true understanding of Christ's presence at the Supper will lead people to experience a deep joy in regularly participating in it. The Lord's Table must be recovered as the sacred place where believers encounter their Savior, are strengthened by his presence, and deepen their fellowship among their brothers and sisters. Olson notes from personal experience that many Baptists adopt their view of infrequently celebrating the Lord's Supper simply to distance themselves from other traditions.[82] Any denomination's practice of communion should not be dictated by what another tradition does or does not do; instead, it must be focused on Scripture itself and seek to be faithful in the eyes of the Lord. Regardless of how often a pastor feels his church should practice the Lord's Supper, the reality is that believers will not grow in grace and experience Christ more fully by practicing the sacrament less frequently. The Scripture is clear that believers have a genuine spiritual benefit to gain from the Supper, which indicates that frequent celebration of the Supper is both biblical and spiritually edifying. Too many churches have starved their members at the Lord's Table and failed to teach them what is truly offered to them in the Supper. When rightly understood, the Lord's Supper is a fresh gift of the glories of God in Christ. It is a powerful experience of Christ drawing near to his people, nourishing and satisfying them for the week ahead. The Lord's Supper ought to be a weekly proclamation of Jesus Christ and a reuniting of believers' hearts to him.

The manner in which the Lord's Supper is administered must also reflect believers' communion with Christ and unity

---

[82] Roger Olson, "The Baptist View," in *The Lord's Supper: Five Views*, ed. Gordon T. Smith (Downers Grove: IVP Academic, 2008), 108.

among the congregation. In some churches, fathers come forward to receive the elements and then serve their families. The goal is to emphasize the role of fathers as the spiritual leaders of the household. Although this practice undoubtedly has good intentions, Paul's emphasis in 1 Corinthians 10 is that the body of Christ spiritually encounters the Lord as one united family, rather than a collection of families.[83] Practicing communion this way could lead the members of the family to focus solely on their own interpersonal relationships rather than their spiritual encounter with Christ and their communion with the rest of the congregation. Similarly, other churches present the elements and allow individuals to come and receive them whenever they choose. As one walks down and takes the elements individually, he or she thereby feels less connected to the rest of the church body. By allowing the members to simply come as they feel led, church leaders are prioritizing the individuals' preferences over the beauty of the body of Christ experiencing him together.

One of the greatest detriments to communion is thinking of it solely in terms of a private encounter between the individual believer and Christ. Although there is a special union between the believer and Jesus, it is meant to be experienced alongside our brothers and sisters. Ciampa and Rosner note that that the Supper is "not merely a ... group of individuals sharing in the redemption found through the breaking of Christ's body, but of a group whose identity is formed in light of that in which they all share together."[84] The church is therefore bound together by their common participation in the benefits of Christ's death on their behalf. As the believers experience Christ together, he draws them closer to himself and deepens their unity. The prominent practice in Baptist churches (as well as other Protestant traditions) is to distribute the elements to each member and wait to eat and drink until each member has received them, which accurately reflects the communal participation in the sacrament that Scripture intends. As every believer eats and drinks simultaneously, they profess

---

[83] Van Neste, "The Lord's Supper in the Context of the Local Church," 377.
[84] Ciampa and Rosner, *1 Corinthians*, 552.

their universal need for Christ and experience his spiritual nourishment. They partake as one united family and each member experiences his sacramental presence. The grace that Christians receive at the Table ought to lead them to walk in closer companionship with their brothers and sisters and to become more mindful of their needs.

Because the Supper is not a private endeavor between the believer and Christ, it should not be administered as such. If we truly believe that there is a divine encounter taking place at the Table, then the location is not superfluous. The Lord's Supper is an ordinance given by God to his Church and thus it should be confined to the local church. To detach the Lord's Supper from the local church's worship service is to remove a key facet of its purpose. The Scriptures are clear that the Supper is not a practice meant to be done privately but as a core element of the church's worship. Thus, pastors should refrain from administering the Lord's Supper to individuals or small groups. A pastor cannot merely take the elements to an individual or a small group of people and recreate the local worship service. The spiritual encounter believers have with the Lord as they participate in the Supper is unique in that it cannot be replicated apart from the gathered body. Communion was ordained by God to give his people a taste of Christ's presence for their edification and should only be practiced where they are gathered for this purpose.

Another central question in regard to the Lord's Supper is the elements that should be used. It is crucial to remember that the emphases of the biblical texts on the Lord's Supper are not on the elements themselves. Neither Jesus nor Paul prescribed what specific type of bread or whether real wine or grape juice must be used. The effectiveness of the sacrament is not in the bread or the cup itself but in the Spirit, who unites the believers' hearts to Christ. However, the New Testament clearly indicates that the practice of the early church was a single loaf and a single cup in communion. That is not to say that there is anything inherently wrong with not using a single loaf and cup, as Scripture does not command it. Nevertheless, the church should seek to align its practice with scriptural examples as much as possible. The manner of celebration that is popular in many Protestant churches is to pass precut bread and individual cups of grape juice in the pews, which removes the significance of breaking a single loaf. Paul writes in 1 Corinthians 10:17 that we are one body because (γαρ) we partake in the one bread. Although the use of one cup was also the common practice during the New Testament era, Paul interestingly makes the point that it is the one loaf that brings about this unity.[85] The Old Testament shows that Yahweh commanded the Israelites to sacrifice a single Passover lamb, which paralleled the single Messiah who would be slain and cultivated unity among the people. In the same way, the single loaf in the Lord's Supper is meant to be a powerful sign of the single body that was broken for the people and their singular identity as his bride. By breaking a single loaf, believers come to the Table more cognizant of their universal need for Christ. Moore rightly argues that the use of one loaf would alleviate much of the individualism that is present in our contemporary celebration of the Supper.[86] The use of a single loaf would also maintain the same symbolism and emphasize the imagery that Paul used and allow for a more intimate experience for believers at the Table. Regardless of whether a church uses a single loaf or a single cup, their practice should ultimately reflect their common union with Christ and one another.

    The beauty of the Lord's Supper is that it does not hinge on believers' works or worthiness, but on the work of Christ which he accomplished on their behalf. It is a display of his glorious grace, which the church is invited to receive at his Table. In many Protestant circles, however, communion has become a remorseful time of focusing solely on one's sins. Many believers fear that they will partake in an "unworthy manner" and therefore "eat and drink judgment on themselves" (1 Cor. 11:27–29). An improper understanding of these verses has led many believers to abstain from participating in communion because they do not feel they have been "good enough" throughout the week to warrant participation. But Paul's warning in 1 Corinthians applies to those who are living in unrepentant sin, not those who are struggling with sin and

---

[85] Van Neste, "The Lord's Supper in the Context of the Local Church," 375.
[86] Russell Moore, "Baptist View," in *Understanding Four Views on the Lord's Supper*, ed. John H. Armstrong (Grand Rapids: Zondervan, 2007), 43.

trusting Christ for repentance.⁸⁷ By neglecting to participate in the Lord's Supper, believers are thus neglecting the benefits that Christ offers them. No one comes to the Lord's Supper with a perfect life or a sinless week behind them. Each member comes with memories of their own shortcomings and the burden of their struggles. The Lord bids believers to come to the Supper not merely to remember that he died for their sins but that he reigns victorious over sin and offers them a taste of that victory through his presence. Just as Jesus invited sinners and outcasts to come and share meals with him during his earthly ministry, he likewise now invites imperfect people to come and experience his life-giving presence at the Table. Believers are not worthy in and of themselves to come to the Table, but Christ counts anyone worthy who comes in faith and repentance. Despite how good or how bad the week has been, the church is invited to dine with the Lord and to draw their strength and encouragement from him alone. When believers realize their desperate need for Christ, that is precisely when the Supper has its full effect. As the participants enter into Christ's presence, they are refreshed, comforted, and strengthened by him. This sacred practice reminds us of the fact that Christ is indeed risen and that we have been given access to the benefits of that resurrection.

    The Lord's Supper also provides an opportunity for participants to respond to the gospel in a tangible way. For those who have struggled spiritually throughout the week, the Lord offers his grace to sustain them by faith. His spiritual presence gives them precisely the spiritual nourishment they need and they are given an opportunity to recommit themselves wholeheartedly to Jesus. Perhaps it reminds church members who are involved in a conflict of the κοινωνία that the church is intended to have and causes them to be reconciled to their brother or sister. For the unbelievers who were not allowed to participate in the Supper, it could prompt them to begin asking what the sacrament truly means and eventually realize their desperate need for Christ. Yet these things are much less likely to occur if the Supper is an infrequently celebrated

---

⁸⁷ Van Neste, "The Lord's Supper in the Context of the Local Church," 386.

afterthought to worship. Elders and pastors must make every effort to anchor the sacrament in the Word and remind the church that it ought to be one of the core facets of our worship. The Supper allows believers to experience Christ more fully and invites them to taste all the benefits he has to offer them at his Table.

As we have seen, the narrative of Scripture clearly illustrates God's unique display of his presence over a sacred meal. When God created Adam and Eve, he provided them with food and invited them to feast in his presence. After man's sin severed this fellowship, by his grace God instituted other sacred meals that allowed mankind to experience his presence, such as the meal with the Israel's elders on the mountain and the Israelites' consumption of the sacrifices in the presence of God. Yet, the Old Testament meals foreshadowed a greater meal, one that would be shared with the Messiah himself. This meal would fulfill every previous meal as a celebration of the forgiveness of sins and a more intimate fellowship with the Lord. The Lord gave us his Supper not simply to bring to mind his sacrifice, which it does, but also to reveal that Christ offers himself to us. In the offer of his presence, there is also the promise of grace and spiritual nourishment that believers will receive as they come to the Table. The sacrament is designed to point believers beyond themselves to the mercies of Christ and beckoning them to enter into a unique fellowship by virtue of their faith. The Lord's Supper is also a meal of hope for the future, as Christ will eventually bring his church into the consummate eschatological meal: the wedding supper of the Lamb (Revelation 19:6–9). At this great banquet meal, the full extent of our union with Christ will be realized. The experience we have of dining with Christ spiritually at his Table will be fulfilled by feasting with him physically forever. The Lord's Supper is the gift of God designed for his people to experience Christ spiritually, know him more intimately, and be united to his church more fully. This fellowship itself is based on the presence of Christ; as the communicants encounter Christ and know him more deeply, it naturally leads to union with the rest of the congregation. Fellowship is not a matter of affection, but a matter of commitment. As the church partakes of the

Lord's Supper and commit themselves to Christ, they likewise commit themselves to one another.

The church today must be reminded of the privilege it is to eat and drink in the presence of the Lord. It is crucial for the church's worship to recover the biblical vision of God dwelling with his people in a special way within a meal in our communion services and to convey to all who participate the joy that we have from being united to Christ. The believer's union with Christ in the Lord's Supper is a mystery that simply cannot be fully explained in human terms. Although we cannot adequately explain it, Christ's presence is real and near to us, designed to bring the church joy in its sacramental practice. Calvin referred to the union of the believer and Christ in the Supper as a mystery "so great that he [Paul] prefers to marvel at rather than to explain it."[88] Like Calvin and Paul, may believers rest in the reality of this union, marvel at its unexplainable nature, and be drawn into more meaningful communion with Jesus Christ because of it.

---

[88] John Calvin, *Institutes of the Christian Religion* (Philadelphia: The Westminster Press, 1960), 4.17.9.

GOD, HIS PEOPLE, AND MISSION TO THE NATIONS: A BIBLICAL-THEOLOGICAL EXPLORATION OF THE THEME OF MISSION IN THE OLD AND NEW TESTAMENTS

Jonathan E. Pope

INTRODUCTION

Though there is a plethora of biblical-theological themes that constitute the complex infrastructure of the narrative of Scripture, few are more far-reaching and multifaceted than the theme and development of the concept of *mission*. More specifically, this is to suggest the importance of the theme of *mission to the nations*. The word "nation(s)" (along with "peoples" and "gentiles") is mentioned over six hundred times throughout the Bible. Not only does this suggest that the theme of "nations" plays a crucial role in understanding the Scriptures, but it also affirms that its use spans multiple contexts. It is not enough, then, to recognize the importance of the theme of the nations within the Scriptures only, but it is equally paramount to observe how the theme functions in any given context.

Therefore, the focus of this paper will be upon the specific context of mission to the Gentiles, for the theme of mission to the Gentiles, in a sense, encompasses God's redemptive plan in history and in the Scriptures. The hope for this exploration is that God's redemptive plan for the nations will be seen as a central thread across the canon. Along with this study of key texts pertaining to the development of the theme of mission to the Gentiles, other questions will necessarily arise with reference to the people of God and ethnic Israel. For example, if mission to the Gentiles is central to God's heart and his Scriptures, why did he specifically choose the Israelites over other ethnic peoples? What is the nature of the relationship between ethnic Israel and other nations? If God has intended mission for salvation to the Gentiles, did ethnic Israel also have an explicit evangelistic mission to the nations? As many scholars have pointed out previously, God's choosing of a specific people group to be his own while not choosing others necessarily requires us to understand, then, the status or connection of God's chosen people with all other nations among whom his people must live.[1] This also raises the question of the nature of the people of God since the coming of Christ, namely, who are the people of God in the New Covenant and what is their relationship to the nations? These questions and others will be addressed throughout this biblical-theological examination.

The theme of mission should also cause us to reflect upon what God's greater plans are in general for the peoples of the earth. Throughout the development of the redemptive story of Scripture, God has shaped and is still shaping a people of his own, a people that is distinctively seeking to live in a way that corresponds to his will and ways. But where do the nations fit into this story? Will all nations be included in this plan? These questions are critical in understanding a proper biblical framework concerning the peoples of the world, but they are also expansive in such a way as to make our topic extremely challenging. In order to achieve this goal, one must examine key texts from the various epochs of redemptive history and see how God's story brings the theme to an ultimate consummation. However, a few caveats must be made. The premise of this project necessitates an overview of this theme and the Scriptures. The intent of this paper is not to give a comprehensive treatment of this theme in its complete biblical theological context, nor is it to give a thorough exegetical investigation of each key text included. The intent is to examine particularly significant texts concerning this theme in order to provide a deeper understanding of how God's mission of salvation for the Gentiles fits into the overall story of the Bible.

---

[1] Charles H. H. Scobie, "The Nations," in *The Ways of Our God: An Approach to Biblical Theology* (Eerdmans, 2003), 509.

MISSION IN THE OLD TESTAMENT
Creation: Genesis 1 and 2

To consider the theme of mission within its biblical theological context one must begin with God's creation of all things in Genesis 1, the first major epoch of redemptive history. Though many biblical commentators have neglected this period concerning its importance for understanding mission, it is foundational in understanding redemptive history. In the opening verses of the Bible, we find a vivid account of the creation of mankind and the world, in which God's authority and divine power are displayed over all the created order. God has not only created all things but all things were created for his purposes.

The creation narrative's importance for mission can be seen in God's creative acts as well as in his cessation from work in chapter two. In 1:3-23 of chapter one, the Lord spoke the universe into existence according to his divine order. From the stars in the sky to the creatures of the earth, all things proceeded from God's divine intentions. God confirms this by affirming each day that what he had made is "good" (vv. 4, 10, 12, 18, 21, 25) and that, after evaluating the whole of his work, it is "very good" (v. 31). Though these appraisals have largely been seen as primarily ethical or aesthetic assessments, a better understanding is that God cis confirming all he had made was in accord with his will and his character: God's world is in accord with God's ways.[2]

God's rest from his work completes this image of creation's corresponding with the will of God, that is, the objective of creation was achieved. This image of resting is not to suggest that God grew physically tired and weak but that he finished his task. God's resting on the seventh day reveals his intention of dwelling with mankind in the new "house" he created. Not only did God create mankind in his likeness to have dominion over the earth but he also invited man to dwell with him in his perfect rest.[3] In other words, God's purpose in creating the world and mankind the way he did was to dwell in

---

[2] Andreas J. Köstenberger, and Peter T. O'Brien, *Salvation to the Ends of the Earth: A Biblical Theology of Mission* (Downers Grove, IL: InterVarsity Press, 2001), 26.

[3] Gen 2:1-3 also seems to affirm this view in that on the seventh day there is no mention of day or night: the day here is seemingly without end. God invites man to dwell with him endlessly. The emphasis is not on literal time but on the nature of God's communion with mankind.

communion with the creation.

Though it may not seem so on the surface, these truths from the creation narrative have much to say concerning the theme of mission. First, this portion of redemptive history reveals that all creation was made and still exists under the divine authority of God. God created all things by the power of his words, and in so doing all things were created in accordance with his divine will. The created order is not synonymous with God, yet all things are dependent upon him for every second of their existence. Therefore, creation as God intended it exists in total submission and harmony with his divine purposes. Second, the goal of God's creating work was to commune with his creation, especially his most treasured creation: humankind. God did not create all things arbitrarily, but he created them in order to commune with his creation. The creation was primarily an act of love, which resulted in bringing him glory. What these two elements mean for the theme of mission is that God's mission has a basis or goal: when one says that God has a mission to the world, it is to bring that creation back into his original design. This implies, then, that the created order does, indeed, need redeeming.

As we will observe with the next redemptive epoch, what God designed did not stay as he intended. God's communion with his creation was distorted and destroyed by cosmic rebellion against his sovereign lordship. But this gives us a glimpse into the nature of God's mission. To speak of God's mission in the world is to speak of his divine purposes in restoring creation to his original design. Though this will be touched on later, it is important and wonderful to see how God's mission is a global focus in bringing his creation into a new creation, which reflects his purposes from the beginning. Just as at the beginning of God's story in Gen 12 God calls Abram with the purpose of blessing the nations, we also see at the closing of God's word in Revelation that he is concerned with redeeming a people from "every nation, tribe, language, and people" (Rev 14:6). "This theme of God's saving purposes reaching the ends of the earth forms a grand envelope that contains the entire story of Scripture."[4]

---

[4] Köstenberger and O'Brien, *Salvation to the Ends of the Earth: A Biblical Theology of Mission*, 26.

The Fall and Hope of Redemption: Genesis 3:14–16

Though Israel is instituted as a people for God in the Old Testament, the beginning of the Bible does not start there. At the beginning of all things in the garden and through Genesis 11, God is proclaimed to be the God of all peoples and over all the created order.[5] This is important because up to this point *no* distinction has been made between "a people of God" and the rest of the peoples of the earth. God is the God of all people.

And what is at the root of God's lordship over all peoples is His care, love, and lordship over all created things. The early depiction of life we find in Genesis (and throughout the entire canon) undoubtedly shows that God is holding together the entire created order: He is the life-giver, life-sustainer, and very force that makes being and the habitability of earth possible. So with this in mind, it is key to see how the early parts of Genesis exemplify God's great love and desire to reconcile peoples from all the earth. And one of the first and primary examples of this heart of God for the nations comes in Genesis 3:14-15:

> The LORD God said to the serpent,
> "Because you have done this,
> Cursed are you more than all cattle,
> And more than every beast of the field;
> On your belly you will go,
> And dust you will eat
> All the days of your life;
> And I will put enmity
> Between you and the woman,
> And between your seed and her seed;
> He shall bruise you on the head,
> And you shall bruise him on the heel."

God's promise to Adam and Eve and the serpent is not simply one to be interpreted for the nation of Israel only. Indeed, the ethnic people of Israel did not exist yet. But God's ultimate plan and promise is for peoples from all Eve's "seed." However, the

---

[5] Scobie, "The Nations," 509.

grammar and interpretation of this verse is problematic, and there are points that need to be made in order to understand what this passage means for mission to the nations. Though these difficulties are multifaceted, for our discussion here it will be fruitful to look at the identity and nature of the meaning of "seed" (or "offspring") and the identity of "he" in the latter half of verse 15.[6] The first important thing to note is that the word "seed" is singular (זֶרַע). Therefore, it makes sense that the subsequent personal pronoun would be in the singular ("he"). However, this does not clarify the main issue of the text: is this word referring to the offspring of the serpent and the woman more broadly or to a singular descendant? Some commentators have interpreted this text as explicitly messianic, pointing forward to a singular descendant who will destroy the devil and the powers of evil.[7] One of the difficulties with this argument, however, is that the number of occurrences in the Old Testament where this word refers to one individual and is singular almost always refers to an immediate descendant rather than a singular descendant in the future (Gen. 4:25; 15:3; 19:32, 34; 21:13; 38:8–9; 1 Sam. 1:11; 2:20; 2 Sam. 7:12).[8] Furthermore, the Old Testament also includes a significant number of references where this word refers to a collection of descendants; in all these examples the word is never plural in the Hebrew (Gen. 9:9; 12:7; 13:16; 15:5, 13, 18; 16:10; 17:7–10, 12; 21:12; 22:17–18).[9]

It seems difficult to argue that this word can be understood in both senses in this context, especially since this is typically the only verse in the Old Testament that is debated in this regard. In other words, there are no other passages adequate for comparison. Still others argue that since both verbs in verse 15 are imperfect iterative verbs, the action denotes an

---

[6] For a general synopsis of the interpretive issues of this passage, consult Victor P. Hamilton, *The Book of Genesis: Chapters 1–17*, NICOT (Grand Rapids: Eerdmans, 1990), 197.
[7] For example, T. D. Alexander, "Further Observations on the Term 'Seed' in Genesis," *Tyndale Bulletin* 48, 363–367; John C. Collins, "A Syntactical Note (Genesis 3:15): Is the Woman's Seed Singular or Plural?" *Tyndale Bulletin* 48, 139–148.
[8] Hamilton, *The Book of Genesis: 1–17*, 198.
[9] Ibid., 199.

ongoing struggle between the offspring of the serpent and the offspring of the woman.[10] In this vein of interpretation belongs a significant amount of support of a long-term struggle between Satan, sin, and death and mankind where a kingly messiah would one day give a final fatal blow to the serpent, the symbol of all forces set against God and his rule, sometime in the future. For example, some the oldest Jewish interpretations within the Septuagint and Palestinian targums seem to argue for this symbolic meaning that would come to a climax with the coming Messiah.[11] Additionally, the New Testament seems to argue for this text as being "broadly messianic" (Heb. 2:14; Rev. 12).[12] Later Christian authors such as Justin (*ca.* 160 A.D.) and Irenaeus (*ca.* 180 A.D.) maintained this text as the first messianic text of the Old Testament.[13]

Regardless of where one lands on this particular issue, the key to understanding this text is to recognize 1) this passage is a curse upon the serpent and 2) the symbolism of the serpent. This passage is not simply an etiology of how men would hate and battle snakes throughout history. This passage describes the serpent's leading mankind astray. And due to the nature of the injuries promised to be inflicted upon the woman's seed and the serpent's seed, it seems most likely that God is pronouncing a future defeat and end to the serpent's raging against man (i.e., the serpent will bruise the man's heel, but the man will bruise the serpent's head). The "bruising" or "crushing" of the serpent's head is surely a fatal blow. Therefore, it is right that Christian commentators have long considered this
passage the "protoevangelium," or the first pronouncement of the God's redeeming purpose in the world in destroying the powers of evil. But how does this necessarily connect to mission? We know from the creation account that God's original design was to dwell with man in the world that he made in accordance with his will and ways. But sin disrupted and

---

[10] Gordon J. Wenham, *Genesis 1-15*, Word Biblical Commentary (Word Books, 1987), 80. Though the iterative nature of these verbs is debatable, many Qal imperfect forms seem to point forward to future events.

[11] Wenham, *Genesis 1-15*, 80.

[12] Ibid., 80.

[13] Ibid., 81.

damaged this design: when Adam and Eve sinned in the garden, they were no longer fit to dwell in God's presence. Therefore, when considering the protoevangelium, it seems most likely that God's pronouncement of judgment upon the "anti-God" forces represented by the serpent and his offspring is the first indication of restoring his original design with mankind. In order for man to dwell with God, as seen in the creation account, man's sin and the powers of evil must be removed.

So, with all that in mind, how does this affect the nations generally? How does God's plan to deal with sin and the devil in the protoevangelium mean good news for mission to the world? Put simply, because God designed at creation that he would dwell with *all* mankind and since the protoevangelium is a proclamation to retrieve this design, Gen. 3:15 should be seen as a promise of hope for peoples of all nations. Neither in the creation narrative nor in the protoevangelium does there exist any ethnic limitation to God's designs and stated intentions. God's plan to crush the evil one, then, has implications for all the world, not simply a single ethnic people. Though much of the Old Testament is indeed focused primarily on Israel, God's attention and plan for the nations is present prior to the choosing of Israel. Israel is often warned not to worship and live as the rest of the nations around them (Deut 12:30, 18:9; 2 Kg 17:15), and many Old Testament proclamations pronounce judgment on the nations (Isa 13-23; Jer 46-51; Ezek 25-32). But these texts teach us that God is primarily concerned about the *holiness* of his people, not simply their ethnic identity. Even so, God is instrumentally involved and intentional concerning the well-being and the salvation of peoples from all nations of the world (Ps 67:2, 98:2; Isa 52:10, 15).[14] Here in the protoevangelium is the revelation of God's purpose to one day destroy the evil one and to crush sin, death, and struggle. This a promise that reaches across all ethnic peoples. And, as we will soon see elsewhere in Genesis, this promise and truth concerning God's care for the nations of the earth from Gen. 3:15 is reiterated and amplified throughout the rest of the Old Testament.

---

[14] A. J. Köstenberger, "Nations," in *New Dictionary of Biblical Theology* (IVP, 2000), 677.

God's Promise for all the Nations: Genesis 12:1-3

The establishment of God's promise in the protoevangelium is the first major movement in redemptive history for the blessing and reconciliation of the nations. But Genesis 12:1-3 is the first explicit instance where God's ultimate plan to reconcile his relationship with man will result in the blessing of all nations:

> Now the LORD said to Abram, "Go from your country and your kindred and your father's house to the land that I will show you. And I will make of you a great nation, and I will bless you and make your name great, so that you will be a blessing. I will bless those who bless you, and him who dishonors you I will curse, and in you all the families of the earth shall be blessed."

This is an astounding text in more than one respect, for God's redemption of all the earth is wrapped up deep within it, which will be revealed as we explore the development of mission through the rest of the story of the Bible. But one key observation that should be made here is that God chooses to bless and build up Abraham and his descendants *for the purpose* of "being a blessing" (v. 2). God's whole purpose is ultimately not for Abraham or his descendants' sakes, but for the blessing of the nations. And as the rest of Scripture attests the nations are blessed for the glory of God.

Notice also the universality of this blessing, a heightening to the promise that was made in Genesis 3:15: "and in you *all the families of the earth* shall be blessed" (v. 3).[15] It is overwhelmingly clear that even though in this text God is beginning to form a specific people for himself that will be distinct from all others, this distinctive people is being formed with a grander and more global purpose in mind. This passage clearly shows that God's ultimate fulfillment of the promise and blessing to Abraham is to be fulfilled in all the nations of the earth.[16]

---

[15] If one interprets Gen 3:15 as describing mankind broadly, even so, this passage pronounces God's promise of blessing to the nations of the world in more definite terms. In other words, this passage leaves no doubt about whom will benefit from the Abrahamic promise.

[16] Scobie, "Israel and the Nations: An Essay in Biblical Theology," *Tyndale Bulletin* 43, no. 2 (1992): 285-286.

God Establishes His People: Exodus 19:3-6

The book of Genesis ends in anticipation of God's fulfilling his promises to Abraham concerning the nations and the land (e.g. Exod. 1:12). The book of Exodus, then, "recounts how the Lord began to fulfil his promise of the land to the assembled multitude of Israel."[17] God's saving of the people of Israel from the hands of the Egyptians marks the creation of something new, a people for God's own possession. This new people of God will soon enter into covenant with him at Mt. Sinai in Exodus 19-20. For this reason, the Exodus out of Egypt was and still is considered the most significant event in Israel's history by the Jewish people. But on an even deeper level, because the Abrahamic covenant is wrapped up in the Exodus and survival of the people of Israel, God's plan for salvation to the ends of the earth is also profoundly intertwined with the Exodus and creation of Israel as a people.[18]

Just as God chose Abraham for the specific purpose of blessing all the nations of the world, he also chose Israel as a people for his own with a specific purpose in mind. God reveals this plan for Israel in Exodus 19:3-6, which is pivotal in understanding Israel's role with respect to mission and the nations:

while Moses went up to God. The LORD called to him out of the mountain, saying, "Thus you shall say to the house of Jacob, and tell the people of Israel: 'You yourselves have seen what I did to the Egyptians, and how I bore you on eagles' wings and brought you to myself. Now therefore, if you will indeed obey my voice and keep my covenant, you shall be my treasured possession among all peoples, for all the earth is mine; and you shall be to me a kingdom of priests and a holy nation.' These are the words that you shall speak to the people of Israel."

This passage represents Israel's call to action. It is here that God indicates the purpose for their election from all the nations. Before giving Israel this purpose, though, he gives the grounding for this purpose. In verse 4 God reminds Moses and the Israelites that their existence as a people and ability to have election

---

[17] Köstenberger and O'Brien, 32.
[18] Ibid.

is only a result of divine deliverance. There is nothing they have done to merit God's favor. This is important to recognize because God is about to make a covenant with them, and if they desire to flourish as his people, they must recognize his divine sovereignty and power in their salvation from bondage.

In verses 5 and 6 God's plan for Israel is outlined in terms of their identity and vocation as a people. If Israel remains faithful to the covenant he is making with them at Sinai, they will be to him a "treasured possession." As the passage suggests in verse 5, "Israel is not the Lord's only possession, but rather a special and treasured possession among all peoples who are his."[19] God will also make them a "kingdom of priests." Though there are nuances here with the Hebrew grammar,[20] the main point of this distinction is that Israel is to reflect God to the other nations around them in the way they live. Their priestly function means that they were to act as representatives of the Lord to the peoples around them much in the same way Aaronic priests function.[21] But just as these priests represented Israel to the Lord, so also are they to represent the nations before God. When these two functions come together, Israel essentially becomes "the possibility of a relationship between the Lord and the nations."[22] God continues along this line by saying they will also be a "holy nation." In a word, "Israel was set apart as

---

[19] W. Ross Blackburn, *The God Who Makes Himself Known: The Missionary Heart of the Book of Exodus*, (Downers Grove, IL: IVP, 2012), 89.

[20] Commentators have debated over how this phrase should be rendered. Some translate it to the effect of "a kingdom set apart like a priesthood" or "kings who are like priests/priest-like kings." Regardless of the wording, John I. Durham, Exodus, Word Biblical Commentary (Word Books, 1987), 263, sums up the basic meaning of the passage well: "Israel as a 'kingdom of priests' is Israel committed to the extension throughout the world of the ministry of Yahweh's presence...they are to be a people set apart, different from all other people by what they are becoming–a display-people, a showcase to the world of how being in covenant with Yahweh changes a people."

[21] Blackburn, *The God Who Makes Himself Known: The Missionary Heart of the Book of Exodus*, 89–92. Here Blackburn gives a helpful overview of the various exegetical issues that arise from this text, but he is most helpful in demonstrating that this election of Israel is not ultimately designed to shut them off from the world but to be a part of his redemptive plans for the world.

[22] Ibid., 92.

a nation for the purpose of rendering priestly service in order to reflect the character of God to the nations."[23]

Deuteronomy 4:1–8

In Deuteronomy 4:1–8 Israel receives a pivotal message from Moses concerning their new home in the promise land, a message which is from the Lord and demands their obedience in order to prosper according to the "treaty" being made with Israel.[24] God gives Israel through Moses a reassurance of the obedience that is expected of them, obedience to the commands that God has given them. God reminds the people what will happen if they do not obey, which is judgment just like they have seen before when God disciplined His people for their idol worship at Baal Peor.[25] On the other hand, obedience will lead to life, prospering, and a possession of the land. But when Moses speaks in verses 6–8, we find God's purpose for their obedience and the outcome that he desires concerning the nations surrounding Israel as a result of their obedience:

> "So keep and do them, for that is your wisdom and your understanding in the sight of the peoples who will hear all these statutes and say, 'Surely this great nation is a wise and understanding people.' For what great nation is there that has a god so near to it as is the LORD our God whenever we call on Him? Or what great nation is there that has statutes and judgments as righteous as this whole law which I am setting before you today?"

Here we see God giving a command to Israel with the intention of seeing the people of their new land recognize God and his anointing of them. More importantly, God wishes to have his law and his glory made prominent in this new land, and he is doing so through the obedience and holiness of Israel. But

---

[23] Ibid. Deut 4:5–8 affirms this purpose and clarifies it, as we will observe later.
[24] J. A. Thompson, *Deuteronomy: An Introduction and Commentary*, Tyndale Old Testament Commentaries, IVP/Accordance electronic ed. (Downers Grove, IL: IVP, 1974), 117–118.
[25] Ibid., 118.

this also means that Israel must conduct themselves in a way in which other nations can recognize their works and why they are doing them. Although Moses does not indicate how this is to occur, it is not unlikely that the people of these other nations were in close enough proximity to the Israelites to observe how they lived. And we know that the people of Israel anticipated this because of verses 6: "for that is your wisdom and your understanding in the sight of the peoples..." This is not an explicit command to proselytize the nations around them; however, it is one of the first major texts in the life of Israel where the people undoubtedly receive a clear command to live and worship rightly before the other nations in order that those peoples may see their righteousness and the power of the one true God. And in seeing their righteousness and the power of the Almighty, these nations will also see a quality of the God of Israel that sets him apart from all others: an intimate God with his people who is completely righteous (v. 8). Just as in Exodus 19:3-6, God's purpose for Israel was a global purpose: God's concern for the whole world established in the garden and in the Abrahamic covenant undergirds Israel's existence.

The Broken Mosaic Covenant: Israel's Failure as a Nation

Though this issue deserves an extended treatment, which cannot be accomplished here, a crucial point concerning the Mosaic covenant and the people of Israel needs to be made in order to rightly understand the theme of mission in this period of the Old Testament. As stated above, God's covenant with Israel at Sinai meant that they would be a specially prized people by God for the sake of revealing God's holy nature to the world. But looking back to both of those crucial texts (Exod. 19 and Deut. 4), Israel was required to obey God's commands if these realities were to become a reality. Israel's obedience to God was essential if they were to see the fulfilment of certain covenantal promises. In a word, the Mosaic covenant was different from the Abrahamic covenant in that fulfillment for certain promises was contingent upon their obedience.
The Mosaic covenant, then, should be viewed as a covenant

of works rather than a covenant of grace.²⁶ Of course, God's covenant at Sinai was grounded upon his divine actions in raising Israel out of Egypt and preserving them with his lovingkindness thereafter in spite of Israel's good deeds or failures, and this theme of God's pouring out of his grace upon them continues through the entire Old Testament. But this does not negate the fact that the covenant contained clear covenant stipulations. Though the formal ratification of the Sinai covenant does not take place until Exodus 24, the covenant stipulations for Israel appear clearly in the aforementioned passages. Additionally, the covenantal blessings and curses described in Deut. 27–30 clearly demonstrate that Israel's obedience was necessary if they were to maintain a covenant with the Lord. Furthermore, as the Mosaic covenant is expanded upon, direct similarities between ancient Near Eastern law codes and this covenant are unavoidably noticeable.²⁷ For example, the *lex talionis* found in Exodus 21:23–25 resembles well the "retaliation laws" found in the Code of Hammurabi.²⁸ To say that this is an inconsequential coincidence or that this correlation is nonexistent is a grave miscalculation.

Though the extent of the influence of these ancient Near Eastern law codes upon the Mosaic covenant is not completely agreed upon, the point here is that the Mosaic covenant contained conditional covenant stipulations. Many scholars resist this notion, asserting that it implies a works-based salvation ethic. But this position ultimately misunderstands the purpose of the Mosaic covenant. The purpose of the Mosaic covenant and subsequent laws was not to instruct the way to work and attain eternal (or eschatological) salvation from the

---

[26] Contra Köstenberger and O'Brien, 33–34, who argue that the covenant made in Exodus 19:3–6 is merely an extension/reminder of the Abrahamic covenant. Put simply, this argument is unsatisfactory due to the literary context and the reality that God's forming of his covenant here is not framed in the same way in Gen. 12.

[27] Cf. J. B. Pritchard, *Ancient Near Eastern Texts Relating the Old Testament*, 3rd ed., ed. J. B. Pritchard (Princeton: Princeton University Press, 1978), 159–223, for similarities between some biblical covenantal stipulations and other ancient Near Eastern law codes.

[28] J. P. Hyatt, *Exodus*, NCBC (Grand Rapids: Eerdmans, 1971), 234. Cited in Paul R. Williamson, *Sealed with an Oath: Covenant in God's Unfolding Purpose* (Downers Grove, IL: IVP, 2007), 98.

eternal consequences of sin. Rather, God gave this covenant in order to show Israel and the world how holy a people must be to be in communion with God (Lev 11:45; 19:2; 20:26). Israel's national covenant reveals a deeper understanding of who God is. But most importantly, as the re-establishment time and again of this national covenant after Israel's constant rebellion indicates, the conditional nature of the Mosaic covenant and law reveals that no one will be fully redeemed from sin due to 1) their fulfilling of the law through good works 2) or because of *any* national or ethnic barrier (Gal 3:7-9; Rom 9-11). Yet, even then, it is clear that the inauguration of national Israel was inextricably linked with the promises made to Abraham, which was not a conditional covenant (Gen. 15). So how do these two fit together? Though this topic will be picked up again in our observations of significant New Testament texts, the covenantal promises of the Abrahamic covenant did not fail with the insufficiency of Israel's disobedience. Rather, God had planned the establishment of a new covenant to follow the old, one that would *fulfill* rather than nullify Israel's election: a final and perfect covenant uninhibited by human inability.[?] This covenant would be manifested through the coming of a Jewish messiah, one who would remove the sins of all who believe in him (Isa. 53:4-5; John 1:29). The Old Testament shifts from this point to a period that surrounds a similar covenant to the one made to Abraham: the covenant between God and King David. And it is in the Davidic covenant where this messiah is revealed and anticipated through the rest of the Old Testament.

The Davidic Kingdom and God's Blessings for the Nations

2 Samuel 7

To begin to understand how the Davidic covenant is deeply intertwined with God's covenantal promises in both the Abrahamic and Mosaic covenants, one must begin with the

---

[?] Paul R. Williamson, *Sealed with an Oath: Covenant in God's Unfolding Purpose*, 192, 194.

establishment of David's kingship in 2 Samuel 7.[30] Second Samuel 7 begins with David's praising God for delivering him from his enemies, and as a result he wants to build a temple for God fit to house the ark of the covenant. However, God denies David this opportunity and reveals that his son Solomon will inherit the gift of building the temple, for the promised land had not yet been granted full peace (vv. 9–13). But God does not leave David there. Instead of granting him the chance to build the temple, God gives him the grand promise of a never-ending reign as king. In verse 13 God says to David concerning one of his descendants, "He shall build a house for my name, and I will establish the throne of his kingdom forever." Here God makes the astounding promise to David that his house will reign for all time. It will not be shaken or destroyed as Saul's kingship or the other rulers of the earth. But there are difficulties with this text. For example, from history we know that the Davidic line of kings was defeated in the fall of Jerusalem in 587/586 B.C. "The answer to this tension appears to be that while the covenantal promises may be withdrawn from individuals of David's line, the line itself will not ultimately fail."[31] At the end of this line, it is the person of Jesus Christ who brings to fulfilment the covenant promises made to David. And consequently, then, it is Jesus who brings to fulfilment the promises of the Abrahamic and Mosaic covenants.[32]

How then does the Davidic covenantal blessings relate to the promises made to Israel and Abraham? And what does 2 Sam 7 and the Davidic kingship mean for our exploration of the theme of mission? First, with reference to the Mosaic covenant, God similarly gives promises to David of "the blessedness of the covenant people, the institution of a theocratic king, the establishment of temple worship, and the centrality of Jerusalem."[33] But there are dissimilarities as well. Unlike within the Mosaic covenant, David is promised a dynasty. David and

---

[30] Köstenberger and O'Brien, 37.
[31] Ibid., 38.
[32] This idea will be developed more as we examine the New Testament, but it is helpful here to recognize that all of these covenantal promises point to the messiah from the Davidic line, who is Jesus Christ.
[33] Willem Vangemeren, *The Progress of Redemption: The Story of Salvation from Creation to the New Jerusalem* (Grand Rapids: Baker, 1988), 235.

Solomon would also introduce specific changes related to temple worship and the identity of the priestly order (i.e., the judgment of Eli's house and appointment of Zadok as high priest). But God did not discontinue the promises made to Israel at Sinai with the Davidic kingship, but rather he fulfilled what God had intended his people to be. In this way as revealed in the context of 2 Sam 7, David is appointed as Israel's representative before God and other nations (cf. Ps. 110:4, which links David's kingship with Israel). "The sonship terms previously applied to Israel (Exod. 4:22) are now predicated of David ('I will be his father, and he shall be my son', 7:14)."[34] Verses 9-11 further demonstrate that the promises to Israel concerning the promised land are to be finally fulfilled through David's line. This is all wrapped up in the reality that in this passage the priestly kingdom expectations of Israel in Exodus 19:6 are now found in the Davidic line: the king is now an embodiment of this reality.

Second, concerning the covenant with Abraham, the most obvious connection between these two covenants is the "reiteration" of God's promises to Abraham in Gen. 12:1-3: namely, that God will make his name great (2 Sam 7:9).[35] There is also a connection in terms of God's promising of a specific place for Israel just as he did for Abraham's descendants (cf. Gen. 15:18). The Davidic dynasty "will set the ideal borders of the Promised Land, which the promise to Abraham had foreshadowed."[36] The inauguration of the Davidic dynasty also reaffirms God's global purpose to bless all the nations, which will be expressed in the global rule of David's descendants (see discussions below).

Lastly, with concern to mission and our discussion here, the Davidic covenant reveals a fulfilment of both the Abrahamic and Mosaic covenants: David's embodying God's original intentions for Israel and his embodying the fulfilment of God's promises to make Abraham be a blessing to all nations. Without the Davidic covenant, these promises would be left incomplete. It

---

[34] Köstenberger and O'Brien, 39.
[35] Ibid.
[36] W. J. Dumbrell, *The Search for Order: Biblical Eschatology in Focus* (Grand Rapids: Baker, 1994), 70. Quoted in Köstenberger and O'Brien, 39-40.

is through this future Davidic King's ruling in God's authority that the God's rule over the all peoples will be realized.[37] As we will observe in the new covenant inaugurated in the New Testament, Jesus of Nazareth will be the ultimate fulfilment of this reality.

Psalm 72:8–11

Before moving on to later Old Testament developments of the theme of mission to the nations and their relationship with Israel, there is a key movement and point of emphasis that also occurs within God's covenant with David, one that was tangentially touched on in the previous section. Within the covenant with David, God makes a promise to David much like the one he made to Abraham, a promise that is intended for all peoples. Psalm 72:8-11 depicts a universal scope of David's rule, a rule that renders tribute from all kingdoms and that subordinates all kings under his rule. But in verse 17 we find a tremendous echoing of God's promise to Abraham: "May his name endure forever, his fame continue as long as the sun! May people be blessed in him, all nations call him blessed." This is important because the two covenants with Abraham and David are being brought together intimately here just as they did in 2 Samuel 7. "Indeed, it is being affirmed that a king in the line of David will be the means through which God's promise to bless the nations will be fulfilled. Those who stand to be blessed through Abraham here stand to be blessed through the Davidic King."[38]

This development is crucial because it shows how God is carrying out his promise and plan that he made all the way back in Genesis, both in the protoevangelium and in his covenant with Abraham. It shows that God did not forsake his plan for the nations, but rather purposed and is purposing now to bring blessings to the nations. But what is the nature of this blessing? We have discussed already that God wishes that all

---

[37] Köstenberger and O'Brien, 40.
[38] Christopher J. H. Wright, "The Span of God's Missional Covenant," in *The Mission of God: Unlocking the Bible's Grand Narrative* (Downers Grove, IL: I VP, 2006), 345.

the peoples worship him and honor him as is fitting, but it is also clear amidst God's working to build up the people of Israel that only those who worship him rightly and have been brought into obedience to God can claim that blessing (e.g., Exod 32). God takes pleasure in righteousness, and unrighteousness conjures his wrath. How can all the nations be included in this blessing, then, if those outside Israel do not know how to worship rightly before God? How can they worship him when they are wicked (Deut. 9:4, 7:1–6, 16)? This raises an issue that often arises with concern to the global blessings of the Davidic covenant and the Old Testament at large: how will God bring about these blessings? As we observed in 2 Samuel 7, this discussion is within the context of national Israel as well. Does Israel have a role to play in this fulfilment like they did in the Mosaic covenant? Particularly, what is the nature of salvation concerning the nations and what is Israel's role in reaching them (if at all)? The rest of the Old Testament, which chronicles the life of Israel, contains several key texts that will clarify these issues. After observing these texts, we will find that mission for the inclusion of the nations in salvation has always *implicitly* been a role and function of God's people. This is normally not a point of contention concerning the New Testament (which has *explicit* commands for mission), but with the Old it seems to be quite debated.[39] We will also realize that these blessings for the whole world are dual in nature corresponding to the Old and New Testaments: the nations were blessed by inclusion *within* Israel in the Old and eschatological redemption *outside* Israel in the New.[40]

---

[39] Eckhard J. Schnabel, "Israel, the People of God, and the Nations," *Journal of the Evangelical Theological Society* 45, no. 1 (2002): 35–57; Craig Blomberg, "Mission in the Bible: Non-Existent in the Old Testament but Ubiquitous in the New?" *Themelios* 32, no. 2 (2007): 62–74; For a discussion of the point of view that Israel had no explicit missionary calling to the nations in the Old Testament and a response to his work, see Schnabel's biblical theological treatment of the theme and Blomberg's response. I will expand on points made in the two works in the section to come.

[40] Köstenberger and O'Brien, 35.

1 Chronicles 16:23–30

Moving forward into the Davidic rule of Israel, we find an interesting text that communicates two main points concerning Israel and the nations: 1) a universal call for all nations (and all of creation) to give praise and honor to the Lord and 2) a call for Israel to declare God's mighty deeds to all peoples.[41]

> Sing to the LORD, all the earth!
> > Tell of his salvation from day to day.
> Declare his glory among the nations,
> > his marvelous works among all the peoples!
> For great is the LORD, and greatly to be praised,
> > and he is to be feared above all gods.
> For all the gods of the peoples are worthless idols,
> > but the LORD made the heavens.
> Splendor and majesty are before him;
> > strength and joy are in his place.
> Ascribe to the LORD, O families of the peoples,
> > ascribe to the LORD glory and strength!
> Ascribe to the LORD the glory due his name;
> > bring an offering and come before him!
> Worship the LORD in the splendor of holiness;
> > tremble before him, all the earth;
> > yes, the world is established; it shall
> > never be moved. 1 Chr. 16:23–30

Particularly there are two prominent exhortations that take place in vv. 23–24 opening this section. All the earth is being called here to worship God. And in the latter half of twenty-three into twenty-four, we see a command to declare "God's salvation from day to day," to display His splendor, and to tell of all His mighty acts among the nations of the earth. Presumably this exhortation is primarily intended for *Israel*, if for nothing else other than the fact that the majority of God's acts in history up to this point have been for the building up and forming of

---

[41] Martin J. Selman, *1 Chronicles: An Introduction and Commentary*, Tyndale Old Testament Commentaries, IVP/Accordance electronic ed. (Downers Grove IL: IVP, 1994), 177.

His chosen people since the time of Abraham. But this text is important because it is an Old Testament call for the people of all the earth to sing and worship God. And this necessarily includes Israel's declaring God's mighty deeds of salvation among the nations. It is a call for all peoples to worship God because God takes delight in the worship of the nations. As vv. 25 and 29–30 expound, it is fitting that all creation worships the Lord because he is "greatly to be praised" and all glory is due his name. He is above all the gods of the nations. And this is why he desires that all the "families of the earth" worship him and give him honor that is rightly owed his name. It is how he intended it to be.

The Psalms to the Prophets: Messages of Israel's Testimony before the Nations

Psalm 96:1–11

Throughout the Psalms there is an ever-present theme of universality: God is the origin and source of all things, creator of the universe; he is the sovereign over all peoples and kingdoms of the earth, and as a result all peoples are commanded to give God the worship he is due (33:8; 66:4; 67; 86:9; 98:4; 100; 138:4; 148:11).[42] Psalm 96:1-11 in particular is one that has a very similar message to 1 Chr 16:23–30. In fact, it uses much of the same language (Ps 96:2–5, 7–13). This passage again is key simply because it demonstrates that it is appropriate and by design that all peoples worship and cry out to the Lord.

But as mentioned before, some would argue that none of the Psalms' "mission" texts should be considered explicit calls to evangelize those outside Israel. Eckhard Schnabel makes the claim, "The prophetic announcement, the historical reality, and the legal stipulations surrounding the exodus indicate that Israel's role as a witness among the nations and to the nations was a passive one at best."[43] This would also include the Deuteronomy text that we discussed earlier. Shortly thereafter

---

[42] Scobie, "The Nations," 521.
[43] Schnabel, "Israel, the People of God, and the Nations," 37.

Schnabel goes on to say, "Neither the Torah nor the prophets contain any hint that Israel has a historical mission to bring members of other nations to a saving knowledge of YHWH."[44] While it is important to recognize that there is no explicit call to proselytize the nations in the Old Testament such as what we see in the New Testament, there is (as we have seen in previous passages) a consistent implicit witness of Israel to the nations. Israel's separateness, in other words, was not one of complete seclusion. This implicit (or passive) witness is profoundly present in the eschatological anticipation of God's inclusion of the nations in the book of Isaiah.

Isaiah

Schnabel is quite correct concerning the lack of evidence to support a strong missionary appeal in the Old Testament such compared to the New Testament, but, as Blomberg points out in his review of Schnabel's work, many scholars and readers have recognized that Schnabel's own examination of some of these specific texts leads directly to an *implicit* mission of Israel to the nations, particularly in the Psalms and prophets.[45] Isaiah in particular presents us a host of passages that carry such a tone. Isaiah 42:6–7 says:

> I am the LORD; I have called you in righteousness;
>   I will take you by the hand and keep you;
> I will give you as a covenant for the people,
>   a light for the nations,
> to open the eyes that are blind,
> to bring out the prisoners from the dungeon,
>   from the prison those who sit in darkness.

This text is key in showing that God is shaping his covenant people Israel for the purpose of being a "light" to the nations. As will be discussed shortly, these later texts of reaching the

---

[44] Ibid.
[45] Blomberg, "Mission in the Bible: Non-Existent in the Old Testament but Ubiquitous in the New?" 65.

nations do have a greatly eschatological view of the inclusion of the nations in salvation (Isa 66:23, 45:14, 60:5, 2:2-3; Zech 8:20-23, 2:11; Mic 7:12).⁴⁶ But that does not dismiss the fact that God also gives these promises in the present for the people of Israel. Isaiah 49:6 again reaffirms this truth, stating again that God desires the worship and salvation of the nations "to the end of the earth." God has made and fashioned a people into his likeness in order that the lost and blind of the world might come to know him and worship him. God anchors this truth in the fact that his name is above every name: he reserves his glory for no other and all praise belongs to him alone.

Jonah: A Pattern of Old Testament Mission?

Throughout the last few decades some scholars have viewed the book of Jonah as the key portion of the Old Testament concerning the theme of mission. For example, John Bright speaks of Jonah saying, "No sterner attack on smug exclusiveness, no more ringing challenge to Israel to take up her world mission, could be imagined than the little book of Jonah."⁴⁷ In this view the book of Jonah should be understood as a foundational basis for Israel's responsibility to share the gospel with the nations, which makes this passage incredibly convenient as a "precursor" to the explicit evangelistic mission found in the New Testament.⁴⁸ However, these viewpoints overstep the scope and purpose of the book and seem to read too much into the text. This is unfortunate because the book of Jonah does have a unique contribution to understanding mission in the Old Testament and in redemptive history.

The main reason why these other viewpoints miss the mark in their estimation of the meaning of the book of Jonah concerning mission is that the idea of explicit evangelistic activity to the Gentiles is depicted in the book as a non-typical concept. In other words, the book of Jonah gives the

---

⁴⁶ Scobie, "The Nations," 518-520.
⁴⁷ John Bright, *The Kingdom of God in Bible and Church*, (London: Lutterworth, 1955), 162-163. For a similar viewpoint see also: R. E. Hedlund, *The Mission of the Church in the World: A Biblical Theology* (Grand Rapids: Baker, 1991), 126.
⁴⁸ Köstenberger and O'Brien, 44.

impression that this kind of mission to Gentiles was both rare and unexpected in the Jewish community of Jonah's day. Jonah is one of the only detailed prophetic books focused on a prophet sent not to preach to Israel but to Gentiles with the hope of their salvation (1:1; 4:2). This is possibly one reason why Jonah's initial response to God's command is not swift obedience but fleeing and a reluctance to preach to the Assyrians (1:3). The whole prophecy itself holds together, in one sense, in the fact that what happens in Jonah's life is contrary to what the Jewish readers would have expected. Therefore, the book of Jonah should not be viewed as an account detailing Israel's duty to evangelizing the nations, nor should Jonah the prophet be seen as a "missionary whose preaching to Nineveh (even if for tragic reasons) is intended to serve as a paradigm for Israel's outreach to the nations."[49]

What, then, exactly is the book of Jonah's unique contribution to the theme of mission if it is not to provide guidance for the aforementioned reasons? To begin with, the purpose of the book of Jonah is to probe the question God raises in 4:11: "Should I not be concerned about that great city?" This question key is in understanding the book, for "The Lord's willingness to save Nineveh (cf. 4:2) shows that his *hesed* ('covenant love') cannot be predicted or confined to Israel."[50] Though Jonah reluctantly obeys God in the end, the Gentiles of Nineveh surprisingly respond in repentance as a result of hearing his preaching. The same grace God repeatedly showed time and time again to Israel he desires to show to those in Nineveh. What this all amounts to is that God desires that his love reaches beyond ethnic Israel. He desires to reconcile people from all over the world to himself, which corresponds to the promised blessing in his covenant with Abraham (Gen. 12:3). Jonah should not be viewed as an explicit precursor for the New Testament's Great Commission, but it should be viewed as an anticipatory narrative that points to God's fulfilling of his promises for blessing the nations.

---

[49] Köstenberger and O'Brien, 45.
[50] Ibid.

Putting the Pieces Together

So why focus on the Old Testament relationship between Israel and the nations? Simply put, in order to understand what God has done and is doing in his redemptive story concerning mission in the Old Testament, the focus upon Israel and her interactions with the nations reveals the future hope of global salvation. Although we find strong passages that describe God's coming judgment upon the nations for their wickedness, we also find a consistent and powerful thread that points forward to God's ingathering of the nations into his covenant people. Indeed, this thread is central to the story of the Bible. Though Israel is commanded to worship God and live distinctly before the surrounding pagan nations, they are also commanded to proclaim God's mighty acts of salvation to them and to rejoice when the foreigner turns to the God of Israel. But all of this is contextualized within the prophetic witness of the Psalms and prophets, which reveal that one day a global unification under God's salvation will come. And it is promised through a future king in the line of the Davidic rule, a ruler who will have dominion over all the earth and over all peoples. This coming king, the Messiah, will deliver Israel from her suffering and will provide salvation for all those who bow the knee to him and confess him as their sovereign Lord.

The implicit call to be a light to the nations hearkens back to God's initial love and desire for the nations, the same desire that he revealed in Genesis 3–12. We also know that the Old Testament teaches that God's promise to bless the nations through Abraham would one day be revealed in "the Servant of the Lord" who will bring the good news of salvation to the Gentiles and carry out justice for the nations (Isa 54:1–2, 52:10, 61:1–2).[51] This brings us to the apex of the development of mission to the nations: the life, ministry, death, and resurrection of Jesus Christ. Indeed, Jesus's entering into redemptive history as a man becomes the center of all human history. All the Old Testament texts discussed so far point toward him, and he is the one in whom the eschatological hope for the ingathering of the nations lies.

---

[51] Köstenberger, "Nations," 677.

MISSION IN THE GOSPELS AND ACTS

Matthew and Luke: The Witness of Christ's Ministry

As mentioned before, Jesus's entering into the realm of men in the form of a man is the ultimate revelation and fulfillment of God's plan of redemption. And when one considers the development of the theme of mission, it must be firmly understood that the New Testament unquestionably views Christ as the sure fulfillment of anticipated blessing to the nations (Abrahamic covenant) and the servant who will bring salvation to the world (messianic texts of Psalms and Isaiah).[52] And according to these prophetic accounts, we know that Christ has authority over all creation. It is in this context that we find the first major texts in the New Testament and in the life of Christ that come to bear on the theme of the mission and bring God's plan from Genesis into effect on the rest of human history.

After Christ's resurrection and immediately before his ascension to the right hand of the Father, Christ gathers the apostles and the other disciples around him and gives final words of instruction that will become the guiding mission of the newly adopted people of God, what the rest of the New Testament writers would recognize as the *church*. Matthew 28:18–20 says:

> And Jesus came and said to them, "All authority in heaven and on earth has been given to me. Go therefore and make disciples of all nations, baptizing them in the name of the Father and of the Son and of the Holy Spirit, teaching them to observe all that I have commanded you. And behold, I am with you always, to the end of the age."

---

[52] Köstenberger, "Nations," 677; see discussion on how Christ is the fulfillment of the key Old Testament that we have discussed so far. We will discuss this development soon taking up Galatians 3:7–9.

This text is the pinnacle of the NT in showing God's purpose for the church's role 1) in the world, 2) in redemptive history, and 3) for the nations/gentiles (see also Matt. 24:14). But as discussed earlier, this is vastly different from Israel's role in the Old Testament because this is a clear and *explicit* call to go to the nations for the sake of seeing non-Jews come to salvation.

Furthermore, Christ spoke to confirm that he is the fulfillment of God's promised blessing for the nations in Luke 24:44–49, and as a result received dominion over all things:

> Then he said to them, "These are my words that I spoke to you while I was still with you, that everything written about me in the Law of Moses and the Prophets and the Psalms must be fulfilled." Then he opened their minds to understand the Scriptures, and said to them, "Thus it is written, that the Christ should suffer and on the third day rise from the dead, and that repentance for the forgiveness of sins should be proclaimed in his name to all nations, beginning from Jerusalem. You are witnesses of these things. And behold, I am sending the promise of my Father upon you. But stay in the city until you are clothed with power from on high."

This new movement in redemptive history represents the fulfillment of the Old Testament Jews' anticipation for the eschatological inclusion of the nations into the people of God. Because of Christ's life, death, and resurrection, the Old Testament promises to Adam and Eve in Genesis 3, to Abraham in Genesis 12, and to David through the Davidic covenant and in the Psalms move from a prophetic future promise to a present reality.

It is also important to note that God is doing something very similar through Christ that he also did through the covenant people of Israel. In the Old Testament, God established Israel for the ultimate purpose of magnifying his wonderful works and to reflect his holiness and glory in the world.[53] In the New

---

[53] J. G. Millar, "People of God," in *New Dictionary of Biblical Theology* (IVP, 2000), 684.

Testament and beyond, God saves and molds Christians in order that they may make other Christ followers throughout the world. This is a heightening, if you will, of God's already outward-looking formation of his people. This is all for the ultimate purpose of the glory of God: that all the rightful worship and praise in the universe might be to God.

The Early Church: Acts 15:1–29

The Jerusalem Council in Acts 15:1–29 is a major point in redemptive history concerning the nations. The apostles and leaders of the early church recognized and understood that Christ's work for salvation undoubtedly is for all peoples. The contention in this passage, however, centers on whether or not one must submit to the Mosaic law (particularly circumcision) in order to become a follower of Christ and to have fellowship with the people of God. This event in particular represented a turning point for the Jewish Christians who were seeking to understand Christ's inclusion of the Gentiles. This key portion of the text in the words of Peter, found in verses 7–11, clearly shows that Christ's saving of the Gentiles does not render them responsible for the law:

> After there had been much debate, Peter stood up and said to them, "Brethren, you know that in the early days God made a choice among you, that by my mouth the Gentiles would hear the word of the gospel and believe. And God, who knows the heart, testified to them giving them the Holy Spirit, just as he also did to us; and he made no distinction between us and them, cleansing their hearts by faith. Now therefore why do you put God to the test by placing upon the neck of the disciples a yoke which neither our fathers nor we have been able to bear? But we believe that we are saved through the grace of the Lord Jesus, in the same way as they also are."

Peter leaves no doubt that the Gentiles are not justified by any work of the Mosaic law but by the saving grace of God through the faith of every true believer.⁵⁴ Therefore, the demand of the Pharisees that these new believers become Jewish proselytes is completely contrary to the work of Christ. And to push the point even further, James reiterates this point explaining how this proper belief in salvation by grace through faith is the perfect fulfillment of the Old Testament (Amos 9:11–12). We can conclude from this text that 1) the gospel inclusion of the Gentiles is not only biblical but is a crucial part of the Old Testament's prophetic eschatological message concerning the salvation of people from all nations, and 2) that true faith in Jesus Christ is by grace alone for all peoples, both apart from works and circumcision. The human heart is at issue more than completing good works or maintaining the ritual components of the law.⁵⁵

MISSION IN PAUL: THE APOSTLE TO THE GENTILES

When considering the New Testament and the era of the newly inaugurated new covenant, no one individual other than Jesus Christ has had more impact upon the Christian understanding of mission than the apostle Paul. The apostle Paul has long been considered "the apostle to the Gentiles" due to his unique role in the infancy of the Christian faith in proclaiming the good news of Jesus Christ to those outside the Jewish community. Indeed, this tradition began with Paul himself, who first described himself as an "apostle to the Gentiles" (Rom 11:13). In fact, it would not be an overstatement to say that this was the defining mark of Paul's ministry. It could also be said that Paul's ministry was one of the primary means by which Gentiles were brought to faith in Jesus Christ, and his epistles are still today leading people to faith in Christ. The writings of Paul have been foundational for evangelicals all around the

---

[54] Eckhard J. Schnabel, *Acts*, Zondervan Exegetical Commentary on the New Testament (Grand Rapids, MI: Zondervan, 2012), 653.
[55] Schnabel, *Acts*, 654–655.

world ever since the Protestant Reformation as well, since it is in his writings that the gospel of justification by faith alone in Christ alone apart from both works and *ethnicity* is most clearly described and celebrated. One cannot help but recognize Paul's zeal for Gentile believers while reading through his letters. This theme is notably shown in Paul's repeated emphasis on the "mystery" revealed in the gospel, which is the gospel to the Gentiles (cf. Rom 16:25-26; Eph 3:1-6; Col 1:24-28). In texts like these Paul speaks of his ministry to the Gentiles as not just as a fulfillment of God's calling on his life but also as a fulfillment of God's promises in the Old Testament. In other words, these passages testify a continuity with all the Bible.

Knowing how important this mission to the Gentiles was for Paul's ministry and that he saw it in conjunction with both the Old Testament and Christ's work on the cross, how exactly did he understand this reality? Or put another way, how did Paul envision his gospel-preaching to the Gentiles as a *necessary* fulfillment and conclusion of the life, death, and resurrection of Jesus Christ and of the teachings of Old Testament Israel? Why did Paul seem to believe that the cultural identity boundaries that had separated Jew and Gentile for so long no longer mattered within his vision of God's redeeming purposes? Related to this question is the continuity of the Old Testament: was gospel-mission to the Gentiles an entirely new phenomenon or a timely completion of what God had planned all along?

Questions such as these are crucial for Christians to answer rightly if they are to have a robust biblical theological understanding of missions and the nature of the church. Understanding the biblical foundations of Paul's mission to the Gentiles will help Christians better understand the relationship between Jews and Gentiles in the Old Testament as well as how they should understand mission in terms of their relationship with non-Christians. The objective of this section is to 1) present a coherent understanding of Paul's development of the "mission" theme, 2) provide a thorough, though not comprehensive, view of Paul's understanding of mission to the Gentiles. This is not intended to present the specific nuances of every text within Pauline literature concerning the mission theme. However, the hope is that by looking at several of the major passages from Paul's letters we might better grasp Paul's essential thought concerning mission to the Gentiles.

The following exposition of texts is organized by content rather than chronology or book. The reason for this is to present and explain the most significant texts for this discussion. The intent is not to provide a comprehensive treatment of Paul's development of this theme but simply to put forward the most clear and helpful passages from Paul's letters. After doing so, the hope is to see a critical portion of the "final chapter" in Scripture's elaboration on mission to the Gentiles, which is the "already not yet" reality of the age to come until Christ's second coming.

Romans 10:5–21

Romans 10:5–21 is a fundamental text for understanding Paul's explanation of mission to the Gentiles. As in all of his letters, Paul firmly grounds his claims in evidence from the Old Testament. This is important to recognize because he is not merely making these arguments based on his own thinking; rather, he is seeking to establish a thoroughly biblical understanding of his topic. Though this passage breaks down into two subunits (5–13 and 14–21), it holds together in its Old Testament foundations regarding 1) salvation through faith and 2) faith that comes from hearing the gospel preached.

Before diving into the passage's significance for our discussion concerning mission, some text analysis is necessary to better understand Paul's flow of thought. Verse 5 begins with a γάρ clause, which serves as a grounding for verse 4. More than likely, though, the γάρ grounds all the content in verses 5–8 to verse 4, which clarifies how Christ is the "end of the law...to everyone who believe."[56] Paul's interpretation of the Old Testament texts here is quite difficult to understand on the surface, specifically the relationship between verse 5

---

[56] See Joseph A. Fitzmyer, *Romans: A New Translation with Introduction and Commentary*, Anchor Bible (New York: Doubleday, 1993), 587; and Thomas R. Schreiner, *Romans*, Baker Exegetical Commentary on the New Testament (Grand Rapids: Baker, 1998), 550.

and verses 6–8.⁵⁷ The most convincing reading is that Paul is simply contrasting the righteousness that comes from faith in Christ and the righteousness that comes from obedience to the law. Paul does not deny that obeying the law perfectly will lead to eternal life and righteousness. Rather, he implies that it is impossible for any man to do so (e.g. Rom 2:1–3:20). Therefore, the contrast is not that the law is bad but that no human being will be justified before God based on his or her adherence to the law. This is why Paul continues in verses 6–8 to explain that no human being will be saved through their own efforts to bring about what only God can do: only God has the power to bring the Messiah to earth and raise him from the dead, which is the purpose of Paul's Old Testament citations here. So the difference between righteousness from the law and righteousness from faith is the difference between "do" and "done." The way to salvation is not to work for God's approval but to respond in faith to what God has already done through Christ.

Verses 9–13 serve to further explain the nature of this faith mentioned in verse 8, which is in God rather than works of the law. Paul explains that true faith demands proclaiming Christ as Lord and belief that he was raised by the Father on the third day.⁵⁸ Verse 10 also clarifies that belief in the heart precedes confession with one's mouth, but the two together are necessary in order to be saved. Paul grounds this in the reality of the final judgment in verse 11, quoting Isa. 26:16, where all will stand before God to give an account. Paul affirms that only those who express genuine faith in Christ will be saved. It is at this point in the text where Paul's focus shifts to the implications of salvation being grounded in faith rather than works, and it is here that these implications aid our understanding of mission in Paul.

In verses 11–13 Paul reintroduces the same Old Testament quotation used in Rom 9:33, but here he adds the word πᾶς.

---

⁵⁷ See Schreiner, *Romans*, 551–560, for a general discussion of the different views on how to interpret this relationship. The most likely understanding, as stated above, is that Paul is refuting the notion that "the law is the source of life" (Schreiner, 555). Or in other words, seeking to attain eternal life and righteousness through perfect adherence to the laws demands is vain.

⁵⁸ Schreiner, *Romans*, 550.

The introduction of this concept at this point in the argument demonstrates the universality of Paul's gospel. Up to this point Paul has contrasted righteousness by faith in Christ with righteousness from works of the law, the law that was given to the Jews. Verse 11, however, shatters any idea that salvation belongs exclusively to the Jews. Verses 12-13 reaffirm this, beginning with another γάρ clause, where Paul explains what he means by "everyone." Bringing back the concept of "distinction" from earlier in the letter (cf. 3:22-23, 29-30), Paul rejects the notion of any kind of superiority in salvation. God's choosing of Israel in the past certainly led many to see a distinction concerning salvation, but Paul counters that there is one basis for salvation for both Jews and Gentiles. He grounds this claim in the reality that there is one Lord over all people: "Since the same Lord is Lord over all, then, both Jews and Gentiles are all equally beneficiaries of his lordship."[59] Paul grounds all of this in verse 13, once again, in the truth of the Old testament that all who call on the Lord in faith will be saved (LXX Joel 3:5). Appealing to the context of this passage, Paul is more than likely showing that he is not introducing some new doctrine that negates all God's works among Israel in the Old Testament. He, rather, is showing that this universality of the gospel is an eschatological fulfillment of what God has planned all along.

This brings us to the significance of this passage for the theme of mission. The natural progression from Paul's explanation of salvation is *how* faith comes about. Verses 14-21 reveal that belief in the gospel comes from hearing the gospel preached, and the gospel is preached when those who believe it are sent to the lost. The context here, though, is surrounding the gospel news that the Gentiles are now included in the promises of God. In verses 16-21 Paul argues that Israel's unbelief in the gospel has long been foreseen and that the inclusion of the Gentiles should have been anticipated. The seemingly implicit statement here, then, is that the reluctance of the Jews to embrace the gospel reveals an ignorance of God's plan all along.

Though it may not seem to be on the surface, this passage is foundational for understanding mission in Paul. There are

---

[59] Schreiner, *Romans*, 561.

several ways that this can be teased out, but there are a few important reasons why this text matters for mission. First, Paul affirms in this text the universal nature of saving faith throughout all of Scripture. As stated above, Paul views this as an Old and New Testament reality. Salvation is by faith in what God has done and no human being will be saved by their own works of the law. Paul applies this truth directly to the conflict between Jews and Gentiles and shows that both Jews and Gentiles are saved on the same basis, namely faith in Jesus Christ (vv. 11–12).

Second, saving faith comes from hearing the gospel preached, and this is true for all people. Paul's understanding that the gospel was intended to be preached and shared to all was based in part on the fact that faith only comes from hearing the gospel. Verses 14–15 are the natural outflow of verses 9–11. Though it is tempting to view this passage (especially verses 14–15) as a special defense of mission to the Gentiles,[60] the focus is still upon "πᾶς," thus emphasizing that all come to faith from hearing the gospel.[61] Because no exclusive group comes to faith apart from hearing the gospel proclaimed, mission to the Gentiles is a necessary part of God's plan as well as Paul's flow of thought.

Third and finally, mission to all people and not just ethnic Israel is a reality foreseen in the Old Testament (vv. 18–21). Paul argues in this text that the Jews should have anticipated the ingathering of Gentiles into the people of God. Quoting the Old Testament, he shows that God had always intended to have people from all the earth to worship Him because God is over all. Though Israel's unbelief in the gospel is lamented here, Paul clarifies later on in Romans that God has utilized the stubbornness and rejection of ethnic Israel in order to engraft the Gentiles into the people of God (Rom 11:11–12).

---

[60] James D. G. Dunn, *Romans 9–16*, Word Biblical Commentary, 38b (Dallas: Word Books, 1988), 620 takes this approach. Though he is not wrong in asserting this has special implications for the Gentiles, the focus contextually is on the fact that both Jews and Gentiles receive salvation through hearing.

[61] Thus, E. Käsemann, *Commentary on Romans*, translated and edited by G. W. Bromiley (Grand Rapids: Eerdmans, 1980), 294; and Schreiner, 566.

Romans 15:8–12

Romans 15:8–12 on the surface does not seem to be particularly relevant for Paul's understanding of mission. Yet, within this section lies wonderful truths concerning the basis for Paul's missionary theology and how we should understand the people of God. This text is key in that it links the preaching of the gospel to Gentiles directly with the Old Testament.

Verses 8–9 function as the ground for Paul's previous command in verse 7, where Paul commands his readers to accept one another just as Christ has accepted them.[62] Many commentators also view verses 7–13 as summary of important themes of the letter,[63] though for our purposes verses 8–12 will be the focus. In verse 8 Paul explains that Christ fulfilled the will of God the Father in order to 1) preserve the truth of God by fulfilling His promises to the patriarchs and 2) cause Gentiles all over the world to glorify God according to His mercy. Upon further investigation, however, it is apparent that these purposes are grammatically and theologically connected in the text. It is clear from passages concerning Abraham in the Old Testament that these covenantal promises included the Gentiles rather than excluded them (Gen 12:3; 18:18; 22:18; 26:4). By nature, then, if these promises are to Abraham and the rest of the patriarchs, they also include peoples from the whole world. [64] The Gentiles, then, would also necessarily be included into God's mercy, which He lavishes on all His people. This is indicated by the word "mercy" (ἐλέους) in verse 9, which also echoes covenantal language and suggests a correlation of mercy to the Gentiles and the Old Testament.[65]

In the remaining section of verses 9–12, Paul offers up Old Testament references that support his previous claim that both Jews and Gentiles are beneficiaries of the same covenant. This is reaffirmed by the καθὼς at the end of verse 9. Though there is no space to break down each of these references individually,

---

[62] Schreiner, 753.
[63] Fitzmyer, *Romans*, 705–706.
[64] Schreiner, 756.
[65] Leon Morris, *The Epistle to the Romans*, Pillar New Testament Commentary (Grand Rapids: Eerdmans, 1987), 504–505.

their implications for this passage are significant. First, the worshipping of Jews and Gentiles together in a harmonious manner stands as a visible fulfillment of God's Old Testament promises that one day people from all the world would gather as God's people for the purpose of worshipping Him (Ps 22:27-31; Zech 2:11; Isa 2:2-4).[66] Second, the Gentiles' joining in with the Jews in worship of God fulfills specific messianic prophecies that further point to God's salvific purposes for the Gentiles (e.g. Isa 11:10).

The overall importance for this passage as a whole for the theme of mission in Paul is that it firmly grounds Paul's preaching of the gospel to the Gentiles in the teachings of the Old Testament. Indeed, often Paul cites the Old Testament directly to describe his ministry to the Gentiles (see Rom 10:11-15 where Paul cites Isa 52:7). It is overwhelmingly apparent that "Paul saw his labors as a missionary to the Gentile world as grounded squarely in the Old Testament vision of salvation of the nations in accordance with the promises of the Abrahamic covenant."[67] Indeed, "the Old Testament quotations strung together in verses 9-12 show that in Christ God had opened up his covenant promises to Gentiles."[68] For Paul, preaching the gospel to the Gentiles was not simply due to his unique apostolic calling. As his understanding of Christ's place in the historical timeline exemplifies (see Rom 9-11), his ministry was based in God's salvific plan for the Gentiles, which was anchored in the truths of the Old Testament and the expectations of Old Testament authors.

Ephesians 3:1-11

One of the most interesting themes throughout all Pauline literature is Paul's elaboration upon the concept of "the

---

[66] Morris, *The Epistle to the Romans*, 505; and Schreiner, 757.

[67] See note 13 in Robert L. Reymond, *Paul Missionary Theologian: A Survey of his Missionary Labours and Theology* (Geanies House, Fearn, Ross-shire, Scotland: Christian Focus, 2000), 310.

[68] Köstenberger and O'Brien, 165; and Köstenberger, "Mission," 666-667.

mystery of Christ" or "mystery" with respect to the gospel. [69] The book of Ephesians specifically has often been referred to by scholars as the "epistle of mystery," because that term is mentioned six times throughout the letter.[70] Ephesians 3:1–11, however, presents the most comprehensive outworking of Paul's development of this theme in all the New Testament. Paul's main purpose in this passage is to inform his readers of the stewardship of the gospel God has given him, namely concerning this mystery that was for generations unknown but has now been revealed.

Though much could be said here exegetically, for there are rich gems here to be mined, it will be most helpful to investigate the nature of this mystery that Paul is stressing. For at the heart of this mystery lies also a key to better understanding Paul's mission to the Gentiles. This mystery (τὸ μυστήριον) is first mentioned in verse 3, and Paul begins by explaining the relationship between God's making him a steward of the work God has given him and "the mystery" God has revealed to him.[71] First, he expounds that God has revealed this mystery to him not as a result of human wisdom. Second, Paul argues that this mystery had long been unknown until God had revealed it to the apostles, undoubtedly a reference to the revelation of Jesus Christ. Third, Paul describes the content of this mystery.[72] The essential content of this message is that Jewish and Gentile believers have become one through the saving power of the gospel. They both have become equal partakers of the promises of God's covenant people. Paul speaks of this union in terms of its dawning in redemptive history. "God has revealed a new and definitive stage in his eternal plan that involves creating a people for himself consisting of Jews and Gentiles united to Christ and joined to one another."[73] Paul precedes and follows

---

[69] Col 1:26–27, 2:2, 4:3; Rom 11:25, 16:25; Eph 1:9, 6:19; 1 Tim 3:16.

[70] Peter T. O'Brien, "Mystery," in *Dictionary of Paul and His Letters* (Downers Grove, IL: InterVarsity Press, 1993), 622.

[71] Frank Thielman, *Ephesians*, Baker Exegetical Commentary on the New Testament (Grand Rapids: Baker, 2010), 189.

[72] The previous description of the sequence of the passage originates from Thielman, *Ephesians*, 189.

[73] Clinton E. Arnold, *Ephesians*, Exegetical Commentary on the New Testament (Grand Rapids: Zondervan, 2010), 180.

these points with the assertion that God has made Paul a vessel and apostle of the truth out of pure grace toward him, for Paul is to be considered no one among the saints (vv. 2, 7–8). In vv. 9–11 Paul reaffirms that he has been called to illuminate for all people the truth of the mystery, which has been accomplished and revealed through the person of Jesus Christ.[74]

The significance for mission in this text, then, is that through the gospel of Jesus Christ, which was anticipated in the Old Testament and realized in the life, death, and resurrection of Jesus, Gentiles now can commune with God. They commune with God alongside the Jews, for there is no distinction.[75] So it seems that in Paul's framework, if Jesus is truly the Messiah and anyone who professes faith in Him can receive eternal life from the Father, it is a logical step to assert that Jesus's message of hope through faith and repentance should be proclaimed among both Jews and Gentiles. Or in other words, assuming there is a command to preach the gospel at all, Paul's understanding shows the necessity of preaching to both Jews and Gentiles.[76] Paul seems to argue this very thing also in Rom 16:25–27.

Colossians 1:25–27, Rom 16:25–26, and Gal 1:15–16 further clarify this mystery of Christ, of which Paul was made a steward. These passages indicate that Paul has been made a minister of the gospel by God's grace in order to see that this mystery be made known among all the Gentiles. Paul understood that this mystery was the "eschatological revelation that now Jews and Gentiles alike were gathered together into one body, the church."[77]

Galatians 3:7–9

Before meeting with the other apostles and elders at the council in Jerusalem, Paul wrote the letter to the Galatians. In it we find an extremely pivotal passage concerning the people of God and the nations. Galatians 3:7–9 states:

---

[74] Benjamin L. Merkle, *Ephesians,* Exegetical Guide to the Greek New Testament (Nashville: B&H, 2016), 94–96.
[75] Arnold, *Ephesians,* 202.
[76] See. Matt. 28:18–20.
[77] Köstenberger and O'Brien, 258.

> Know then that it is those of faith who are the sons of Abraham. And the Scripture, foreseeing that God would justify the Gentiles by faith, preached the gospel beforehand to Abraham, saying, "In you shall all the nations be blessed." So then, those who are of faith are blessed along with Abraham, the man of faith.

If one stops to think about this passage, it contains a startling truth: God's promise to Abraham was to be ultimately fulfilled in the *nations*. The reason this is startling is the same reason the Jews in John 8 could not understand why Jesus boldly declared that they were not sons of Abraham but of the devil. The Jews had always viewed themselves as the true sons of Abraham, and ethnically this is true. But what Christ teaches us in that passage and what Paul is teaching here is that one's ethnic heritage, obedience to the Mosaic and ritual laws, or any other merit-based effort do not entail genuine faith in God or genuine sonship in Abraham. Children of Abraham have faith in God like Abraham did, for Abraham was counted righteous before the giving of the law.[78] The true sons of Abraham are the ones who have the faith of Abraham, and it is through faith in Jesus Christ that all the nations are blessed in Abraham.

But this has significant implications for how we interpret the meaning of the word "Israel." The New Testament speaks of the church as the "Israel of God" (Gal 6:16), or in another way the new Israel of God. Recognizing that the nation of Israel was the people of God in the Old Testament, the New Testament writers viewed the Christian church not as a replacement of the people of God in the Old Testament but a fulfillment and eschatological completion of God's plan from the beginning (Matt 19:28; Luke 22:30; Heb 4:9).[79] So in one sense there is a strong typological relationship between the Christian church and Old Testament Israel. Israel was a type of God's people to come: whereas Israel was an unfinished and small portion of God's chosen people, Christians represent the full people of God from all corners of the earth. In the same way the term

---

[78] Thomas R. Schreiner, *Galatians*, Zondervan Exegetical Commentary on the New Testament (Grand Rapids, MI: Zondervan, 2010), 193.
[79] Millar, "The People of God," 686.

"nations" also has a typological shift. The nations in the Old Testament represented those who were other from the Israelites, who lacked the holiness and religion of the one true God. In the New Testament and beyond the nations are those around the globe who have not accepted the gift of salvation by placing their faith in Jesus Christ alone, and so they cannot take part in the redemption of God. The shift in mission to the nations by the people of God, however, also experienced a heightening from the Old Testament to the New: what was once an implicit call to evangelize the unbeliever has become an explicit imperative for Christian believers.

But in another sense, the true Israel as Paul describes here in Galatians 3 has always been present in the people of God. Across the history of the earth and of redemption righteousness by faith has always been the only way to salvation in God. Old Testament saints were not saved by their works, as one might think, and New Testament Christians are saved by faith in Christ. Paul clearly demonstrates here that Abraham was not justified by earning God's favor by works. So it is by faith in both the Old Testament and in the New that we are made right with God.[80] The true Israel has always been justified by faith, either by looking forward to the promised messiah or as Christians do today by looking back at Christ. There has always been one true Israel, one true people of God.

Concluding Mission in Paul

Though this exposition does not represent a completely comprehensive presentation of missional texts in Pauline literature, it does put forward the larger and more significant texts that reveal the backbone of Paul's understanding of mission to the Gentiles. Within these passages lie crucial truths that illuminate Paul's calling as the apostle to the Gentiles. They also give us the foundational theological reasons for understanding why the Gentile faith is even a possibility in a Jewish Messiah.

One of these foundational truths is that Paul's mission to

---

[80] Schreiner, *Galatians*, 196.

the Gentiles functions as a fulfillment of God's promises from ages past to form a unique people for Himself. Pauline mission to the Gentiles within these passages is deeply interwoven with the message of the Old Testament. As mentioned earlier concerning specific passages within Genesis and God's covenant with Abraham, the worldwide nature of all those who will worship God eschatologically simply cannot be denied. God's plan from the beginning, long before ethnic Israel had been established, was to bless all the nations of the world for the purpose of bringing Him glory. God planned for this to happen through the lineage of Abraham. But what these passages reveal is that God's fulfillment of this promise did not occur the way the Jews had anticipated. Instead of building up divisions between Jews and Gentiles, God united them together.

In one sense this misconception seems to be caused by an inability to understand the context in which Paul affirms this covenantal fulfillment. As briefly mentioned beforehand, Paul truly did view the ingathering of Gentiles into the people of God and his ministry as fulfillment of an eschatological reality.[81] Therefore, it must be noted that one of the keys to understanding mission in Paul is to grasp that he connects preaching the gospel to the whole world with the second coming of Christ where Jesus will once and for all vindicate His people and destroy the evil one. This is important because it directly connects mission to the Gentiles (and Jews, for that matter) with the person of Jesus Christ and His personal mission as the Messiah. The two must be seen in tandem with one another.

It is not hard to see, then, some of the more important implications that these passages have for the church today in its understanding of mission to the Gentiles. First, because the church too remains in the "last days" ushered after the resurrection of Jesus, the work of mission around the world is also deeply eschatological. In other words, the church's mission today is focused on and looking to the second coming of Christ when Jesus will finally redeem all his people. The Christian work of mission is not a light or temporal thing: it is consumed with the weighty eternal task of seeking after souls to be rescued from God's wrath at the eschatological judgment and instead to

---

[81] Reymond, *Paul Missionary Theologian*, 529–530.

lead them to find life and joy in God. Just as Paul envisioned the gospel for every person despite race, ethnicity, or background because of Old Testament eschatological expectations, so too the church should view its preaching of the gospel. Though much time has passed since the New Testament era, the gospel of Jesus Christ remains the same and will remain the same until Christ's second coming. Second, the inclusion of the Gentiles does, indeed, represent a shift or heightening theologically. This is clear from these passages in how Paul refers to the mystery of the gospel (i.e., the uniting of the Gentiles and Jews into one covenant people of God) as formerly being unknown to many who had gone before but has now been revealed through Jesus Christ to the apostles and saints.

Third and finally, passages like these should cause those in the church, especially Gentile believers, to be humbled and awestruck at the grace of God. This mystery of the gospel that benefits both Jew and Gentile is purely by God's grace. There is nothing special about being a Gentile that impresses God (see Rom. 11:17–22). In fact, before Christ's coming, Gentiles were alienated from the people of God. Without Christ they are helpless. But Christ has come and He has made a way for Gentiles and Jews alike to receive salvation from the wrath of God at the coming judgment. The depth of the mercy and grace of God in these passages should cause the church to respond in no manner other than in repentance and faith, living lives of obedience to Jesus Christ.

THE CONSUMMATION OF GOD'S MISSION TO THE WORLD

The Goal of Mission: Revelation 5

Redemptive history concludes God's plan for the nations in the ultimate consummation of all things in the book of Revelation, where God will finish for all eternity the story he began in Genesis. In one of the most beautiful chapters in all of Scripture, God brings to a completion of every text we have discussed thus far and brings into reality the purpose he intended in the garden of Eden: the gathering of all creation and men from *every* nation eternally worshipping God. Revelation 5:8-9 says:

> When He had taken the book, the four living creatures and the twenty-four elders fell down before the Lamb, each one holding a harp and golden bowls full of incense, which are the prayers of the saints. And they sang a new song, saying, "Worthy are You to take the book and to break its seals; for You were slain, and purchased for God with Your blood *men* from every tribe and tongue and people and nation.

This is the manifestation/result of the promise of the gospel and the promise made to Abraham: all peoples of the earth gathered around the throne of God worshipping Him. The ultimate blessing of the nations, which God promised to Abraham is the eternal life of all who place their faith in God alone, and they will worship in the presence of God forever. And this is a result of salvation in Christ (the Lamb), who was from the beginning purposed for all the nations.

Although the fall of man in Genesis has resulted in pain, suffering, and bitter darkness in this world, the theme of mission in redemptive history gives Christians hope that God will 1) be faithful to His promises as he has time and again (e.g., in fulfilling the Abrahamic covenant, the Davidic covenant and through the life, death, and resurrection of Christ), and 2) one day reconcile all things to himself, including peoples from all nations of the earth. But this also reveals that mission is not the goal of redemptive history in itself. Mission is not and end but a means to an end: namely, "a total focus on the worship and the glory of God in our Lord Jesus Christ."[82] The perfect communion with God in the garden will be restored in the New Jerusalem for all eternity for those who belong to Christ.

---

[82] Köstenberger and O'Brien, 262.

THE VOTARY OF THE BLUE FLOWER: A HISTORICAL REFLECTION ON HOPE IN THE LIFE AND THOUGHT OF C.S. LEWIS

Seth Reid

I must keep alive in myself the desire for my true country, which I shall not find till after death; I must never let it get snowed under or turned aside; I must make it the main object of my life to press on to that other country and to help others to do the same.

–C.S. Lewis, *Mere Christianity*

Introduction: A Life of Hope

Early in his life, C.S. Lewis began to long in a way that gripped him for a lifetime. As a child, his longing was delightful but was elusive: he knew not what he longed for. It was also fickle: he could not just summon the longing whenever he liked. Despite not knowing what he longed for, he enjoyed the feeling of longing and he tried to trigger the feeling as often as he could. As he matured, his understanding of this longing and the possible object of the longing changed. He began to portray the object of his longing as being deeply real and solid. In his early thirties, in his conversion to Christianity, he recognized the object of his longing was God. In his conversion, his longing became fuller, taking on the firmer characteristics of hope. The portrayal of his hope continued to develop, being portrayed in his earlier Christian writings in primarily apologetic ways. His hope was still for something real and solid, but he knew it was God, the source of all reality. Another shift in portrayal came following a debate with Elizabeth Anscombe in 1948 when he started portraying his hope in more imaginative ways. As a child, C.S. Lewis longed for what he did not know through unbidden moments of romantic delight, but his longing matured into a romantic and rational hope for Christ to bring the solid and glorious New Creation where pain is redeemed, harmony is perfect, and people are united with God.

Lewis cared deeply for his longing and his Christian hope because they both connected him to a greater reality than merely the physical. In his longing, Lewis connected—albeit momentarily and in a vague manner—with a reality beyond himself. In his hope, Lewis connected with this greater reality by looking forward, past the merely physical, to the coming of this greater reality. This connection to a greater reality gave Lewis purpose, and therefore, the hope and longing were important to him. Further, Lewis's hope brought implications for his life and thought. Since his Christian hope was a fundamentally communal hope, involving many humans together moving towards God, his hope thus had implications for both the way he interacted with people and the way he thought about God, such as enabling him to properly grieve his wife's death and hoping for the redemption of sinful people before a just God.

There is substantial literature on C.S. Lewis's life and thinking, but a historical approach to the development of his hope is lacking. His biographers have done exceptional work chronicling Lewis's life and the shifts of his thinking. This thesis will draw particularly Alister McGrath's *C.S. Lewis: A Life* and Alan Jacobs's *The Narnian*. Further, Adam Barkman, in *C.S. Lewis & Philosophy As A Way of Life*, has done terrific work tracking the progress of his romantic longing and his rational thinking. His work, however, attempts to track them separately and does little work to place them in the context of Lewis's circumstances. Marc Watney's dissertation "Perplexed by Joy: Sehnsucht in C.S. Lewis's Pagan Writings" tracks the development of Lewis's longing from his childhood to early adulthood, but the scope of the work does not include Lewis's Christian life or writings. This thesis will fill this void in the literature, arguing that his romantic longing was an early form of his Christian hope and tracking the progression of this longing and hope within the context of his life's circumstances.

Youth: Beginning to Long

Lewis was born in 1898 in Belfast, Ireland. Before he was six, when he was still spending time in a nursery, he began to long for the hills beyond his nursery window—what he and his brother called the "Green Hills." They were not far, he later reflected, but they were out of reach for a young boy. Reflecting later, he wrote, "[the hills] made me for good or ill, and before I was six years old, a votary of the Blue Flower."[1] Lewis was invoking a symbol from the German Romantics, which, according to Michael Ferber, represented a "primordial harmonious realm, accessible only in a dream."[2] Presumably, Lewis did not know as a six-year-old that the blue flower was a symbol that stood for unattainable longing, but even at this young age, Lewis already had begun to long beyond his grasp.

Sometime later, Lewis had a sequence of three encounters with similar longing for the unknown and unattainable.[3] The first came on a summer day, when Lewis, standing beside a bush, was struck "as if from a depth not of years but of centuries" by the memory of his brother's toy garden. This toy garden was not much, but Lewis later wrote that as "long as I live my imagination of Paradise will retain something of my brother's toy garden."[4] This memory came with a sensation that Lewis, years later, had difficulty putting into words. The longing was triggered by the memory of the toy garden, but his longing was not for the toy garden. While not for the toy garden, the longing was also not for anything else Lewis could identify, and as quickly as the desire came, it was gone. "It had taken only a moment of time; and in a certain sense everything else that had ever happened to me was insignificant in comparison."[5] It was when he stared out the window to the "Green Hills" that Lewis first remembered longing, but this moment, by Lewis's reflection, played a different kind of role. It was here that he was first overwhelmed by longing and was delighted by it.

The second instance of what Lewis called "glimpses," came when he was reading *Squirrel Nutkin* by Beatrix Potter. The book sparked a longing for what he could only describe as "the

---

[1] C.S. Lewis, *Surprised by Joy: The Shape of My Early Life* (New York: Harcourt, Brace, 1956), 7.
[2] Michael Ferber, *A Dictionary of Literary Symbols* (Cambridge, UK: Cambridge University Press, 1999), 76.
[3] Lewis's autobiographical dating lacked precision in his early years.
[4] Lewis, *Surprised by Joy*, 7.
[5] Ibid., 16.

Idea of Autumn." He later reflected that "in this experience also there was the same surprise and the same sense of incalculable importance [as the surprise and importance of the longing that arose from the bush]."[6] He wrote that this feeling of longing was different from ordinary pleasure and something one might say was "in another dimension."[7] The longing was a glimpse at something not fully present or material.

The final encounter came when Lewis was reading Henry Wadsworth Longfellow's translation of the Swedish poet Esaias Tegner. Lewis read the words, "I heard a voice that cried, / Balder the beautiful / Is dead, is dead", and reflected that "I knew nothing of Balder, but instantly I was uplifted into huge regions of northern sky, [and] I desired with almost sickening intensity something never to be described (except that it is cold, spacious, severe, pale, and remote)." The moment passed just as quickly as the others, leaving him unable to reenter his longing.[8]

The delight of these encounters was not satisfaction, for there was none. Instead, it produced a longing that was itself delightful. After his encounters passed, he found himself not longing for satisfaction, but "longing for the longing."[9] This insatiable longing that concerned Lewis was not like other earthly desires. This desire had come without being summoned and left without being permitted. Alister McGrath writes that "as frustrating and disconcerting as they have been, they suggested to him that the visible world might only be a curtain that concealed vast, uncharted realms of mysterious oceans and islands."[10]

These experiences of desire came early in his life, perhaps age six to eight.[11] These images—the green hills beyond his nursery window, Lewis's brother's toy garden, the "idea of autumn," and "Balder the beautiful / is dead, is dead"—were Lewis's first

---

[6] Lewis, *Surprised by Joy*, 17.
[7] Ibid.
[8] Ibid., 16-17.
[9] Ibid.
[10] Alister E. McGrath, *A Life: Eccentric Genius, Reluctant Prophet;* (Carol Stream, Ill.: Tyndale House Publishers, 2013), 20.
[11] Lewis, *Surprised by Joy*, 15.

moments of romantic longing and, as Corben Carnell points out, were all before the death of his mother.[12] In his preface to the third edition of the *The Pilgrim's Regress*, Lewis defined his romanticism as a "particular recurrent experience which dominated my childhood and adolescence and which I hastily called 'Romantic' because inanimate nature and marvelous literature were among the things that evoked it."[13]

Adam Barkman argues that Lewis's romanticism was "the product of both his own personal experiences and, it can hardly be denied, the larger Romantic Movement."[14] This is evidenced by Lewis's own reflections on his early childhood. His moments of longing tended to come from reading a book (often in the vein of the Romantics) or a personal experience with nature. Yet, this longing would remain inexplicable until his conversion to idealism in the mid-1920s, and it would not be fully explained until his conversion to Christianity in 1932. In the meantime, he was delighted by the feeling of longing and wanted to recover it as often as he could.

The time when Lewis experienced these longings was a time of great stability for the Lewis family.[15] However, the stability of the Lewis home all but vanished on August 23, 1908 when Lewis's mother died. Lewis was only ten-years-old and with his mother's death, all "settled happiness, all that was tranquil and reliable" disappeared from his life.[16] The Lewis family also suffered the loss of C.S. Lewis's grandfather and uncle the same year. In the wake of three deaths, Albert Lewis, C.S. Lewis's father, failed to provide the stability and comfort his two sons needed. Instead of purposing the time following these deaths to be a time for family intimacy, Albert thought it was best to send his two sons away to school. Only two weeks after the death of Lewis's mother, Lewis was sent to Wyvern

---

[12] Corbin Scott Carnell, *Bright Shadow of Reality: C.S. Lewis and the Feeling Intellect* (Grand Rapids, Mich: Eerdmans, 1974), 36.

[13] C.S. Lewis, *The Pilgrim's Regress: An Allegorical Apology for Christianity, Reason, and Romanticism* (Grand Rapids, MI: Bantam Books, 1981), VII.

[14] Adam Barkman, *C.S. Lewis & Philosophy as a Way of Life: A Comprehensive Historical Examination of His Philosophical Thoughts* (Wayne, Pa.: Zossima Press, 2009), 73.

[15] McGrath, 21.

[16] Lewis, *Surprised by Joy*, 21.

Preparatory School in England, away from his home in Ireland and away from his father. Lewis had lost the stability and safety of his early childhood.

As a child, Lewis grew up in the Christian faith, but in his early teens, his affirmation of Christianity started to wane. When he was thirteen, while attending school at Wyvern Preparatory School, he was introduced to the occult. Lewis did not offer much information of what his encounters with the occult entailed, but he described it as a spiritual lust that, "like the lust of the body it has the fatal power of making everything else in the world seem uninteresting by comparison."[17] Lewis did not know where his romantic longing came from or what it was for, but he knew that it often arose in him when he read myths and fairy tales. In the occult, he found some of the same characters that he thought could only be found in fiction. Lewis, reflecting on this, wrote:

> I had loved to read of strange sights and other worlds and unknown modes of being, but never with the slightest belief; even the phantom dwarf had only flashed on my mind for a moment. It is a great mistake to suppose that children believe the things they imagine....But now, for the first time, there burst upon me the idea that there might be real marvels all about us, that the visible world might be only a curtain to conceal huge realms uncharted by my very simple theology.[18]

The idea that there was something beyond what he could see—that there was a curtain separating this world from a world of things unseen—was an idea that, unbeknownst to young Lewis, belonged to the Christian faith of his childhood. When he first encountered longing, he did not know what he was longing for, but when he was introduced to the occult, he began to contemplate the idea that there may be mysterious and glorious things that he could not see with his naked eye. The language he used to describe it is revealing: "...the visible

---

[17] Ibid., 60.
[18] Ibid., 59-60.

world might be only a curtain to conceal huge realms uncharted by my very simple theology."[19] In the occult, he was hoping for something more than what the visible world offered.

As a thirteen-year-old, there were two things working against Lewis's faith in Christianity. One was his fascination with the occult. Another was a "deeply ingrained pessimism." This pessimism was the opinion that the "universe was, in the main, a rather regrettable institution."[20] He attributed this pessimism to several things. Most prominently was the clumsiness of his hands, which gave Lewis a "sense of resistance or opposition on the part of inanimate things" or, as Lewis clarifies, a "settled expectation that everything would do what you did not want it to do." Another factor contributing to this pessimism was that, as a child, Lewis was told, or at least inferred, that "adult life was to be an unremitting struggle in which the best I could hope for was to avoid the workhouse by extreme exertion."[21] Finally, the books that Lewis read when he was young situated in his imagination "the vastness and cold of space, the littleness of Man."[22] The Christian idea that a sovereign and good God created and ruled the world seemed to Lewis to be contradictory to his experiences and understanding. Lewis further entertained the "Argument from Undesign," which argued that, if God did design the world, it would not be so "frail and faulty as we see." Lewis was becoming opposed to Christianity, partly due to this pessimism and partly due to his interactions with the occult.

Yet, these dual emphases of pessimism and the occult proposed a contradiction in Lewis's narrative. On one hand, he was obsessed with the occult—fascinated by the idea that there was some great mysterious force or reality lying beyond the eye's perception. On the other hand, he was also firmly pessimistic towards a higher being, which, presumably would be necessary for there to be some truth to the occult. Lewis acknowledged this paradox, and wrote: "I do not think I achieved any logical connection between [the 'Argument from Undesign' and his interactions with the occult]. They swayed me in different

---

[19] Lewis, *Surprised by Joy*, 60.
[20] Ibid., 63.
[21] Ibid., 64.
[22] Ibid., 65.

moods, and had only this in common, that both made against Christianity."[23] The "Argument from Undesign" represented, more broadly, his rational thinking and his interactions with the occult were a part of his attempts to recover romantic longing.

In his autobiography, Lewis left a gap of undefined time when he felt no care for his old romantic longing. The longing had disappeared from his life "so completely that not even the memory or desire of it remained."[24] Yet, when he was in the schoolroom at Wyvern, he glanced and saw the Christmas edition of *The Bookman* from December 1911, which featured the caption "Siegfried and the Twilight of the Gods" and an accompanying illustration by Arthur Rackham. Seeing this image and reading the caption, he found himself lifted up again into the old romantic longing which had for so long disappeared from his life. His romantic longing often hinged on memory. The longing was often experienced as a moment where Lewis remembered a feeling, but in the remembering itself he experienced a longing. In this moment, Lewis experienced "almost like a heartbreak, the memory of Joy [delightful romantic longing] itself, the knowledge that I had once had what I had now lacked for years, that I was returning at last from exile and desert lands to my own country." This moment sent him to a new terrain of imaginative thought, but in connection with the memory of his old imaginative thought.

This moment of longing caused Lewis to become enamored with "Northernness," as he named it. Northernness, for Lewis, was a catch-all word to describe Norse mythology, Wagnerian opera, and the northern skies. For Lewis, this Northernness became more important than anything else, and taught him what true religion ought to feel like. This love of Northernness led to "a reading of all the Norse mythology he could get a hold of... [and to] writing poems about Mime, Siglinde, and Fafner."[25] He spent his pocket money on recordings of Wagner's operas and bought "a copy of the original text from which the Rackham

---

[23] Ibid., 66.
[24] Ibid., 72.
[25] Carnell, 41.

illustrations had been extracted." [26] He spent the summers of 1912 and 1913 writing *Loki Bound,* a poem in Greek verse about the gods of Norse mythology.[27] His love of Northernness also taught him to love nature, which though initially tied to Northernness, developed to be independently valuable and later became a consistent reminder of his longing. His love for Northernness developed in secret, discussing it with his close confidant, Arthur Greeves, but otherwise it was a private longing which he attempted to separate from his public life.

When Lewis saw that image with the caption of "Siegfried and the Twilight of the Gods," his "secret, imaginative life began to be so important and so distinct" that when telling his life story, he had to tell two different stories. "Where there are hungry wastes, starving for Joy [his delightful and romantic longings], in the one, the other may be full of cheerful bustle and success; or again, where the outer life is miserable, the other may be brimming over with ecstasy." Until Lewis converted to Christianity, he lived in the tension of two different and imposing values. He attempted to live this tension by keeping his life of longing secret and the life of rational thought public. Lewis wrote that his was a "story of two lives. They have nothing to do with each other."[28] Lewis exaggerated here, but this point in his life is representative of the growing dualism he lived. His moments of longing were so intimate and hard to express that they were not often a part of his outward life. This dualism might have also been caused by his attempt to seem like a Christian to his father, while abandoning the faith himself. Simultaneously, he was beginning to wonder about the occult, something he could never acknowledge to his father. It is hard to determine how much of this dualism was brought about by Lewis's effort. The way that Lewis himself describes it is as primarily accidental, not intending to separate the intimate personal life from the external life, but his circumstances, unbeknownst to him, produced a dualistic life. It was a dualism he struggled with his entire life, but the origins of the struggle traced back to this time in Lewis's life.

---

[26] McGrath, 29.
[27] C.S. Lewis, *The Collected Letters of C.S. Lewis, Volume I: Family Letters 1905-1931,* ed. Walter Hooper (San Francisco: HarperSanFrancisco, 2004), 20.
[28] Lewis, *Surprised by Joy,* 119.

Studies with Kirkpatrick: The Tutor of Rationalism

His romantic longing and rational thought did not coexist in harmony. They rivaled each other, and in 1914, when Lewis was 16, he began an education that temporarily gave one the upper hand. Lewis had survived boarding schools, which he claimed were the darkest times of his life. After these schools, Lewis's father put him under the private tutelage of William Thompson Kirkpatrick. Kirkpatrick taught Lewis to rely on rationalism, only accepting arguments constructed within reason. Lewis was trained to have a defense for any claim he made. Marc Watney writes that Lewis, while under Kirkpatrick, was trying to bury "his implacable and inconsolable yearnings deep in his flesh, and face the world with a stoical indifference to both fairies and gods."[29] While he was still struggling to understand the longing he had felt in the past, Kirkpatrick taught Lewis to submit his experiences of longing to his supreme rationality. In the rivalry between romanticism and rationality, the latter gained a tutor in Kirkpatrick.

According to Lewis, Kirkpatrick "was great on *The Golden Bough.*"[30] *The Golden Bough* was Sir James Frazer's study of ancient religious practices and in it he argued that the "dying-god myths" found in religions simply developed out of the cycle of seasons. This emphasis of Kirkpatrick on *The Golden Bough* gave Lewis more ammunition against Christianity and undermined the importance of his romantic longing. It provided Lewis ammunition against Christianity by explaining away any validity to the "dying-god" myth of Christianity, in which Jesus, who claimed to be the son of God, died.

Simultaneously, however, the emphasis on *The Golden Bough* undermined his romantic longing. Besides the Christian "dying-god" myth, Lewis knew of one other, that of Balder, which he found full of meaning even if he had not believed it factually true. Balder was a Norse god and his myth concerned his dramatic death at the hands of another god. This was the myth

---

[29] Mark Cedric Watney, "Perplexed by Joy: Sehnsucht in C.S. Lewis's Pagan Writings: Spirits in Bondage (1919) and Dymer (1926)" (Dissertation, The University of Texas at Dallas, 2006), 21.
[30] Lewis, *Surprised by Joy*, 139.

that Lewis read of as a child that caused him to be "uplifted into huge regions of northern sky, [and] I desired with almost sickening intensity something never to be described." This myth was specifically attacked by Frazer in *The Golden Bough*. According to Alan Jacobs, "Frazer explores at great length his belief that the myth of Balder is closely associated with the many different 'fire-festivals' practiced throughout Europe; he comes to the conclusion that Balder is a personification of the oak tree."[31]

Likely, reading Frazer did not change any of Lewis's intellectual affirmations of the accuracy of the myth of Balder. Prior to reading Frazer, Lewis did not argue that Balder was true as an historical fact. However, Frazer was a direct assault on whether the myth of Balder had some greater meaning. Lewis was learning from a man "great on *The Golden Bough*" and *The Golden Bough* attacked the validity of Balder. As Lewis tried to compartmentalize these two emphases into separate parts of his life, an emphasis of romanticism and an emphasis of rationalism, the emphasis of rationalism began to attack the romantic value Lewis had for the myth of Balder.

The effect of this assault is seen in a letter Lewis wrote to Arthur Greeves just about a month after beginning his instruction with Kirkpatrick:

> You ask me my religious views: you know, I think that I believe in no religion.... All religions, that is, all mythologies to give them their proper name are merely man's own invention—Christ as much as Loki. Primitive man found himself surrounded by all sorts of terrible things he didn't understand—thunder, pestilence, snakes etc: what more natural than to suppose these were animated by evil spirits trying to torture him. These he kept off by cringing to them, singing songs and making sacrifices etc. Gradually from being mere nature—spirits these supposed being[s] were elevated into more elaborate ideas, such as the old gods: and when

---

[31] Alan Jacobs, *The Narnian: The Life and Imagination of C.S. Lewis* (San Francisco: HarperSanFrancisco, 2005), 48.

> man becomes more refined he pretended that these spirts were good as well as powerful.... Superstition of course in every age has held the common people, but in every age the educated and thinking ones have stood outside it, though usually outwardly conceding to it for convenience.[32]

This letter reveals Lewis's frame of mind in at least two ways. First, he used the term "mythology" here to dismiss the meaningfulness of religion. Not only are religions not true, they are more accurately called mythologies. This conflicted with the value Lewis had for northern myths. Lewis's rationality declared the myths he valued void of truth. Second, he accepted that the "common people" would be led astray by superstition, but he did not count himself among that group. He was not among the common people, but was of the "educated and thinking ones" who have stood outside it. And when he wrote that these educated people concede to the superstition "for convenience" he was speaking of himself, whether consciously or not; at this time, he was still putting on his façade of faith for his father. Lewis's time with Kirkpatrick was largely a time of sharpening his reason.

While he was a student of Kirkpatrick, Lewis was accepted to Oxford University. However, he did not spend much time at Oxford before being drafted into the British army to fight in "The Great War." Before he went off to war, Lewis made what he called a "treaty with reality." In effect, he told his country: "You shall have me on a certain date, not before. I will die in your wars if need be, but till then I shall live my own life. You may have my body, but not my mind. I will take part in battles but not read about them."[33] Whether he was fully successful in standing by this treaty, in keeping the war from affecting his mind, is difficult to determine. What does seem plain is that years later, reflecting on the war, Lewis believed he had stood by his treaty. Reflecting later on the whole of his experience in the war, including "the frights, the cold, the smell of H.E., the

---

[32] Lewis, *The Collected Letters of C.S. Lewis: Volume I*, 230-31.
[33] Lewis, *Surprised by Joy*, 158.

horribly smashed men still moving like half-crushed beetles, the sitting or standing corpses, the landscape of sheer earth without a blade of grass, the boots worn day and night till they seemed to grow to your feet," Lewis considered them all "in a way unimportant."[34]

Lewis's assessment is suspect for at least two reasons. First, in 1939, Lewis wrote in a letter to a friend: "My memories of the last war haunted my dreams for years. Military service, to be plain, includes the threat of *every* temporal evil... the flesh is weak and selfish and I think death [would] be much better than to live through another war."[35] Lewis was known to be reserved in commenting on his personal struggles; it is sensible, then, that Lewis would have attempted to disregard the importance of his time in war. Yet, the statement in this letter might give a glimpse at how deeply his time in combat affected him.

The second reason his assessment is suspect is because it was after the war that Lewis's writing began taking on a distinctive anger towards God. Lewis published *Spirits in Bondage: A Cycle of Lyrics* in 1920, shortly after returning from war. In this series of poems, Lewis talked of the pain of humanity and the massive destruction seen in war. His writing in these poems reveal two realities about Lewis's reaction to World War I. First, he was not as unaffected by war as he later wanted to portray himself. In his eleventh poem, *In Prison*, Lewis begins "I cried out for the pain of man / I cried out for my bitter wrath / Against the hopeless life...."[36] In the very next poem, Lewis seems to be thinking directly of his historical context and the effects of World War I.

> Four thousand years of toil and hope and thought
> Wherein man laboured upward and still wrought
> New worlds and better, Thou hast made as naught.

---

[34] Ibid., 196.
[35] C.S. Lewis, *The Collected Letters of C.S. Lewis, Volume II: Books, Broadcasts, and the War 1931-1949*, ed. Walter Hooper (San Francisco: HarperSanFrancisco, 2004), 258.
[36] C.S. Lewis, *Spirits in Bondage: A Cycle of Lyrics* (Champaign, Ill: Project Gutenberg, n.d. *eBook Collection (EBSCOhost)*, EBSCOhost (accessed November 14, 2017), 7.

> We built us joyful cities, strong and fair,
> Knowledge we sought and gathered wisdom rare.
> And all this time you laughed upon our care,
>
> And suddenly the earth grew black with wrong,
> Our hope was crushed and silenced was our song,
> The heaven grew loud with weeping. Thou art strong.
>
> Come then and curse the Lord. Over the earth
> Gross darkness falls, and evil was our birth
> And our few happy days of little worth.[37]

Before World War I, the idea was prevalent that humanity was getting better and more civilized. Given the advances of the Industrial Revolution, bringing food, shelter, and amenities to greater amounts of people than ever before, people began to think that ultimate progress in all things was possible. It was starting to seem that the economic pie could continually get bigger, and with it, the necessity of poverty and destitution would surely get smaller. If Lewis agreed with this idea before he went to war, it was thoroughly crushed in the trenches. World War I affected Lewis deeply and particularly affected his narrative of hope.

In these post-war poems, Lewis longed to escape to the western forests and to escape from the wrath of God. These were two different types of longings, although they were expressed together. In one, he longed to escape from the wrath of God and the horror of nature. This longing was his attempt to escape, and not firmly connected to his romantic longings of delight. Yet, what he longed to escape to was a form of his delightful longing. In longing for the western forests, there was delight. His romantic, delightful longings and God, in *Spirits in Bondage,* were in tension. If there was an object, it was not God, but for something other. He allowed that God might exist—a development from his avowed atheism under Kirkpatrick—but was sure that if God existed, he was completely

---

[37] C.S. Lewis, *Spirits in Bondage: A Cycle of Lyrics* (Champaign, Ill: Project Gutenberg, n.d. *eBook Collection (EBSCOhost),* EBSCO*host* (accessed November 14, 2017), 7.

evil. Lewis conveyed the central idea of the collection of poems in a letter to Greeves, writing that "nature is wholly diabolical & malevolent and that God, if he exists, is outside of and in opposition to the cosmic arrangements."[38] Yet, despite his growing animosity towards God, he still delighted in longing. "If you could flee away / Into some other country beyond the rosy West, / To hide in the deep forests and be for ever at rest / From the rankling hate of God and the outworn world's decay."[39] In this passage there was both delightful longings to be "beyond the rosy West…. for ever at rest", but there is also a longing to escape from God. The first is a precursor to his fuller Christian hope, while the second resists a theistic conversion.

In this passage, there seems to be a contradiction. On one hand, he wrote to Greeves that "nature is wholly diabolical," and yet on the other hand, he longed to "hide in the deep forests." For Lewis, there was a third category, that of Faery, which often felt like the things of nature, but had distinctive differences. Jacobs writes that he himself does "not know of anything harder to explain than the land of Faery."[40] Yet, Jacobs's explanation is helpful. The land of Faery is an alternative but similar Britain. Similar in that the land of Faery depends on the "gentleness of British landscapes—their greenness…their lack of outsize mountains or dramatic weather, their essential homeliness."[41] However, in the land of Faery, nature is sentient, taking on a will and power. There are fairies in the land of Faery, and they are simply "nature embodied in human or humanlike forms." But, above all, the land of Faery is a "world equally capable of enchanting us and destroying us."[42] When Lewis was longing to hide in the forests, he was longing for something like the land of Faery. In saying that nature was diabolical, he was likely thinking of earth, not the land of Faery, although either interpretation could stand. In these poems, he still longed, but his longing was exclusive from God and from the nature that the Christian God—or, for that matter, any other God—created.

---

[38] Lewis, *The Collected Letters of C.S. Lewis: Volume I*, 397.
[39] Lewis, *Spirits in Bondage*, 6.
[40] Jacobs, 15.
[41] Ibid., 16.
[42] Ibid., 16-17.

His understanding of God needed to develop before he would connect this longing with the God of Christianity.

Spirits in Bondage gives a hint at what Lewis was longing for. It lacked definition, but it was beginning to take on patterns of description. First, it looked something like the land of Faery, although it was not explicit. Further, at least two places in *Spirits in Bondage* point to an attribute that Lewis associated with his longing, that of a firmer and more solid reality somewhere out there, beyond his grasp. In the sixteenth poem, Lewis writes, "… who shall pierce with surer eye! / This shifting veil of bittersweet / And find the real things…."[43] The twenty-fourth poem in the collection is titled *In Praise of Solid People* and the twenty-fifth poem contains a verse where Lewis describes the place of his longing, where "the real flowers are blowing."[44] Whatever the object of Lewis's longing was—he did not yet know—it had a certain quality of heightened reality.

His romantic longing was put on hold, however, when Lewis returned to Oxford after the war and adopted what he termed the "New Look." For Lewis, this meant that there was to be "no more pessimism, no more self-pity, no flirtations with any idea of the supernatural, no romantic delusions." In Lewis's later estimation, it was a flight from "all that sort of romanticism which had hitherto been the chief concern of my life."[45] He had abandoned thinking about the secret life of imagination to focus on the rational and clear.

The Long Conversion

When he returned to Oxford, he began a relationship with Janie King Moore, a relationship Alan Jacobs called "the great mystery of C.S. Lewis's life."[46] The relationship, especially its origin, was shrouded in mystery. Moore was the mother of Lewis's roommate at Oxford before he went to war. The roommate, Paddy Moore, and Lewis made an agreement that if either of them died in the war, the other would take care of

---

[43] Lewis, *Spirits in Bondage*, 9.
[44] Ibid., 13.
[45] Lewis, *Surprised by Joy*, 201.
[46] Jacobs, 93.

the deceased's remaining parent.⁴⁷ After Paddy Moore died in combat, Lewis began living with Mrs. Moore. The primary mystery of the relationship regards the level of intimacy that Lewis and Moore engaged in and whether that was the reason for their common living arrangements. Regardless of the answer to this question, Lewis continued living with Mrs. Moore until her death in 1951.

Lewis's other relationships were primarily male friendships. These friendships often challenged Lewis to think differently and to examine his own position critically. Before his post-war arrival at Oxford, his friendships mainly consisted of his brother and Arthur Greeves. When he arrived at Oxford he met Owen Barfield, the man to whom he would later dedicate *The Allegory of Love*, dubbing him the "wisest and best of my unofficial teachers." Barfield played an important role in bringing Lewis out of his "New Look."

Lewis described himself during his "New Look" as being a realist in the technical sense, meaning he only accepted "as rock-bottom reality the universe revealed by the sense."[48] This, of course, left no room for his romantic longing. Barfield convinced Lewis that if matter was all there was, it would be inconsistent to claim that logical abstract thought could give indisputable truth.[49] Lewis was forced to abandon his New Look "realism." He began to think and talk of what he called the "Absolute", but it was so impersonal that Lewis admitted it "cost nothing." Lewis thought of it as being "there" and did not think it would come "here." With the Absolute, there "was nothing to fear; better still, nothing to obey."[50]

Lewis's dual narratives of longing and rationalism had reappeared, but with a difference. His hope that there was something more to reality than what he could feel with his hands and see with his eyes had returned, but it now had a loose connection with his rationalism. Not only did he rationally allow for the existence of something beyond himself, he believed in it. In Lewis's autobiography, he confessed that the "Norse gods

---

[47] McGrath, 66.
[48] Lewis, *Surprised by Joy*, 208.
[49] McGrath, 103
[50] Lewis, *Surprised by Joy*, 210.

had given me the first hint of [the great glory of God]; but then I didn't believe in them, and I did believe... in the Absolute."[51] His two paths were converging through two questions. First—the one that had followed him since he was a child—was he longing for something real? Second, what was this "Absolute" that he believed in? He found part of the answer through a recognition of how his longing fit into his philosophy.

Barfield forced Lewis to give up the realism of his New Look, but Lewis had not given up the whole New Look philosophy.[52] It was while Lewis was re-reading Euripides' *Hippolytus* in March of 1924 that Lewis abandoned the rest of the New Look.[53] In reading it, he remembered all the romantic images he had been forced to renounce in his New Look. He attempted to patronize the memories of these romantic images, and thus maintain his philosophy. But the next day, he was "overwhelmed" and gave up his New Look completely. Finally, "the long inhibition was over, the dry desert lay behind, I was once more into the land of longing, my heart at once broken and exalted."[54]

The renunciation of the New Look marked Lewis's conversion to idealism, defined by Barkman as the "philosophical docrine that says reality is mind-coordinated or that the objects constituting the 'external world' are not independent of minds, but exist only correlatively to mental operations."[55] His idealist thinking would take several different nuanced forms, but this definition encapsulates the view broadly.

His renunciation of the New Look marked a new phase of longing for Lewis. While he maintained his New Look philosophy, there could be no acknowledgment of longing, and after the New Look had fallen away, longing flooded back.

---

[51] Lewis, *Surprised by Joy*, 211.
[52] It is challenging to date some of Lewis's readings and changes of philosophy, particularly in aligning the order of events in *Surprised by Joy* to the diary and collected letters of Lewis. Barkman presents this same challenge, writing that Lewis's "letters and journal are a more accurate account of the particulars of his life" (Barkman, 114). Considering this, it is best to recognize the significance of certain moments as presented in *Surprised by Joy*, while relying on the letters and journal of Lewis for the particular dates.
[53] Entries March 4th and March 7th of Lewis's journal (published as *All My Road Before Me*) both mention reading *Hypolytus*, but the former entry gives more significance to and indicates more delight in the reading.
[54] Lewis, *Surprised by Joy*, 217.
[55] Barkman, 42.

Reflecting after, he noted that his time living by the New Look was a time of inhibition, a time of drought and not of joy.

The importance his longing played in his life, up to this point, was of delight. It did not primarily speak to truth as much as pleasure. Therefore, he continually tried to regain the longing, which was a delight in itself. This perspective changed through reading Samuel Alexander's *Space, Time and Deity*. Lewis wrote of reading this on March 8, 1924.[56] He realized that he could not try and recover the feeling of longing, but must long after the object of his longing. Lewis wrote that you "cannot hope and also think about hoping at the same time; for in hope we look to hope's object and we interrupt this by (so to speak) turning around to look at the hope itself."[57] Lewis learned that all his watching for longing was vain, for longing implies an object, and that object should have been his focus. This clarified the issue. After this discovery there was no longer a question of how he could get the longing back and it was exclusively a matter of finding the object.

After he realized that the object was the important part of his longing, he began to connect his longing, and thus the object, with his rational understanding of reality. In his words, this was the when he saw that his longing would "fit in."[58] In his rationalism, he believed that humans were "appearances" of the Absolute. Thus, his longing was to be united with the Absolute. This abstract understanding of longing would become clearer and fleshed out in Christianity but the core continued from this abstract longing to his hope in Christianity. His compartmentalized emphases of longing and rationalism had found their way to a unified expression. His rationalism required the existence of some kind of absolute, and he now knew that the object of his longing was the important piece, not the longing itself, and the object was being unified with the Absolute.

Lewis, however, was a tutor at Oxford and found the term "Absolute" to be too abstract a term to be helpful to his students.

---

[56] C.S. Lewis, *All My Road Before Me: The Diary of C.S. Lewis, 1922-1927*, ed. Walter Hooper (San Diego: Harcourt Brace Jovanovich, 1991), 301.
[57] Lewis, *Surprised by Joy*, 218.
[58] Ibid., 221.

So, from 1928 to 1929, he began phasing out the term "Absolute" for "Spirit."[59] He was, however, clear to distinguish this Spirit from the "God of popular religion."[60] This Spirit was not personal and people could no more have a relationship with him than a character in a play could meet the playwright. Lewis attempted to live out this new philosophy by bringing his "acts, desires, and thoughts... into harmony with universal Spirit." He found that he could not do this without consciously returning his mind to reflect upon the Spirit, which Lewis later admitted was not so different from praying to God.

Through trying to live in harmony with the Spirit and returning his mind to dwell on the Spirit repeatedly, Lewis realized that the Spirit was not passive or indifferent. It was not even comparable to the playwright as he thought it was. Rather, it was personal, and the Spirit said to Lewis, "I am the Lord."[61] It was not too long afterward that during the Trinity Term (approximately April 20 to July 6) of 1929 Lewis "gave in, and admitted that God was God, and knelt and prayed."[62] This was Lewis's conversion from idealism to theism.

The next part of Lewis's narrative in his autobiography presents what seems to be a paradox. He writes that in this God that he submitted to, which was not yet exactly the Christian God, he did not think "that there ever had been or ever would be any connection between God and Joy."[63] When he converted to theism, it was not because of any hope to find the object of his longing. In fact, he even thought that this new deity might demand he give up his longing. Yet, one of his important realizations when he was an idealist was that his longing was to be united with the Absolute, that his moments of longing were "the moments of clearest consciousness we had, when we became aware of our fragmentary and phantasmal nature and ached for that impossible reunion which would annihilate us."[64] Earlier, he realized that his longing would fit in with his idea of the Absolute, but when he converted to theism, he did not hope

---

[59] Barkman, 49.
[60] Lewis, *Surprised by Joy*, 227.
[61] Ibid.
[62] Ibid., 228.
[63] Ibid., 230.
[64] Ibid., 222.

for a connection of this kind. This is best understood by making a distinction between Lewis as a theist and as an idealist, where his idealism allowed for longing, but this allowance did not immediately transfer when he converted to theism.[65]

Lewis had progressed from thinking that there was nothing beyond material reality to believing in the Absolute, then to believing in the Spirit, and then to a theistic God. Yet, in Lewis's theism, there was still a gap between his longing and his rational belief in God. As Barfield pulled Lewis out of his New Look, another friend would enable Lewis to see the connection between his longing (provoked by myths) and his rationalism (belief in God).

For much of his life, he had found myths, especially northern myths, to be the stories that filled him with delight, engaging his romanticism. But, as yet, he did not have the clarity to know how these myths worked into his faith. The answer to this question of myths would come in part through a friendship with John Ronald Reuel (J.R.R.) Tolkien, whom Lewis met in 1926.[66] Tolkien helped Lewis resolve this tension by uniting his romanticism and his rationalism in the Christian God.

Lewis had to confront two prejudices he had in Tolkien. Growing up in the Protestant part of Ireland, he did not trust Roman Catholics, and upon entering the English faculty at Oxford he was informed never to trust a philologist. Tolkien was both these things.[67] However, due in large part to a mutual love for myth, especially Scandinavian myths, Tolkien and Lewis grew close. In his love for ancient languages and Scandinavian myths, Tolkien founded a study group he named "Kolbitar" to study these old languages and stories and Lewis joined the group. Kolbitar is an old Icelandic word which Lewis translated "old cronies who sit round the fire so close that they look as if they were biting the coals."[68] Lewis and Tolkien would talk late into the night about myths and their wonder.

Perhaps the most important of these conversations was on the night of September 19, 1931, when Lewis had invited

---

[65] An Idealist, according to Lewis, was his identity as a believer in the Absolute.
[66] McGrath, 128.
[67] Ibid., 216.
[68] Lewis, *The Collected Letters of C.S. Lewis: Volume I*, 701.

both Tolkien and another friend, Hugo Dyson, over for dinner. Lewis had been thinking about different religions and, while he thought Christianity was possibly true, he had difficulty figuring out what the death of a man in Jerusalem, two thousand years before his time, had to do with him. In their conversation that night, Tolkien made no complaint about Lewis's reasoning, but he argued that Lewis was not engaging with the material in the right way. His issue was a failure to imaginatively engage with Christianity. Lewis had long allowed himself to engage with and be engaged by pagan myths which he knew to be false. He understood that they inspired feelings of great joy, but he never acknowledged them as possibly having happened. In his theism, he acknowledged the factuality of god, but could not imaginatively engage with Christianity. Tolkien argued that Lewis needed to approach the New Testament with the same imaginative engagement that he brought to the pagan myths.[69]

Lewis wrote his friend Arthur Greeves on October 18, 1931, soon after his conversion: "The story of Christ is simply a true myth: a myth working on us in the same way as the others, but with this tremendous difference that it really happened."[70] Myths had often provoked Lewis's feelings of longing and he now knew why. Myths were glimpses at truth, and the myth of Christ was a true myth, in fact, truth itself. Before his conversion, Lewis had difficulty fully reconciling his longing and his rationalism. They had not been fully reconciled in his theism, and they only found reconciliation in his idealism, in Lewis thinking of himself as a projection of the Absolute, an idea which faded. However, after his conversion, his rationalism and romantic longing both became fully alive in the narrative of Christianity. Lewis grew up loving stories and particularly mythological stories of the Norse gods. Finally, in Christianity, he found the most perfect myth, but it was true. In the narrative of Christianity, Lewis's romanticism found an incredible story and his rationalism found the truth. Tolkien had helped Lewis realize that his rational understanding of the theory was fine,

---

[69] McGrath, 153.
[70] Lewis, *The Collected Letters of C.S. Lewis: Volume I*, 977.

but he had an "imaginative failure to grasp its significance."[71]

The letter referenced above is the second that Lewis wrote to Greeves referencing a belief in Christ at some level. A few weeks prior, on October 1, Lewis wrote to Greeves that he had "just passed on from believing in God to definitely believing in Christ—in Christianity."[72] The conversion itself was an extended process, and just how extended it was is newly up to debate. Biographers have tended to date the beginning of the conversion process as September 19, 1931, when Lewis had his conversation with Dyson and Tolkien. The conclusion of the conversion process is typically dated as October 1 when Lewis wrote that first letter to Greeves. In his biography, Alister McGrath argues that the actual dating of his conversion is more ambiguous. He proposes that the concluding date of his conversion may have been June 7, 1932. For the sake of consistent dating through this thesis, I will use McGrath's date. Given McGrath's arguments, it is best to hold this date of conversion with a loose grip, understanding that regardless of the specific length, the conversion can be described as an extended process that resulted in the most significant turning point of Lewis's life.[73]

The Apologist: Arguing from Hope

In Christianity, Lewis's longing found both a framework to understand his longing and it, his longing, matured into Christian hope. The framework was the narrative and rational nature of Christianity which enabled him to trust the experience of longing as a rational and valid experience. Further, by understanding the purpose of this longing and its context within the Christian narrative, this longing matured into Christian hope. No longer was it isolated or abstract, but it was a feeling of delight that pointed him to the promises of Christianity. It was in this connection to specific promises that Lewis's longing matured into hope. The line between longing

---

[71] McGrath, 149.
[72] Lewis, *The Collected Letters of C.S. Lewis: Volume I*, 974.
[73] McGrath, 154-156.

and hope is not distinct, but where his longing was vague and frustrating (albeit delightful), his hope was rooted in the specific promises of Christianity (New Creation, redemption, Christ's second coming, and others).

Before he knew the object of his longing, he knew that longing was important. Despite often causing him deep frustration and despair, it also gave him meaning. It was a struggle that drove him forward. Before his conversion, Lewis's longing was vague and mysterious, but not meaningless. As is characteristic of much of Lewis's conversion, his longing was not eliminated in his conversion, but transformed into hope. He did not acknowledge Christianity as true and then replace all that he had come to believe in prior in his life. Rather, the reality that Lewis longed for became more specific. The longing and rationalism that Lewis struggled and wrestled with before his conversion did not become irrelevant, but rather found their fulfillment in the Christian faith. In his conversion, his longing found its full meaning through understanding more clearly the object of his hope.

Just as Lewis's pre-conversion life can be organized into phases, so can his post-conversion life. Two phases stand out in his post-conversion life, the division between the two being marked by a scholarly debate that occurred near the end of the 1940s. The division marked a shift from writing primarily apologetic works to primarily pastoral works. In the first phase of his converted life, Lewis published *The Problem of Pain, Mere Christianity, The Abolition of Man,* and *Miracles*. Additionally, his Space Trilogy, while imaginative, is often focused on convincing his readers of a certain viewpoint. *The Great Divorce* engages his and his audience's imagination, but for the case of a certain position. They were not exclusively concerned with apologetics, but that was the primary push.

Jacobs argues that when Lewis became a Christian, he seemed to "have entered his maturity as a Christian and a thinker almost overnight."[74] Before his conversion, Lewis struggled to gain publishers and decent reception to his works. He also maintained a slow writing process. He published *Spirits in*

---

[74] Jacobs, 162.

Bondage in 1919 and *Dymer* in 1926, separated by the span of seven years. After his conversion, he published six books in the same span of time.[75] Further, his works found success in a variety of genres, from imaginative children books to academic textbooks. His newfound quickness of writing is illustrated well in his first published work post-conversion. While Lewis was visiting Greeves in Belfast, Ireland from August 15 to August 29, 1932, he wrote his first novel, *The Pilgrim's Regress*. Depending on when his conversion was complete, this might have been just a few months or almost a year after he became a Christian.

In some ways, *Pilgrim's Regress* was a fictional form of the autobiography he later wrote. In the allegorical novel, Lewis primarily looked backward, telling the story of his life up to his conversion. Near the end of the book, the protagonist, John, had a conversation with History. At that point in the story, John had traveled far and through many different arguments, pulled the entire way by a longing for the Island. The Island was a place he saw visions of as a child, and being stirred by it, began a journey to find it. When he met History, he began to learn the deeper nature of this desire and who sent it. History taught John that his desire for the Island was a picture sent from the Landlord—the allegory's version of God—and different people had received different pictures.

But this worried John: "Perhaps what troubles me is a fear that my desires, after all you have said, do not really come from the Landlord—that there is some older and rival Beauty in the world which the Landlord will not allow me to get." This was the worry that Lewis confessed to have directly after his conversion in his autobiography. He was worried that the longing which he had treasured for so long would in fact conflict with his new Christian faith and he would have to renounce it. It seems by the time he wrote *The Pilgrim's Regress*, however, that this fear had been resolved to some degree. At the very least, Lewis was confident that the source of this longing was God. Directly after the above quotation, John asked History:

---

[75] *The Pilgrim's Regress* (1933), *The Allegory of Love* (1937), *Out of the Silent Planet* (1938), *Rehabilitations and Other Essays* (1939), *The Personal Heresy* (1939), and *The Problem of Pain* (1940).

"How can we prove that the Island comes from him?" History responded by arguing proof of the Island comes from the fact that every other desire had proven itself a failure.[76]

History also taught John something about the nature of this desire. John was worried because the sweet desire "wears out," and if it was truly from the Landlord, that should not be so. History responded by comparing it to human love: "First comes delight: then pain: then fruit. And then there is joy of the fruit, but that is different again from the first delight. And mortal lovers must not try to remain at the first step; for lasting passion is the dream of a harlot and from it we wake in despair."[77] It is not that the longing of his youth, John's or Lewis's, was vain and needed to be discounted, but that it matures and grows through pain, which leads to fruit.

When History said that there is pain that leads to fruit, it is likely that he was referencing a lesson he previously gave John. In this lesson, John learned that there were both pictures and Rules. John lived his life in pursuit of a picture (the Island). His friend Vertue, who had walked much of the journey with him, was an example of someone who lived by the Rules, the moral law. When Lewis wrote that delight comes first, then pain, then fruit, he certainly had the Christian journey towards sanctification in mind, sanctification that was pulled toward the object of his hope. Having learned the nature of his desire, both who it came from and thus who it was for, Lewis understood his journey toward the object of his hope must consist of living by both the pictures and the Rules, a task that was impossible without the Landlord's Son. Lewis wrote that alone, the rules were dangerous, and that alone, the pictures were dangerous, but it was best "to live from infancy with a third thing which is neither the Rules nor the pictures and which was brought into the country by the Landlord's Son. That, I say, is the best: never to have known the quarrel between the Rules and the pictures."[78] It was in the Landlord's Son—Jesus Christ—that the Rules (moral law) and the pictures (his longing) were in harmony, not quarrelling with each other.

---

[76] Lewis, *The Pilgrim's Regress*, 164.
[77] Ibid., 165.
[78] Ibid., 155.

In *The Pilgrim's Regress*, Lewis wrote of himself as a pilgrim, and as a pilgrim he was learning about the nature of both his journey and destination. When he first started on his pilgrimage as a child who felt a deep longing, he did not know whether it was a longing for anything real, let alone what that reality could be. In his conversion, he learned that there was a true reality he was longing for. In *The Pilgrim's Regress*, Lewis suggested what it would take to arrive at his destination. To attain the object of his hope he had to move forward into reality. After John discovered the truth, he had to regress back to his original land. On his way back, everything looked different. Where before he saw a road and on either side, houses and land, on his regress he saw only a "long straight road" with narrow crags on one side and swamps and jungles on the other side. John never doubted that it was the same country and after standing and beholding it, he was told by another that he was "seeing the land as it really is."[79] For Lewis, part of being a Christian meant seeing things and interacting with them as they really were.

This ability to see things as they really are began, for Lewis, upon conversion. According to the roughly autobiographical account given in *The Pilgrim's Regress*, it was only after Lewis understood the truth of his longing and recognized who God was that he began to see things as they really were. John only began to see things as they really were after he understood who the Son of the Landlord was and began his journey towards the Landlord. In *The C.S. Lewis Encyclopedia*, this theme is termed "Undeception and Recognition," where one has the lies removed from his eyes (undeception) and sees reality as it really is (recognition).[80] In the Christian faith, this theme rhymes—although it is not identical—with the doctrines of new birth, or regeneration. John Frame, in his *Systematic Theology*, writes that the "new birth brings life out of [spiritual death]. Without this new birth, we cannot even see the kingdom of God."[81] The *Evangelical Dictionary of Theology* writes under "Regeneration"

---

[79] Ibid., 183.
[80] Colin Duriez, *The C.S. Lewis Encyclopedia: A Complete Guide to His Life, Thought, and Writings* (Wheaton, Ill: Crossway Books, 2000), 216.
[81] John Frame, *Systematic Theology: An Introduction to Christian Belief* (Phillipsburg, NJ: P&R Publishing, 2013), 166.

that regeneration "enlightens the blinded mind to discern spiritual realities."[82] Although not equivalent, Lewis's view that upon conversion, Christians have the ability to see things as they really are is similar to the doctrine of regeneration in which believers are given eyes to see spiritual realities.

In 1938, five years after he published *The Pilgrim's Regress*, Lewis published *Out of the Silent Planet*, his first novel. In it, the protagonist Ransom is kidnapped and taken on a spaceship. When he comes to his senses, he begins to experience "space." Except it was not space as he thought. Lewis describes Ransom bathing in the pure color of brightness, an immersion that left him feeling "his body and mind daily rubbed and scoured and filled with new vitality."[83] Lewis was not trying to describe heaven, but he was imagining one way it might be like. After Ransom had escaped the limitations of his fallen world, he began to experience a kind of heaven.

Lewis was careful in how he viewed the relationship between imagination and reality. He did not consider imagining as a way of truly grasping heaven. As he wrote a few years later, in *Mere Christianity*: "All scriptural imagery (harps, crowns, gold, etc.) is, of course, a merely symbolical attempt to express the inexpressible."[84] Lewis understood that images were useful in suggesting a deeper truth which is not expressible as things are. Lewis contended that the harps of heaven were mentioned because music "most strongly suggests ecstasy and infinity." Likewise, crowns were mentioned because they suggested the glory that Christians are promised in unification with God and gold because it showed the timelessness and preciousness of heaven. Lewis thought it helpful to imagine but not to try and understand precisely what a thing is, only suggesting a deeper truth that cannot be fully explained. When Lewis wrote that Ransom experienced a bath of pure color, he was hoping through his imagination. He was suggesting to himself and to his readers a possible characteristic of heaven. Lewis thought that it was possible and good to learn to want heaven, and part

---

[82] *Evangelical Dictionary of Theology*, 3rd ed. (Grand Rapids, MI: Baker Academic), s.v. "Regeneration."
[83] C.S. Lewis, *Out of the Silent Planet* (New York, NY: Scribner, 1938), 34.
[84] C.S. Lewis, *Mere Christianity* (New York, NY: HarperCollins, 1952), 137.

of this training took place in the imagination.

Two years after he published this novel, Lewis released *The Problem of Pain*, the first of his apologetic works. In it, he writes that it is "safe to tell the pure in heart that they shall see God, for only the pure in heart want to."[85] Lewis wanted to see God. That was his hope. He yearned for it. In his chapter on heaven in *The Problem of Pain*, his hope was for understanding. Lewis wrote: "Be sure that the ins and outs of your individuality are no mystery to him…. Your soul has a curious shape because it is a hollow made to fit a particular swelling in the infinite contours of the divine substance."[86] Lewis longed to know the one who created him and to be completely and ultimately known.

The hope that Lewis wrote in this work was not of being assimilated into God, but being united with God. He made a distinction between Christianity's hope of unification with God and pantheism's understanding that god was all things. Further, in unification, the self became more fully itself. Lewis understood this to be simply the nature of reality. At reality's core is the trinity, and the trinity is the three persons in the godhead giving themselves to each other in a "continual self-abandonment."[87] Regarding the unification of the self with God, Lewis writes that the "self exists to be abdicated and, by that abdication, becomes the more truly self."[88] He had a deep hope that the end of man was to be unified with God, not losing his own soul's uniqueness, but becoming more fully himself in the giving away. Lewis hoped for unification with God.

In 1941, one year after he published *The Problem of Pain*, Lewis was invited to preach the evening prayer in Oxford University Church of St. Mary the Virgin. This sermon was published as *The Weight of Glory*. In it, he teaches that Christians ought to desire glorification as the proper reward of a soul oriented toward God. What he called himself and his listeners to was a certain understanding of glory. Doubtless considering his

---

[85] C.S. Lewis, *The Problem of Pain* (New York, NY: HarperCollins Publishers, 1940), 149.
[86] Ibid., 152.
[87] Ibid., 156.
[88] Ibid., 157.

pre-conversion longings, Lewis said that glory, "as Christianity teaches me to hope for it, turns out to satisfy my original desire and indeed to reveal an element in that desire which I had not noticed."[89] What Lewis had not noticed before his conversion was that all his insatiable longing really felt like a message not meant for him, but something he overheard. That meant isolation, not being known or "taken into the dance." But glory means being noticed by God. This theme, touched on in *The Problem of Pain*, was continued in *The Weight of Glory*, as Lewis longed to be known by God.

In 1943, two years after he preached *The Weight of Glory*, he wrote *Christian Behaviour*. In it, he recognized that we need to learn how to hope. Hoping was a virtue that could be developed by focusing on the right horizon. When we set our vision on earthly goods and possessions, we fail because earthly things were never meant to be our highest aim. Instead, we "must learn to want something else even more."[90] We need to set heaven on our horizon, the place where we are moving toward. This is difficult because "we have not been trained."[91] Lewis recognized that he needed to want heaven more and that it was a faculty that could be trained. Lewis trained his ability to want heaven through his imagination and his rationality.

When Lewis wrote imaginatively of heaven (or, such as in *Out of the Silent Planet*, the heavens), he was suggesting something about heaven, not trying to make a specific argument for what heaven will be. Yet, there were at least a few concepts about heaven to which Lewis seemed deeply committed. He was committed to the understanding that his pre-conversion longings were not meaningless, but rather found their source in God, and they would be satisfied in heaven. He was committed to the idea that heaven meant unification with God. He was also committed to the idea that heaven was even more real, even more firm and solid, than the reality we experience now. Although once a realist "in the technical sense", where he

---

[89] C.S. Lewis, *The Weight of Glory: And Other Addresses* (New York, NY: Harper Collins Publishers, 1949), 39.
[90] C.S. Lewis, *Christian Behaviour: A Further Series of Broadcast Talks* (NY: Macmillan Company, 1943), 56.
[91] Ibid.

thought that reality was simply matter, in Christianity (and in many other stages of his philosophical progression) he saw reality as being more than matter. It included the spiritual as well.

This idea that heaven was more real than the reality humans currently inhabit was implied in his old longing. For a period before he became a Christian, he attempted to live in submission to the Absolute, which in his conversion he realized was God. God was the absolute, not dependent on this world, but the source of all things and all reality. This has been noted in *The Pilgrim's Regress*, when John begins his return journey home and sees all things as they really are. The lies had crumbled away and John saw the truth. The journey toward heaven is a journey toward greater reality. This had implications for Lewis's life on earth, too. It was not only looking forward to unification with the absolute, but understanding that the absolute still existed before he arrived at unification with it.

His hope for unification with God entailed a belief in objective truth. He was hoping in the coming perfection of the world—and of himself—that would usher in "heaven", which is ultimate reality. Ultimate reality was not compatible for Lewis with a relativist opinion of truth. In 1943—the same year he wrote the *Christian Behaviour* chapter on hope—Lewis gave a series of lectures in response to an invitation to lecture at the University of Durham, which were published as *The Abolition of Man*. The book was Lewis's direct assault on relativism. In *The Abolition of Man*, Lewis argued for the "Tao", which, Lewis argued, was present in all cultures. It was a universal truth, a "doctrine of objective value, the belief that certain attitudes are really true, and others really false, to the kind of thing the universe is and the kind of things we are." [92]

Lewis argued that it was in conforming to the Tao that humans become most fully real. This was not a conforming that happened by intellectually affirming its existence. This conforming happened over a long period of time, as one became closer in character and being to the real and the good and the

---

[92] C.S. Lewis, *The Abolition of Man, or, Reflections on Education with Special Reference to the Teaching of English in the Upper Forms of Schools* (New York: Harcourt, Brace, 1956), 18.

perfect. It was not a flip of a switch, but a journey. The Tao was the way "which every man should tread in imitation of that cosmic and supercosmic progression, conforming all activities to that great exemplar."[93] In these lectures, Lewis was not attempting to make an argument for Christianity (at least, not directly), but for Lewis, this conforming to the Tao meant conforming to the perfect one, Jesus Christ, which was the process of sanctification.

This conforming to the Tao, sanctification, was a challenging endeavor. Lewis wrote of this difficulty in a chapter of *Mere Christianity*.[94] Lewis wrote, "[Jesus] says, 'if you let me, I will make you perfect.... Whatever suffering it may cost you in your earthly life, whatever inconceivable purification it may cost you after death, whatever it costs Me, I will never rest, nor let you rest, until you are literally perfect."[95] However, despite the difficulty of this conforming process, it was what was necessary for the ultimate good. Later in *Mere Christianity*, he writes that if "[you] submit with every fibre of your being... you will find eternal life.... Nothing in you that has not died will ever be raised from the dead."[96] It was only in submitting, dying, and becoming as Christ through sanctification (conforming to the Tao) that Lewis thought people could be raised from the dead to glory and eternal life.

Lewis's hope opposed two perspectives: modernism and progressivism. Modernists claimed that the full truth of reality could be understood through rational thought. Progressives claimed that the full potential of humanity could be achieved through humankind's efforts. Both these stand in opposition

---

[93] C.S. Lewis, *The Abolition of Man, or, Reflections on Education with Special Reference to the Teaching of English in the Upper Forms of Schools* (New York: Harcourt, Brace, 1956), 18.

[94] *Mere Christianity* reprinted three books together, but "left the text much as it had been" (*Mere Christianity*, VII). The writings this section deals with would have come from *Beyond Personality*, which was originally published a year after *The Abolition of Man*, in 1944. In preparing this thesis, I was unable to directly consult *Beyond Personality*. Despite these references coming from a book published a decade after *The Abolition of Man*, the original text was written just after *The Abolition of Man*.

[95] Lewis, *Mere Christianity*, 202.

[96] Ibid., 227

to the theological virtue of hope, and, specifically, the hope that Lewis expressed. Thomas Aquinas, considering the theological virtue of hope, wrote that hope "observes the mean between presumption and despair... as a man is said to be presumptuous, through hoping to receive from God a good in excess of his condition; or to despair through failing to hope for that which according to his condition he might hope for. But there can be no excess of hope in comparison with God, Whose goodness is infinite."[97]

By the standards of Aquinas's definition, both modernists and progressives fell into the vice of presumption. On the one hand, modernists presumed that through their rational efforts they could understand the fullness of reality. On the other hand, progressives thought they could achieve the full potential of human life through human effort. Although neither fell into the vice of despair, they both practiced the vice of presumption. Opposing both these presumptuous philosophical perspectives was Lewis's hope.

Lewis's hope fit well into Aquinas's definition of the theological virtue of hope. Aquinas wrote that hope "attains God by leaning on His help in order to obtain the hoped for good" and the hoped for good was "eternal life, which consists in the enjoyment of God Himself."[98] Lewis hoped for a difficult good which he could not achieve on his own, requiring the aid of God ("...the Christian thinks any good he does comes from the Christ-life inside him. He does not think God will love us because we are good, but that God will make us good because he loves us"[99]), whereas modernists and progressives presumed to have obtained or be able to obtain a good by their own means. Lewis put forth his belief in an objective reality in *The Abolition of Man*, but this belief was connected to his hope, which was present throughout his writings.

In 1945, two years after Lewis published *The Abolition of Man*, he published *The Great Divorce*. In the book, he imagined what it would be like to take a visit from hell (or purgatory,

---

[97] Thomas Aquinas, *Summa Theologica* I-II, Q. 64, Art. 4, Reply 3.
[98] Thomas Aquinas, *Summa Theologica* II-II, Q. 17, Art. 2, Answer.
[99] Lewis, *Mere Christianity*, 63.

depending on if you stay) to heaven. The book is a fictional work, but it was not fully a story, lacking much plot development. Lewis acknowledged this when he wrote to a friend on May 10, 1945. The collected letters of Lewis lack the letters Lewis received, but he seems to have received a sort of critique about the book failing to "satisfy". He asks whether the friend thought "the failure to satisfy is due to lack of real *unity* or development? I mean that the dialogues succeed one another arbitrarily and might have come in any other order and might have gone on a longer or shorter time?"[100]

Despite lacking the structure of a story, *The Great Divorce* portrayed what Lewis was imagining about heaven. Two characteristics that Lewis suggested are worth noting. First, Lewis described heaven in this work as being tremendously solid. Walking there was difficult and the narrator explains that the grass was "hard as diamonds to my unsubstantial feet, made me feel as if I were walking on wrinkled rock, and I suffered pains."[101] Further, the people visiting from hell were described as ghosts, contrasting the solid spirits of heaven. The second characteristic of heaven in *The Great Divorce* was that heaven is a place where pain is redeemed. The narrator tried to understand whether a soul could stay in heaven and learns from his guide that for those who stay in heaven, hell was not hell, but purgatory. Even more, if a soul remains in heaven, heaven will work "backwards and turn even that agony [temporal suffering] into a glory" and someday those who reside in heaven will say: "We have never lived anywhere except in heaven."[102] Lewis, in *The Great Divorce*, described heaven as a solid place where suffering is redeemed and turned into glory.

A Shift: Imagined Hope

In his academic work, Lewis was a noted scholar for his work on medieval literature. However, despite this recognition, he often faced difficulties in his life as an academic. From 1947

---

[100] Lewis, *The Collected Letters of C.S. Lewis, Volume II*, 648.
[101] C.S. Lewis, *The Great Divorce* (New York, NY: Macmillan Publishing Company), 31.
[102] Lewis, *The Great Divorce*, 67-68.

to 1951, Lewis failed to obtain three chairs or professorships for which he was a strong candidate.[103] He remained as a tutor, a job for which he had little love and cost him much energy. He was exhausted from his work as both a tutor and in taking care of Mrs. Moore and was making little progress in any major academic endeavor.

Lewis published *Miracles: A Preliminary Study* in 1947, the same year he failed to obtain the Merton Professorship of English. On February 2, 1948, one of the chapters in the book was brought to debate by Elizabeth Anscombe, a rising star in philosophy. Anscombe critiqued the reasoning behind Lewis's argument against naturalism. Lewis acknowledged that she was right, or at least that he could make his point better, and subsequently revised the chapter in the 1960 edition. This debate has been explained differently, but at minimum it marked a change in Lewis's writings. Best understood, the debate ushered in a shift that Lewis was already moving toward, a shift from a primarily rational defense of the faith to a primarily imaginative one.[104]

It could also be characterized as a shift from apologetic defenses of Christianity to pastoral care of Christians. This can be seen by contrasting the books that Lewis wrote before and after the shift. Before 1948, he wrote *Mere Christianity*, *The Problem of Pain*, *The Abolition of Man*, and *Miracles*. After the Anscombe debate, Lewis wrote the whole of *The Chronicles of Narnia*, *Till We Have Faces*, *Reflections on the Psalms*, *The Four Loves*, and *Letters to Malcolm: Chiefly on Prayer*. The shift was not strictly from rational to imaginative writings. Before the shift, he wrote the Ransom Trilogy, *The Great Divorce*, and *The Pilgrim's Regress*. Yet, the focus in each of the pre-debate works was typically toward a rational understanding, where after the debate his writings were marked by pastoral and imaginative concerns.

These post-debate works were still down the road, however. In the late 1940s and early 1950s Lewis persisted through some of his most challenging years. His professional difficulties have been noted. He was also responsible for taking care of

---

[103] McGrath, 242-244.
[104] McGrath, 254-260.

Mrs. Moore, who had been declining in health for some time, and his brother Warnie, who was fighting a "losing battle with alcohol addiction."[105] Through the hardships of life, Lewis was growing weary. He was fifty and losing steam. After receiving encouragement from a friend to write more, Lewis replied in January of 1949:

> I would not wish to deceive you with vain hope. I am now in my fiftieth year. I feel my zeal for writing, and whatever talent I originally possessed, to be decreasing; nor (I believe) do I please my readers as I used to. I labour under many difficulties. My house is unquiet and devastated by my women's quarrels.... My aged mother [Mrs. Moore], worn out by long infirmity, is my daily care.[106]

Five months later, in June, Lewis collapsed. He was taken to the hospital and put on a regiment of penicillin injections every three hours. In the aftermath of this collapse, Warnie convinced Mrs. Moore to allow Lewis a month-long vacation.

Lewis was thrilled at this idea and arranged for his vacation to be with Arthur Greeves in his home of Belfast, Ireland.[107] However, a few weeks later, in July, Lewis wrote to Greeves to cancel this vacation. He wrote to Greeves that Warnie had been struggling with "drink" and after finally convincing Warnie to go into a nursing home, the nursing home announced that "he is out of control and they refuse to keep him." The blessing of vacation had been taken away from him, and he was now responsible for both an aging and irritable woman and a brother struggling with alcoholism. In the same letter to Greeves, Lewis assured Greeves he did not "doubt for a moment that what God sends us must be sent in love and will all be for the best if we have grace to use it so. My *mind* doesn't waver on this point: my *feelings* sometimes do."[108] Lewis was struggling, but he rested in his confidence of God's love and plan. He was

---

[105] McGrath, 245.
[106] Lewis, *The Collected Letters of C.S. Lewis, Volume II*, 905-906.
[107] Ibid., 945.
[108] Ibid., 953.

sure that, in God, the trials he was facing were sent in love and "will be all for the best." Lewis's hope was not abstract. In the physical trials of his life, he hoped in God's assurance that all trials will be redeemed in the future.

Despite this worry that he had lost all steam, Lewis began to write again. Amid Lewis's personal and professional struggles, he wrote five of his seven children's books. Dissecting Lewis's hope as depicted in *The Chronicles of Narnia* cannot be done in the pages allotted here. However, a few scenes can be touched on. Particularly, scenes from *The Lion, the Witch, and the Wardrobe* and *The Last Battle*.

The Lion, the Witch, and the Wardrobe was published in 1950. In it, Lewis portrays hope primarily as an expectation of salvation. The land had been in winter for 100 years, under the cruel dominion of the White Witch. And yet, true Narnians had hope for Aslan's return. When Susan Pevensie asked who Aslan was, Mr. Beaver responds, "Why, don't you know? He's the King. He's the Lord of the whole wood, but not often here, you understand. Never in my time or my father's time. But the word has reached us that he has come back. He is in Narnia at this moment. He'll settle the White Queen all right." Mr. Beaver further quoted an "old rhyme":

> *Wrong will be right, when Aslan comes in sight,*
> *At the sound of his roar, sorrows will be no more,*
> *When he bares his teeth, winter meets its death,*
> *And when he shakes his mane, we shall have spring again.*[109]

The Beavers had never seen Alsan. Neither had Mr. Beaver's father. Yet, this rhyme that they would utter during the dark times of the winter offered hope. Beyond these lines, there were also prophecies regarding the Pevensie children and how children of Adam would come and set things right in Narnia. Despite the gloom, they looked forward to future promises. It is difficult to see directly how the hope got the Narnians through the winter, since *The Lion, the Witch, and the Wardrobe*

---

[109] C.S. Lewis, *The Chronicles of Narnia* (New York, NY: HarperFestival, 2010), 146-147.

begins at the end of this period of darkness, but from these scenes and from the whole book, it can be inferred that Aslan's return was not a shock. It was not something that confused the Narnians. Rather, it was the final return that they had longed for. It was the very deliverance they had place their hope in for a hundred years.

In *The Lion, the Witch, and the Wardrobe*, Lewis's hope was far more full than the longing he had in his early life. In his pre-conversion life, he longed for an abstract object that brought him delight, but in this children's book, his longing is much more vivid and fleshed out. The hope was not abstract, it was specific both in the context of hoping and in the object of the hope. The Narnians—and Lewis, who was then struggling through his own personal circumstances—were living in pain and depending on the old promises of rescue from Aslan. Lewis knew the promises of scripture, that all would be made well in the end, and those were likely on his mind when he wrote this book.

Before Lewis wrote *The Last Battle*, several important events took place. First, Mrs. Moore died in 1951. Lewis had been faithful to the end in taking care of her, but her death also freed his life considerably. In 1954, he was elected to the Chair of Medieval and Renaissance Literature at Cambridge, finally allowing him to take on the role of professor and not be responsible for tutoring as he had been since 1924. Despite these positive changes in Lewis's life, his brother Warnie continued to struggle with alcoholism. Two years after being elected to this position, Lewis wrote *The Last Battle*.

At the end of The Last Battle, the land of Narnia is destroyed as the followers of Aslan are ushered into Aslan's Country. In Aslan's Country, old friends were reunited (the old kings and queens of Narnia with the creatures of Narnia), wounds were healed (Digory said that he and Polly "felt that we'd been unstiffened"[110]), the food's taste was so good that the "nicest things in this world would taste like medicines after it," people were redeemed (Aslan said to Emeth, who worshipped a false

---

[110] Lewis, *The Chronicles of Narnia*, 743.

god, "Son, thou art welcome"111), and the country was more solid than the last (Aslan's country "was a deeper country [than Narnia]: every rock and flower and blade of grass looked as if it meant more."112). This vision of heaven built on themes present in The Great Divorce. First, Aslan's Country was described as being more real than life is now, similar to the descriptions of heaven's solidity in The Great Divorce. Lewis, by suggestion and not exact speculation, described heaven as being more real than the material world that currently exists. Second, Aslan's Country was described as becoming more and more solid as people moved forward, just as people moved toward the mountains in The Great Divorce. Aslan's Country, heaven, was imagined as a journey into greater and greater realities. This description is striking, reflecting a shift in Lewis's own life.

He wrote *The Lion, the Witch, and the Wardrobe* while in the tumultuous times of Mrs. Moore's infirmities, Warnie's alcoholism, and general exhaustion, such that he was afraid that he might never regain his zeal for writing. Contained in that writing was his hope that winter would be ended and springtime would come again. After Mrs. Moore's death and his move to a more sustainable work environment, his hope began to look different. In *The Last Battle*, he was looking forward to the adventure of heaven, of going "further up and further in." He looked forward to the eternal adventure of moving toward God. This was an energetic hope of a man excited by possibilities, not one exhausted seeking rest. Depending on his circumstances, his hope was adopting different emphases.

Will Heaven be Good?

In Lewis's hoping, he was not only moving toward the object of his hope, he was moving into it. And so, while a characteristic or theme might be present in Lewis's life early on, it would become more visceral over time. This is seen in Lewis's view towards forgiveness. He writes to Sister Penelope in June of

---

[111] Lewis, *The Chronicles of Narnia*, 757.
[112] Ibid., 760.

1951 saying that he realized he had "never really believed (tho' I thought I did) in God's forgiveness... I now feel that one must never say one believes or understands anything: any morning a doctrine I thought I already possessed may blossom into this new reality."[113] He echoes this idea in his letter on December 26, 1951 to a priest, Don Giovanni Calabria:

> For a long time I believed that I believed in the forgiveness of sins. But suddenly... this truth appeared in my mind in so clear a light that I perceived that never before... had I believed it with my whole heart. So great is the difference between mere affirmation by the intellect and that faith, fixed in the very marrow and as it were palpable, which the Apostle wrote was substance.

Lewis had understood the idea of forgiveness for a long time, but it was only recent to this letter that he began to understand it more deeply in a way that was "palpable." Forgiveness had become deeper and more immediate to him as he progressed in his pilgrimage. In that same letter to Sister Penelope he asked her for prayers because he was "travelling across 'a plain called Ease'. Everything without, and many things within, are marvelously well at present."[114] Lewis acknowledged that there was a certain danger with all things going well. It is impossible to say what the relationship is between this request for prayer amid good things and the tragedy that struck a decade later.

In April of 1956, Lewis entered into a civil marriage with Helen Joy Davidman. At first, the marriage was primarily a matter of expediency, allowing Davidman, an American, to stay permanently in England. However, through the course of a year, the relationship got deeper and the two were married in Christian marriage in March of 1957.[115] Lewis attributed part of the decision to get married in Christian marriage to the cancer that had been afflicting Davidman throughout their civil marriage. Lewis wrote to a friend on June 25, 1957, saying

---

[113] C.S. Lewis, *The Collected Letters of C.S. Lewis, Volume III: Narnia, Cambridge, and Joy 1950-1963*, ed. Walter Hooper (New York, NY: HarperCollins Publishers, 2007), 123.
[114] Ibid.
[115] Jacobs, 278.

that "a rival often turns a friend into a lover. Thanatos [Death], certainly (they say) approaching but at an uncertain speed, is a most efficient rival for this purpose.... We soon learn to love what we know we must lose."[116]

During this year of civil marriage, Lewis published *Till We Have Faces*. The novel was autobiographical, but in less direct ways than *The Pilgrim's Progress* or his actual autobiography, *Surprised by Joy*. In the novel, two sisters, Orual and Psyche, live as daughters of a king in the fictional kingdom of Glome. Early in the book, in a conversation between a priest and the king, the priest says that holy "places are dark places. It is life and strength, not knowledge and words, that we get in them. Holy wisdom is not clear and thin like water, but thick and dark like blood."[117] This captures the essence of the book well. It was a depiction Lewis's wrestling with the interaction of "clear and thin" rationalism and the "thick and dark" numinous, the powerful mysterious source of his longing.

In the novel, the land of Glome experiences a terrible drought and Psyche is required as a sacrifice to the local god, Ungit, which would take place in the mountains. However, Psyche did not give in to despair. Rather, as she explains in a conversation with her sister just before she was to be sacrificed, Psyche saw it as an opportunity to fulfill the deepest longings of her life. "'Orual,' [Psyche] said, her eyes shining, 'I am going, you see, to the Mountain. You remember how we used to look and long?'" After a little conversation, Psyche continues, "The sweetest thing in all my life has been the longing—to reach the Mountain, to find the place where all the beauty came from.... Do you think it all meant nothing, the longing? The longing for home?"[118] Soon after this conversation, Psyche was "sacrificed"—bound to a tree for the son of Ungit, the Shadowbrute, to be the "bride of Ungit's son" and the "Brute's Supper", which might be the same thing, according Ungit's priest—but in the days following, Orual climbed to the mountain and found Psyche among the trees, blissful and healthy. However, they each saw different surroundings: Psyche saw a palace that she called home, and

---

[116] Lewis, *The Collected Letters of C.S. Lewis, Volume III*, 861-2.
[117] *Till We Have Faces*, 50.
[118] Ibid., 75-76.

Orual saw trees in a mountain. Psyche explained that she was married to a god, which Orual concluded was "sheer raving."[119] Orual had been trained to think rationally, and what Psyche said made no rational sense. Orual left, but upon her return, convinced Psyche to light a lamp at night and see the god, which was forbidden. Psyche was cast into exile, and Orual was visited by the god who told her that she also "shall be Psyche."[120]

In her exile, Psyche was commanded to do a set of tasks. Orual later saw these tasks through paintings, but saw that in some of them, it seemed that there "was no despair" and she saw Psyche laughing and singing.[121] But, in the same years that Psyche had been accomplishing these tasks, Orual had, according to her teacher, "bore the anguish. But [Psyche] achieved the tasks."[122] Eventually, Orual did become as Psyche, just as told by the god. It came after Orual realized that all her life she had possessed people with her love, most of all Psyche. Seeing Psyche again, Orual proclaimed: "Oh Psyche, oh goddess.... Never again will I call you mine; but all there is of me shall be yours."[123] In her selfless realization, she had become beautiful, as Psyche was beautiful. In this encounter with Psyche, who was likened to a goddess, Orual thought she had "come to the highest, and to the utmost fullness of being which the human soul can contain."[124]

Till We Have Faces was one of Lewis's most subtle and difficult books. This was intentional, because wisdom was not "clear and thin like water, but thick and dark like blood." In this book, Lewis dwelled on the mystery and difficulty of his hope. When Psyche was preparing to be sacrificed, she did not long for the mountain without doubt. After Orual told Psyche that she thought Psyche had no fear in her at all, Psyche responded that she was afraid of only one thing: "Supposing... how if there were no god of the Mountain and even no holy Shadowbrute, and those who are tied to the Tree only die, day by day, from thirst and hunger and wind and sun."[125] Psyche longed for the mountain through doubt, persevering in longing through her uncertainty.

---

[119] *Till We Have Faces*, 126.
[120] Ibid., 174.
[121] Ibid., 299-300.
[122] Ibid., 301.
[123] Ibid., 305.
[124] Ibid., 306.
[125] *Till We Have Faces*, 70.

Further, Lewis described what would be required to achieve his hope. Psyche and Orual both had to die to themselves to, as Orual reflected on her experience, come to the "utmost fullness of being." Psyche died, first as a sacrifice in the mountain, and then again through her tasks. Orual, through the anguish she bore. Lewis recognized that to come to the destination of hope, it would require dying to oneself.

Finally, Lewis described what achieving this hope would be like. As a great god came to judge Orual, she felt the "air growing brighter and brighter about us; as if something had set it on fire. Each breath I drew let into me new terror, joy, overpowering sweetness. I was pierced through and through with the arrows of it. I was being unmade."[126] This was one of Lewis's final suggestions of what the presence of God might feel like. It cannot be made too specific, but for Lewis, approaching God would bring terror, joy, and overpowering sweetness; it would unmake him. Beyond what it meant for the individual, Lewis reflected on a general eschatology through the voice of Orual's teacher: "Only this I know. This age of ours will one day be the distant past. And the Divine Nature can change the past. Nothing is yet in its true form."[127] Lewis avoided getting into technical debates on theology, leaving it to the "professional theologians", as he would say. But, despite not giving a specific stance on how the last things would play out, he was committed to the belief that the world was in an age that will not last forever, and will one day "be the distant past." *Till We Have Faces* was a deeply imaginative retelling of an old myth. Myths, for Lewis, had often been able to suggest truths deeper than mere argument through words could convey. In Lewis's last novel, he suggested much about his hope.

Several years later, after *Till We Have Faces* was published and Lewis and Davidman had been joined in Christian marriage, Davidman died on July 13, 1960. In Lewis's fifty-eight years, he had only been in a romantic relationship with, potentially, one other woman (Mrs. Moore) besides Davidman. The next year, in 1961, Lewis published *A Grief Observed*. It was a cry of honest pain and struggle. In the wake of his wife's death, Lewis needed a way to grieve and he began writing as a way to process and

---

[126] Ibid., 307.
[127] Ibid., 305.

grieve. For a man who was typically reticent to discuss matters of his personal life, it is notably and passionately personal.

In *A Grief Observed,* Lewis turned to his pen and tried to settle a similar question that he posed in *The Problem of Pain* twenty-one years prior. But, now, the question of how evil could exist with a perfect God was not a matter of rationality, but a visceral question. It was a question of many things, but one of them regarded his hope. He had placed all his hope in this Christian God, who took away the wife he loved. Could he trust God to deliver on the promises in which Lewis placed his hope?

Lewis wrote, "go to Him when your need is desperate, when all other help is vain, and what do you find? A door slammed in your face, and a sound of bolting and double bolting on the inside."[128] Reflecting on how he had grown since his marriage to Davidman and how he had learned to be more intimately connected with another person, he cried "Oh God, God, why did you take such trouble to force this creature out of its shell if it is now doomed to crawl back—to be sucked back—to it?"[129]

In the *Problem of Pain,* which he published in 1940, twenty-one years before *A Grief Observed,* Lewis argued that God's goodness, and therefore his love, must mean more than kindness.[130] What God's love means is that He seeks to make His children good and thus God is "the consuming fire Himself, the Love that made the worlds, persistent as the artist's love for his work and despotic as a man's love for a dog, provident and venerable as a father's love for a child, jealous, inexorable, exacting as love between the sexes."[131] He continued, writing that we were made so "that God may love us, that we may become objects in which the Divine love may rest 'well pleased.'"[132] In *The Problem of Pain,* Lewis argued that God's love implies that He will discipline and craft His people into what He wants them to be, even if it is painful.

However, twenty-one years later, when his wife died, these

---

[128] C.S. Lewis, *A Grief Observed* (New York, NY: HarperCollins Publishers, 1961), 6.
[129] Ibid., 19.
[130] Lewis, *The Problem of Pain,* 35.
[131] Ibid., 39.
[132] Ibid., 41.

arguments did not help Lewis. In *A Grief Observed*, Lewis wrote that if "God's goodness is inconsistent with hurting us, then either God is not good or there is no God: for in the only life we know He hurts us beyond or worst fears and beyond all we can imagine. If it is consistent with hurting us, then He may hurt us after death as unendurably as before it."[133] Although he was content in *The Problem of Pain* to make a rational argument for understanding God's goodness as something greater than kindness, this goodness seems questionable to Lewis in the pain of his wife's death. Continuing, Lewis wrote: "What reason have we, except our own desperate wishes, to believe that God is, by any standard we can conceive, 'good'? Doesn't all the *prima facie* evidence suggest exactly the opposite?"[134] In Lewis's pain and grief, there was a certain visceral reality which rejects rational explanations of suffering, such as his explanation in *The Problem of Pain* that God's goodness is why He disciplines and provides trials to His children.

Not only does it confront his rational explanation in *The Problem of Pain*, but it confronts the exact promise of God, which Lewis had placed his hope. It was not only a temporary pain that Lewis was struggling through, it made him wonder whether God would "hurt us after death as unendurably as before it."[135] In other words, Lewis was wondering if heaven was going to be all that great. Perhaps it was all a lie. To make matters worse, Lewis wrote to Arthur Greeves on August 30, 1960 and mentioned that his brother had gone away on an Irish holiday and "drunk himself into hospital."[136]

Lewis turned a corner in his grief when he took a decidedly rational approach to the issue. "Feelings, and feelings, and feelings. Let me try thinking instead."[137] He took stock of his former faith and life. He asked what new factor was introduced through Davidman's death: "What grounds has it given me for doubting all that I believe?"[138] He acknowledged that he had

---

[133] Lewis, *A Grief Observed*, 27-28.
[134] Ibid., 30.
[135] Ibid.
[136] Lewis, *The Collected Letters of C.S. Lewis, Volume III*, 1181-82.
[137] Lewis, *A Grief Observed*, 36.
[138] Lewis, *A Grief Observed*, 36.

never understood the depths of pain which he had attempted to explain in books such as *The Problem of Pain*. He explains that if he had really cared "about the sorrows of the world, I should not have been so overwhelmed when my own sorrow came."[139]

Through his process of grief, he began to realize some of what God was doing in his life. He described his prior faith as a house of cards that got blown down through Davidman's death. He realized that he and Davidman were both patients that God was working on to cure of sinfulness and that the "more we believe that God hurts only to heal, the less we can believe that there is any use in begging for tenderness."[140] It would not do to beg God to be tender. Lewis recognized he needed God's healing and that was only going to be accomplished through painful sanctification.

Lewis began to think again on where this sanctification was going. Recognizing that he may have been moving back in his affection for God as a means of seeing Davidman again, he rebuked the method. "If you're approaching Him not as the goal but as a road, not as the end but as a means, you're not really approaching Him at all," Lewis concluded.[141] This means that the end goal of sanctification is ultimately nothing but God. This was not intellectually new to Lewis. He had known since the beginning of his Christian life that his end goal, his hope, was God. Yet, he found himself in a situation begging to meet Joy again, realizing that he was thoroughly wrong. He had to return to his former understanding of the Christian life. He knew that neither Davidman or anything on this earth could satisfy his desires, yet, in her death he had made her his greatest desire. He had to correct that and turn his eyes back to God, the source of all things and the object of his hope.

Conclusion

When he was a child, Lewis longed for an unknown through unbidden moments of romantic delight, but his longing matured

---

[139] Ibid., 37.
[140] Ibid., 43.
[141] Ibid., 68.

throughout his life, first taking on firmer characteristics in his time as a young adult, and then maturing in his conversion to Christianity into a romantic and rational hope for Christ to bring the solid and glorious New Creation where pain is redeemed, harmony is perfect, and people are united with God. He lived in tension between romanticism and rationalism. He treasured the romantic longings that first gripped him as a child and yet grew pessimistic about whether there was a God, and if there was, whether he was good. This dualism resulted in a longing for neither God nor things of earth, but for the land of Faery; a longing that he articulated in the post-war poems, *Spirits in Bondage*. Through both his rational thought and his romantic longing, Lewis moved through his post-war "New Look" realism to being an idealist—believing in the Absolute—and from idealism to theism, and from theism to a faith in the God of Christianity.

The first sixteen years (1932-1948) of Lewis's life after converting to Christianity were spent arguing for Christianity as an apologist. This typically took place within essays and lectures, and books of apologetics, but it also took imaginative and fictional forms, such as the Space Trilogy, *The Great Divorce*, and *The Pilgrim's Regress*. However, the fiction was used less often and, when present, was typically used to make rhetorical points. After a debate in 1948 with Elizabeth Anscombe, Lewis made a noticeable shift to focusing on narratives as a way of expressing meaning. Through narrative, Lewis was able to both write of the feelings experienced by people and make rational points, because in a narrative, these often overlapped. In *The Lion, the Witch, and the Wardrobe*, when Mr. Beaver told the Pevensie children that some "say Aslan is on the move" they began to feel "quite different." They did not know who Aslan was, but at his name they each "felt something jump in its inside. Peter felt suddenly brave and adventurous. Susan felt as if some delicious smell or some delightful strain of music had just floated by her. And Lucy got the feeling you have when you wake up in the morning and realize that it is the beginning of the holidays."[142] In this scene, Lewis emphasized his

---

[142] Lewis, *The Chronicles of Narnia*, 141.

characters' experiences of feelings, and, in the same story, he later emphasized the rational importance of Christ's sacrifice through telling the story of Aslan's sacrifice. In narrative, both the feelings Lewis wanted to express and the rational points he wanted to make complemented each other.

Six years later, Lewis wrote *The Last Battle*. In this tale, Lewis vividly portrayed his hope as heaven, a place of solid reality with overflowing energy and reunited friends, going further up and further in. It was one of the fullest expressions of his hope, but the way it described heaven and New Creation was not entirely unique. Throughout his writing, such as in *The Great Divorce* and some lines from *Spirits in Bondage,* he longed for a reality that was more objective and more solid than his current reality. In Lewis's work, his hope matured and became fuller as he lived.

This pattern of becoming progressively fuller was best seen in his book, *A Grief Observed*. In it, he was forced to confront his younger arguments for the goodness of God and the purpose of pain. In his wife's death, he was forced to confront the truth on a visceral level, requiring his entire being to face the reality of his wife's death and his pain. After facing the pain, he did not abandon his hope, but found that it was renewed. He renewed this hope by turning to God, who he was hoping for and whose promises he trusted.

EATING IS MEETING – CALVIN AND THE REAL PRESENCE

Ryan Sinni

SECTION I: INTRODUCTION

The scope of a thesis about the real presence offers little space to discuss the communal nature of the Lord's Supper. In a paper about communion, however, it seems fitting to thank the intellectual community that has made this paper possible. Two particular Union University students—Zach Clemmons and Kelsie Edgren—presented senior theses that influenced my project: Zach's in Christian Thought and Tradition and Kelsie's in English. I also took an Introduction to Philosophy course with Dr. Justin Barnard during my freshman year that encouraged me to reflect on the essences of things and not merely their component parts. Though I do not have space for a detailed thank-you, I am grateful to the Union University Honors Community for shaping my heart and mind in more ways than I can count, particularly by ingraining in me a more sacramental view of the world. My thesis about communion could not have been produced apart from this intellectual koinonia.

During the spring of my sophomore year at Union University, I heard Zach Clemmons present his thesis on the real presence of Christ in the Lord's Supper. Zach compared those who separate the elements from the realities they signify to food critics who talk about a menu but never taste the food. After hearing Zach present, I became convinced that a memorialist view of the Lord's Supper misses its most central element: the real, living, and personal presence of Jesus Christ himself. In his thesis, Zach encouraged evangelicals to look to Alexander Schmemann, an Eastern Orthodox theologian, for a more robust view of the real presence of Christ in the Lord's Supper. Though I was intrigued by Zach's thesis, I did not want to leave my own Reformed tradition for the sake of a richer experience of the

Lord's Supper, as many of my friends have chosen to do. Writing on Calvin's view of the Lord's Supper has allowed me to explore the resources within my own tradition for understanding the real presence.

In exploring Calvin's view of the real presence, I hoped not only to refine my understanding of the Lord's Supper, but to adopt a different posture toward the world. Hearing Zach present highlighted something I recognized already: both my understanding of the Lord's Supper and my posture toward the world were insufficiently sacramental, insufficiently suffused with the presence of God. I recall one particular moment that helped reveal my lack of wonder at the world. In Introduction to Philosophy during the spring of my freshman year, Dr. Barnard quoted from C.S. Lewis's *The Voyage of the Dawn Treader*. In the episode Dr. Barnard quoted, the English child Eustace meets a retired star named Ramandu. Eustace is puzzled by Ramandu: "In our world," said Eustace, "a star is a huge ball of flaming gas."[1] Ramandu replies, "Even in your world, my son, that is not what a star is but only what it is made of."[2]

Ramandu's response to Eustace exposed my disenchanted view of the world. I, like Eustace, often viewed things as the sum of their physical constituents—their quarks, their atoms, and their molecules. To my impoverished imagination, what a thing is *was* what it is made of. Lewis showed me that things are more than the sum of their parts.[3] When I look at a star, I should not regard it as primarily a flaming ball of gas, but as the workmanship of a benevolent creator, who designed it to illuminate the sky and image forth his glory. To discover what a thing is, I needed to look beyond physical reality to the glory of God that suffuses all things.

During the semester in which I heard Zach defend his thesis on the real presence, I also heard Kelsie Edgren defend her thesis on Gerard Manley Hopkins. Kelsie argued that Hopkins,

---

[1] C. S. Lewis, *The Voyage of the Dawn Treader* (New York: Macmillan, 1988), 175.
[2] Lewis, 175.
[3] Careful readers may note that in the above passage, Lewis articulates an Aristotelian metaphysic, the metaphysic that undergirds a Roman Catholic understanding of the Lord's Supper. I cite this passage not to indicate that Lewis encouraged in me a belief in transubstantiation, but to suggest that he opened up for me a more sacramental understanding of the world.

who sees the world as "charged with the grandeur of God,"[4] offers a model for re-enchanting a disenchanted universe. (Or, more precisely, for regarding this enchanted world with the wonder it deserves). Hearing Kelsie present helped me put words to my false perception of the world and inspired me to write about enchantment and disenchantment. Although I did not instantly gravitate toward writing on the Lord's Supper, I eventually began to regard it as a subspecies of the question of enchantment. If enchantment means seeing the glory of God even in apparently mundane things, then, on a real presence view, the Lord's Supper is the most enchanted event in the cosmos—communion with Christ through bread and wine. I wondered whether my failure to see God's presence in the natural world might be connected with my failure to acknowledge his presence in the Lord's Supper.

Calvin was a particularly helpful figure to write about for a couple of reasons. First, whether his view of the Lord's Supper should be considered a real presence view is a matter of scholarly debate. Second, writing about Calvin allowed me to explore a theologian within my own tradition who did not hold to a memorialist view of the Lord's Supper. Although I had become skeptical of a memorialist view, I did not want to become Lutheran, Catholic, or Eastern Orthodox. Thus began my exploration of the resources of my own tradition.

Seeing some of my friends leaving Reformed churches made the search for such resources personally significant. I suspected that some of my friends left the traditions in which they had been raised because they sensed in their traditions the same deficiency I did: an insufficient theology of the sacraments and of God's presence in the world. Though I sympathized with their flight, I questioned whether the deficiency my friends saw in their churches was really a deficiency in the Reformed tradition itself. Might the Reformed tradition account for the sacramental, enchanted manner by which my friends and I felt compelled to view the world? Although my thesis addresses a much narrower question—whether Calvin's view of the Lord's

---

[4] Gerard Manley Hopkins, "God's Grandeur." in *The Poems of Gerard Manley Hopkins*, edited by W.H. Gardner, and N.H. MacKenzie, 4th ed. (London: Oxford University Press, 1967), 66.

Supper is a real presence view—my larger question of the relationship between the Reformed tradition and an enchanted view of the world still remains in the background.

Determining whether Calvin's view of the Lord's Supper should be considered a real presence view requires answering two main questions. First, what is Calvin's view of the Lord's Supper? Second, what does it mean for Christ to be really present in the Lord's Supper? In "Section II: The History of the Real Presence," I offer an overview of various approaches to the question of real presence in order to provide context for Calvin's view. In "Section III: Calvin's View of the Lord's Supper," I explicate the salient points of Calvin's doctrine as it relates to the real presence. In "Section IV: Calvin and Real Presence," I return to Calvin's view and examine it in light of the question of real presence.

My central claim about Calvin's doctrine of the Lord's Supper is that it should be considered a real presence view, but not on the basis of substance metaphysics. Unlike the Lutheran and Roman Catholic views of the Lord's Supper, in which Christ is in, near, or identified with the physical elements, Calvin's view remains agnostic about where Christ meets the believer during the celebration of the Lord's Supper. Given that Calvin believes that Christ's body is contained in heaven, he rejects any view that locates Christ's body on the communion table. Given his reading of New Testament passages like John 6, however, Calvin affirms that the flesh of Christ nourishes believers by means of the physical elements. Therefore, the real presence of Christ asserted by Calvin is best understood not as a substance that resides in the elements but as an event that takes place during the Supper. I hope that my exegesis and analysis of Calvin's view provides an alternative for those desiring to hold to both the Reformed tradition and a sacramental worldview.

SECTION II: HISTORY OF THE REAL PRESENCE

"The cup of blessing that we bless, is it not a participation in the blood of Christ? The bread that we break, is it not a

participation in the body of Christ?" (1 Corinthians 10:16)[5]

"This is my body" (1 Corinthians 11:24)

"Whoever feeds on my flesh and drinks my blood has eternal life, and I will raise him up on the last day." (John 6:54)

Introduction

Throughout its history, the church has wrestled with how to understand passages of Scripture that seem to speak of Christ's presence in the Lord's Supper. Each period of history tends to view Christ's presence in the Supper through the predominant philosophical lens of its day: Neoplatonism for the early church, "thingly realism"[6] for the early medieval church and Aristotelianism for the late medieval church. Even so, there is often great diversity within each period. Sometimes this diversity of opinions is tolerated, as in the early church; sometimes it leads to division, as in the time of the Reformation. In almost every period, however, there is widespread agreement that Christ is present (in some way) in the Eucharist. These diverse opinions on the Lord's Supper can largely be classified into two main groups: metabolic and nonmetabolic real presence views.[7] Metabolic real presence views argue that Christ's body is present in or around the physical elements. Nonmetabolic real presence views argue that Christ engrafts believers more deeply into himself even though his body is not locally present.[8] The following chart places each major thinker discussed in this section into either

---

[5] All Scripture quotations are from the English Standard Version.
[6] Edward Kilmartin, *The Eucharist in the West: History and Theology*, ed. Robert J. Daly (Collegeville, MN: The Liturgical Press, 1998), 79.
[7] The terms "metabolic presence" and "nonmetabolic presence" come from John Riggs, *The Lord's Supper in the Reformed Tradition: An Essay on the Mystical True Presence* (Louisville: Westminster John Knox, 2015), 15. I do not claim to be classifying each view exactly as Riggs would; he does not present a chart like the one below. I am nonetheless indebted to Riggs for these terms and for many of my applications of them to particular views.
[8] Riggs, *Reformed Tradition*, 34.

the metabolic or nonmetabolic real presence category.[9]

Era and Worldview	Metabolic Real Presence	Nonmetabolic Real Presence
The Fathers (Neoplatonism)	Early Antioch	Late Antioch; Augustine
Early Medievals ("Thingly Realism")	Radbertus	Late Antioch; Augustine
High Medievals	Berengar's opponents	Berengar of Tours
Late Medievals (Aristotelianism)	Thomas Aquinas (synthesis)	Thomas Aquinas (synthesis)
Reformation (Nominalism)	Luther	Bucer; Calvin

The following case studies of the Early, Medieval, and Reformation church offer context for understanding Calvin's view of the Lord's Supper.

Before examining these case studies, it may be helpful to define more precisely what constitutes a "real presence" view. A real presence view of the Lord's Supper is any view of

---

[9] It is unclear whether Origen and Tertullian (in his later teaching) held to the real presence of Christ in the Supper, so they do not appear in the following chart. For Tertullian, see Kilmartin, *West*, 9. For Origen, see Gary Macy, *The Banquet's Wisdom: A Short History of the Theologies of the Lord's Supper* (Mahwah, NJ: Paulist Press, 1992), 39.

the Lord's Supper that posits that Christ is present in a unique way. In other words, for a view of the Lord's Supper to be a "real presence" view, the presence of Christ in the Lord's Supper must amount to something more than his presence with believers at all times or even his presence with believers during the rest of corporate worship. A real presence view does not require the bodily presence of Christ, whether "in" the bread and the cup or mediated through them. Although Calvin's view does posit that the body of Christ nourishes believers, a view that could specify a unique way in which Christ is present without reference to his body would still count as a real presence view. It would simply be a different kind of presence than the one Calvin posits. What does not count as a real presence view is any view that ultimately reduces to Christ's presence with his people at all times in all places. Under my definition, every theologian in the chart above holds to a real presence view. A full-fledged memorialist view, which would not count as a real presence view, does not appear to have arisen until the time of the Reformation with the Anabaptists.

The Patristic Era

Although the first treatise on the Lord's Supper was not written until the ninth century, the Fathers often spoke about the Supper in works not dealing with the Eucharist as the main theme. The Patristics almost universally affirmed the real presence of Christ, but they affirmed it in different ways. Although there are many ways to approach the rich diversity of views present among the Fathers, this essay will examine the Fathers' positions by a case study of two contrasting schools of thought: the Antiochene school and the Neoplatonic school.[10]

The Antiochene school can be divided into two subgroups: Antioch up to the fourth century and Antioch after the fourth century.[11] Early Antioch is represented by such figures as John Chrysostom and Theodore of Mopsuestia;[12] the Western

---

[10] Kilmartin, *West*, xxiii. Macy identifies the Antiochene school with Aristotle, so it could perhaps also be termed the Aristotelian school. Macy, *Wisdom*, 39. In contrast to the Neoplatonic school, which is simply a school of thought, the Antiochene school is an actual school with a history dating back to the 2nd century.

[11] Kilmartin, *West*, 35.

[12] Ibid., 35.

theologians Hilary[13] and Ambrose[14] followed the theology of the early Antiochene school. Late Antioch is represented primarily by Nestorius and Theodoret of Cyrus.[15] The main representative of the Neoplatonic school was Augustine.[16]

The Antiochene School

The doctrines of the early and the late Antiochene schools can be best understood by examining two contrasting passages: one from an early Antiochene theologian and another from a late Antiochene theologian. Representing the early Antiochene school, Theodore of Mopsuestia wrote: "He (Jesus) did not say: 'This is the symbol of my body and blood,' but: 'This is my body and blood.' In this way he taught us not to look at the nature of what lies before us, but that this is changed into the body and blood through the accomplishment of the thanksgiving."[17] Compare this with the statement of Theodoret:

> "For he wished the partakers in the divine mysteries not to give heed to the nature of the visible objects, but, by means of the variation of the names, to believe the change wrought of grace. For He, we know, who spoke of his natural body as grain and bread, and, again, called Himself a vine, dignified the visible symbols by the appellation of the body and blood, not because He had changed their nature, but because to their nature He had added grace."[18]

These passages highlight the key point of contention between early and late Antioch: the doctrine of Eucharistic change. Theodore, the early Antiochene theologian, argued

---

[13] Kilmartin, *West*, 11.
[14] Ibid., 15.
[15] Ibid., 35.
[16] Ibid., xxiii.
[17] Theodore of Mopsuestia, *In Evangelium Matthaie*, Fragment 26, qtd. in Kilmartin, *West*, 39. I have omitted the Greek that Kilmartin includes for some terms.
[18] Theodoret, *Eranistes*, Dialogue 1, in New Advent, http://www.newadvent.org/fathers/27031.htm (accessed December 11, 2017).

that a change of being occurs in the elements: they become the very body and blood of Christ. By contrast, Theodoret, the late Antiochene theologian, argued that the elements do not undergo a change of being. Rather than becoming the body and blood of Christ, the visible elements instead possess "an intrinsic relation to the divine grace."[19] Theodore, however, bridged the gap between sign and signified not by appealing to a relationship between the elements and divine grace, but by positing "the unity of being of the sign and the thing signified."[20] For Theodoret, the grace of God bridges the gap between sign and signified; for Theodore, the sign becomes united with the thing signified.

The Neoplatonic School

Though other theologians such as "Justin Martyr, Athenagoras, and Aristedes were Platonists before their conversion,"[21] Augustine is the primary representative of the Neoplatonic school. A basic understanding of Plato's philosophy is necessary for understanding the Neoplatonic Eucharistic school. To that end, the most important aspect of Plato's philosophy to understand is that "the most 'real' things were those grasped by the mind; the least 'real' things were those things that were sensed. 'Essences' (or 'substances' or 'forms') were *always* more real than sense data."[22]

Understanding that Platonists considered the forms to be more real than sense data helps explain what the Neoplatonic school emphasized about the Eucharist. The Neoplatonic school not only rejected the doctrine of Eucharistic change[23] but also sometimes sharply distinguished between the sense data perceived in the Eucharist and the reality which the sense data signified. Augustine exemplified this distinction in his explanation of how to teach catechumens about the sacraments: "[I]t is first to be well impressed upon his notice

---

[19] Kilmartin, *West*, 40.
[20] Ibid.
[21] Macy, *Wisdom*, 39.
[22] Ibid., 41.
[23] Kilmartin, *West*, 48.

that the signs of divine things are, it is true, things visible, but that the invisible things themselves are also honored in them."[24] Augustine distinguished here between the sign, which is visible, and the thing signified, which is invisible. Augustine made an even sharper distinction when he wrote, "These things, my brothers, are called sacraments for the reason that in them one thing is seen, but another is understood. That which is seen has physical appearance, that which is understood has spiritual fruit."[25] Augustine speaks here in Platonic categories: he contrasts what is seen (sense data) with what is understood (essence). Similarly, in the second sentence of this passage Augustine makes a distinction between the physical and the spiritual.

Augustine not only distinguished between the sensible and the intellectual but also explicitly denied that the body of Christ is consumed by the partakers of the Supper. Augustine wrote, "What you see is transitory, but the invisible reality signified does not pass away, but abides…Is the body of Christ consumed?…Not at all!"[26] Augustine thus apparently denied what the early Antiochene school would have affirmed: that believers consume the physical body and blood of Christ. What then does it mean to eat and drink the body and blood of Christ? In his commentary on John 6, Augustine wrote, "This it is, therefore, for a man to eat that meat and to drink that drink, to dwell in Christ, and to have Christ dwelling in him."[27] Augustine draws a conclusion from this statement:

> Consequently, he that dwells not in Christ, and in whom Christ dwells not, doubtless neither eats His flesh [spiritually] nor drinks His blood [although he may press the sacrament of the body and blood of Christ carnally and visibly with his teeth], but rather does he eat and drink the sacrament of so great a thing

---

[24] Augustine, *On the Catechizing of the Uninstructed*, 26.50, in New Advent, http://www.newadvent.org/fathers/ (accessed December 11, 2017).
[25] Augustine, *Sermon 272*, in Boston College Libraries, https://newspapers.bc.edu/?a=d&d=bcctor20110901-01.2.14 (accessed December 11, 2017).
[26] Augustine, *Sermon 227*, qtd. in Macy, *Wisdom*, 52.
[27] Augustine, *Tractates on the Gospel of John*, 26.18, in New Advent, http://www.newadvent.org/fathers/1701026.htm (accessed December 11, 2017).

to his own judgment, because he, being unclean, has presumed to come to the sacraments of Christ, which no man takes worthily except he that is pure.[28]

For Augustine, merely consuming the visible elements does not imply a true partaking. Rather, only those in whom Christ dwells, or (which is a different way of saying the same thing) those who are "pure," partake of the sacrament in a salutary way.

Tertullian, at least in his earlier teaching,[29] appears to have stood in the Platonic tradition.[30] In response to Marcion, a heretic who believed the body of Christ was not a real human body, Tertullian wrote, "Then, having taken the bread and given it to His disciples, He made it His own body, by saying, 'This is my body,' that is, the figure of my body. A figure, however, there could not have been, unless there were first a veritable body. An empty thing, or phantom, is incapable of a figure."[31] Tertullian's argument is simple: every figure points beyond itself to some real thing. If Christ did not have a real human body, he could not have used the bread as a figure for his body. Like Augustine, Tertullian works within Platonic categories: the visible elements participate in the greater reality of the Incarnation.[32]

The Early Medieval Period: Radbertus and Ratramnus

Because of barbarian invasions, very little was written on the Eucharist from the sixth to the ninth century.[33] The most important development in the doctrine of the real presence during the ninth century was the debate[34] between two medieval

---

[28] Augustine, *Tractates on the Gospel of John*, 26.18. in New Advent, http://www.newadvent.org/fathers/1701026.htm (accessed December 11, 2017).

[29] Kilmartin notes that Tertullian's later teaching (during his Montanist or Montanist-like stage) placed less emphasis on the real presence of Christ. Kilmartin, *West*, 9.

[30] Kilmartin, *West*, 8. Macy links Tertullian more closely with Stoicism. Macy, *Wisdom*, 39.

[31] Tertullian, *Against Marcion*, 4.40, in New Advent http://www.newadvent.org/fathers/03124.htm (accessed December 11, 2017).

[32] Kilmartin, *West*, 9.

[33] Macy, *Wisdom*, 68.

[34] The word "debate" is actually a bit of a misnomer, since there was never a formal debate between these two men.

monks: Radbertus and Ratramnus. Paschasius Radbertus, a monk at the monastery of Corbie, wrote *The Lord's Body and Blood* for the education of the Saxon monks.[35] It was the first theological work written exclusively on the Eucharist.[36] Radbertus affirms that the body of Christ in the Eucharist is "nothing different, of course, from what was born of Mary, suffered on the cross, and rose again from the tomb."[37] Radbertus explains why believers must partake of Christ's flesh: "[T]hat, through God the Word made flesh, the flesh might progress to God the Word, the Word's flesh, of course, becomes food in this mystery."[38] In other words, believers partake of Christ's flesh in the Supper because partaking of his flesh was the very reason for his Incarnation. Christ partook of human flesh in order that human beings might partake of divinity.[39]

Ratramnus offered a view of the Supper that differed from the one presented by Radbertus. As a monk under Radbertus (the abbot of Corbie by the time Ratramnus wrote), Ratramnus wrote *Christ's Body and Blood* in response to a letter from the emperor Charles the Bald, who had received (and probably read) a copy of Radbertus' *The Lord's Body and Blood*.[40] In his letter to Ratramnus, Charles asked two questions: "whether that which in the church is received into the mouth of the faithful becomes the body and blood of Christ in a mystery or in truth"[41] and "whether it is that body which was born of Mary, suffered, died, and was buried, and which, rising again and ascending into heaven, sits on the right hand of the Father."[42]

Ratramnus responded to the first question as any skilled debater would—by defining the terms. Ratramnus argued that "'figure' means a kind of overshadowing that reveals its intent

---

[35] Macy, *Wisdom*, 70.
[36] Ibid.
[37] Paschasius Radbertus, "The Lord's Body and Blood (Selections)," in *Early Medieval Theology*, ed. and trans. George E. McCracken (Louisville: Westminster John Knox,1957), 94.
[38] Radbertus, *Medieval Theology*, 96.
[39] Macy, *Wisdom*, 70.
[40] Ibid., 72.
[41] Ratramnus, "Christ's body and blood," in *Early Medieval Theology*, ed. and trans. George E. McCracken (Louisville: Westminster John Knox: 1957), 119.
[42] Ratramnus, *Medieval Theology*, 119.

under some sort of veil."[43] Ratramnus seems to mean something like metonymy when he talks about figure, because he uses Jesus' vine and branches discourse as an example of figure and argues that the Scriptures he has quoted as illustrations of figure "say one thing and hint at another."[44] That Ratramnus includes metonymy under his definition of figure becomes clearer when he states that with truth, in contrast to figure, "nothing here is adumbrated by concealing metaphors."[45] Ratramnus defines truth as "representation of clear fact, not obscured by any shadowy images, but uttered in pure and open, and to say it more plainly, in natural meanings."[46] As an example, Ratramnus refers to "when Christ is said to have been born of the Virgin, suffered, been crucified, died, and been buried."[47] Truth is that in which "Nothing else may be understood than what is said."[48]

Under these definitions, it is not surprising that Ratramnus concluded that Christ is present in figure rather than in truth. Sounding like Augustine, Ratramnus wrote that "that bread which through the ministry of the priest comes to be Christ's body exhibits one thing outwardly to human sense, and it proclaims another thing inwardly to the minds of the faithful."[49] If there were nothing hidden in the Supper, Ratramnus argued, there would be no mystery and hence no need for faith.[50]

In response to the second question, whether Christ's body is the same as that born of Mary, Ratramnus argued that it is not the same body. Instead, "a great difference separates the body in which Christ suffered...from this body which daily in the mystery of the Passion is celebrated by the faithful."[51] Of what body then do believers partake in the Supper? Ratramnus wrote that "that bread and that drink are Christ's body or

---

[43] Ratramnus seems to use this interchangeably with "mystery."
[44] Ratramnus, *Medieval Theology*, 119.
[45] Ratramnus, *Medieval Theology*, 120.
[46] Ibid.
[47] Ibid.
[48] Ibid.
[49] Ibid.
[50] Ibid., 121.
[51] Ratramnus, *Medieval Theology*, 137.

blood, not with respect to what they seem, but with respect to the fact that they spiritually support the substance of life."[52] Consciously following Ambrose while also anticipating Calvin, Ratramnus linked the presence of Christ with the work of the Spirit: "Clearly [Ambrose] shows with respect to what it is held to be Christ's body, namely, with respect to the fact that the Spirit of Christ is in it."[53] Following John 6:63, Ratramnus brings these two previous statements together: "We therefore see that that food of the Lord's body and that drink of his blood, with respect to which they are truly his body and truly his blood, are so, namely, with respect to spirit and life."[54]

In distinguishing the literal body of Christ from the Eucharistic body, Ratramnus argued that the literal body of Christ is a physical body, whereas the Eucharistic body of Christ is a spiritual body. Citing Luke 24:39, Ratramnus argued that Christ's physical body is "capable of being touched or visible even after the resurrection."[55] Commenting on Augustine, Ratramnus sums up the distinction between the two bodies:

> The former is whole, not cut into parts, nor concealed in any figures; the latter, which is contained on the Lord's Table, and is a figure because it is a sacrament, has also, as it outwardly seems, a corporeal appearance which feeds the body, but inwardly understood it has spiritual fruit which quickens the soul.[56]

The resurrected body of Christ is a physical human body. By contrast, the Eucharistic body is physical only in the sense that it has a physical outward appearance; it is ultimately spiritual, since it feeds the soul of the partaker.

In a conclusion that aches for the Second Coming, Ratramnus adds an eschatological dimension to his argument. He distinguishes between the two bodies of Christ not only by contrast between the physical and the spiritual, but also by

---

[52] Ratramnus, *Medieval Theology*, 137.
[53] Ibid., 136.
[54] Ibid., 142.
[55] Ibid., 143.
[56] Ibid., 145.

contrast between the present and the future. The two bodies "are separated from each other by as great a difference as exists between the pledge and the thing on behalf of which the pledge is handed down, and as exists between appearance and truth."[57] Ratramnus writes that the body of Christ in the Eucharist is "both a pledge and an appearance, but that body[58] is truth itself. This body shall be practiced until that one is reached; but when it is reached, this one will be taken away."[59] Ratramnus reasons that the *telos* of the church is to experience the body of Christ in truth. The Eucharist is therefore "what is done on the way,"[60] and the body present in it is the figure, not the reality. Otherwise, the great hope of the church would already be attained.[61]

The controversy between Radbertus and Ratramnus demonstrates an underlying shift from the worldview of the Fathers to the worldview of the medievals. Edward Kilmartin summarizes this shift of philosophical lenses: "Whereas the idea of participation of the image in the prototype was taken for granted in the ancient Greek worldview, the image now took on the role of signaling a reality to which it can be related only externally."[62] Radbertus and Ratramnus share the assumptions of this "thingly realism," as Kilmartin calls it; they simply take different sides of the dilemma produced by their shared presuppositions.[63] Both Radbertus and Ratramnus assume

---

[57] Ratramnus, *Medieval Theology*, 143.
[58] That is, Christ's glorified body.
[59] Ratramnus, *Medieval Theology*, 143.
[60] Ibid.
[61] In a telling historical foreshadowing, Ratramnus concludes his argument by quoting John 6:63, the text which would become the *sine qua non* of Zwingli's Eucharistic teaching.
[62] Kilmartin, *West*, 79. Kilmartin suggests that the "practical materialism" of the medieval West may have a sociological cause, "the unsettled situation of migratory people throughout northern Europe from the fourth to the ninth century."
[63] Kilmartin, *West*, 79. Kilmartin sees the Western Eucharistic controversies and the Western condemnation of icons as resulting from the same worldview shift. In the iconoclastic controversy, the nuances of Neoplatonic philosophy allowed the Eastern church to affirm various kinds of veneration between *latreia* and idolatry, whereas the Frankish theologians rejected icons as purely material aids to memory and therefore not worthy of any degree of veneration. Kilmartin, *West*, 79-82.

the Supper must be either figure or reality; neither argue that the figure might be a *"reality of a particular kind."*[64] Although Ratramnus's view can still be considered a real presence view in the sense that believers receive life from Christ, the dichotomy between metabolic and nonmetabolic views of the Lord's Supper was greater in this debate than in most of the differences the patristic era.

Radbertus and Ratramnus Rehashed: The Berengarian Controversy

Although Ratramnus' spiritual presence view was not officially condemned during his lifetime,[65] Radbertus' literalist view became the dominant position. The issue did not become terribly controversial until Berengar, an eleventh century teacher at the choir school of Tours,[66] expressed a view similar to Ratramnus' position.[67] Though Radbertus' *The Lord's Body and Blood* was the first treatise on the Lord's Supper, the controversy surrounding Berengar was "the first major discussion concerning the Eucharist in the history of Christianity."[68]

The Berengarian controversy reveals a further separation of symbol and reality. Berengar wrote during a time when extreme realism dominated the theological milieu.[69] In contrast to his opponents, Berengar argued that the bread and wine never cease to be bread and wine; rather, "the body and blood of the Lord are contained there in a manner that is true but hidden."[70]

---

[64] Kilmartin, *West*, 84. Emphasis original.
[65] By the time of the controversy between Berengar and his opponents, Ratramnus' work was apparently attributed to John Scotus Erigena. It was condemned and destroyed by Berengar's opponents at a synod in Vercelli in 1050. Jaroslav Pelikan, *The Growth of Medieval Theology (600-1300), vol. 3 of The Christian Tradition: A History of the Development of Doctrine* (Chicago: University of Chicago Press, 1978), 186.
[66] Macy, *Wisdom*, 75.
[67] Ibid., 76.
[68] Ibid., 81.
[69] Kilmartin, *West*, 97.
[70] Guitmond of Aversa, *On the Reality of the Body and Blood of Christ in the Eucharist*, qtd. in Pelikan, *Growth*, 199. Guitmond is explaining his understanding of Berengar's view. Pelikan notes that much of Berengar's thought must be reconstructed from the work of his opponents. Pelikan, *Growth*, 187.

In his day, Berengar's view was called "impanation."[71] Berengar touched on many of the same themes as Ratramnus: the two bodies of Christ,[72] the physicality of Christ's ascended body,[73] and a metonymic understanding of figure.[74]

The response of Berengar's opponents demonstrates the increasing divide between symbolic and materialist views. Gary Macy summarizes the reasoning of Berengar's opponents: like Radbertus, they argue that "the physical...body of the risen Lord must be present in the sacrament, because it is the natural contact with this glorified body which saves us."[75] Some, such as Rupert, argued that contact with Christ's glorified body was so integral to salvation that the Old Testament saints would have to receive the Eucharist before they could enter heaven.[76]

Unlike Ratramnus, Berengar saw his views condemned during his lifetime. His opponents forced him to take an oath that illustrates the extremes of eleventh-century metabolic views of the Supper:

> ...the bread and wine which are laid on the altar are after consecration not only a sacrament but also the true body and blood of our Lord Jesus Christ, and they are physically taken up and broken in the hands of the priest and crushed by the teeth of the faithful, not only sacramentally but in truth.[77]

The medieval Roman church could hardly have affirmed metabolic presence any more strongly. The oath not only uses "truth" language reminiscent of the controversy between Radbertus and Ratramnus but also describes the physical presence of Christ in the most graphic of terms.[78]

---

[71] Pelikan, *Growth*, 199.
[72] Ibid., 192.
[73] Ibid.
[74] Ibid., 201.
[75] Macy, *Wisdom*, 78.
[76] Ibid., 79.
[77] Berengar, *Fragments*, qtd. in Macy, *Wisdom*, 77.
[78] Macy also notes that a dualistic sect known as the Cathars probably used Berengar's teaching on the Supper to support its positions, which suggests how dualistic Berengar's position may have seemed. Macy, *Wisdom*, 84.

The Scholastic Era: Thomas Aquinas

The eleventh and twelfth centuries saw the development of the schools and, with it, the advent of the scholastics. This period produced a flood of work on the Eucharist.[79] Thomas Aquinas attempted to synthesize symbolic and materialist views using the philosophy of Aristotle, and must therefore be understood in light of Aristotelian categories. In contrast to Plato, Aristotle argued that matter and form are not independent of each other. With Plato, however, Aristotle argued that "the form or essence of a thing was still the most important part of anything."[80] Aristotle taught that things consist of substance and accidents. The substance of a thing is "the essence of any particular thing, grasped by the mind alone."[81] The accidents of a thing are "sense data which change from individual to individual without changing the substance."[82]

Aquinas used these Aristotelian categories to explain what happens in the Eucharist. In the Eucharist, the bread and wine undergo *trans-substance*-iation: their substance is transformed from ordinary bread and wine into the body and blood of Christ. Yet their accidental properties—their color, shape, size, and (if Aquinas had lived in the modern world) their molecular composition—remain the same. An analogy may help explain. If I took a baseball bat and painted it green, its accidents (namely, its color) would change but its essence (its being a bat) would remain the same. Putting a bat through a wood chipper, on the other hand, would change the bat's essence (it would no longer be a bat).[83] What happens to the elements in the Roman Catholic view is the opposite of painting the bat green. The accidents remain the same, but the substance changes. In all its physical properties, the consecrated bread is identical to ordinary bread. But in its essence, the consecrated bread is the body of Christ. Aquinas'

---

[79] Macy, *Wisdom*, 85. According to Macy, "In one recent study of this period, over one hundred and fifty different works treating the eucharist were identified."
[80] Macy, *Wisdom*, 105.
[81] Ibid., 106.
[82] Ibid., 106
[83] I borrow this illustration from Dr. Aaron O'Kelley.

doctrine of transubstantiation paved a middle way between a crudely conceived substantialism and a nonmetabolic view. It avoided crude substantialism because substance is an entity perceived by the mind; it avoided a nonmetabolic view because it regarded the substance of the elements as becoming the body of Christ.[84]

One particularly relevant medieval critique of transubstantiation comes from John Peter Olivi. Olivi argued that Aquinas misunderstood Aristotle's definition of quantity and, therefore, if Christ's body is to be present in the Eucharist, it must have quantity. Otherwise, it would be a ghost or a spirit, like the Christ of the Docetist heretics.[85] This challenge is particularly relevant because, like the controversy between Radbertus and Ratramnus, it anticipates the debate between Luther and Calvin over the nature of the resurrected body of Christ. Although Luther rejected transubstantiation, he affirmed the physical presence of Christ in the Lord's Supper. Luther explained this presence by arguing that Christ's body, because of the communication of divine attributes to the human nature, can be in multiple locations at once. To this Calvin offered the same response that Olivi offered to Aquinas: if Christ's body can be everywhere at the same time, it is not a human body. Despite objections like Olivi's, transubstantiation became the dominant view of the medieval church.[86]

The Reformation: Luther, Zwingli, and Bucer

The Lutheran view of the Lord's Supper is often labeled "consubstantiation": Christ's body and blood are present "in, with, and under" the elements. This language suggests that the body and blood are not identical with the bread and wine, but are united with it in such a way that each can be distinguished

---

[84] Macy, *Wisdom*, 107.
[85] Ibid., 112.
[86] Macy, *Wisdom*, 104. There were some medieval theologians who suggested alternative ways of understanding the conversion of the elements, including consubstantiation (in which the body and blood are added to the bread and wine) and annihilation (in which the bread and wine are cease to be bread and wine at the moment of consecration). Kilmartin, *West*, 145-46.

from the other, like water in a sponge.[87] Perhaps a better term for the Lutheran doctrine of the presence of Christ in the Lord's Supper would be *unio sacramentalis* (sacramental unity), a term Luther himself used.[88] Because the bread and wine are united with the body and blood of Christ, both believers and unbelievers partake of Christ in the Supper. Although Luther's position may seem similar to the Catholic position, Luther rejected the Catholic position for two reasons.[89] First, he thought it relied too much on Aristotelian philosophy. Second, he viewed it as unnecessarily complex. The bread and wine need not cease to be bread and wine in order for Christ to be present.

The Zwinglian view of the Lord's Supper is often termed the "memorialist" view, but this term, like "consubstantiation" is somewhat misleading. Zwingli's view is called a memorialist view because Zwingli taught the Lord's Supper is a memorial, or remembrance, of the death of Christ. Luther stressed "This is my body"; Zwingli stressed "Do this in rememberance of me."[90] But in emphasizing the memorial nature of the Supper, Zwingli did not deny that Christ is present; he simply denied the physical presence of Christ espoused by Luther and Rome (and, in some sense, by Calvin). For Zwingli, Christ is present in the Supper in a special way, not by being physically present, but because the tangible nature of the Supper aids believers' faith. Because the Lord's Supper is a remembrance of Christ's work rather than a physical partaking of Christ, the benefit of the Supper comes only by believing.

The Reformer who came closest to Calvin's view before Calvin himself was Martin Bucer. Calvin admired Bucer's skill as an exegete, claiming that "No one has to our knowledge exerted himself so precisely and diligently in biblical exegesis."[91] Bucer, eighteen years his senior, wrote to Calvin expressing his desire to meet and discuss the "entire administration of the teaching

---

[87] I borrow this illustration from Dr. Aaron O'Kelley.
[88] Bernhard Lohse, *Martin Luther's Theology: Its Historical and Systematic Development*, trans. Roy Harrisville. (Minneapolis: Fortress Press, 1999), 309.
[89] David Steinmetz, *Luther in Context* (Bloomington: Indiana University Press, 1986), 72.
[90] 1 Cor. 11:24 (ESV).
[91] John Calvin, *Joannis Calvini Opera quae extant Omnia* Xb, col. 404, qtd. in Willem Van't Spijker, "Bucer's Influence on Calvin: Church and Community," in *Martin Bucer: Reforming Church and Community*, ed. D.F. Wright (Cambridge: Cambridge University Press, 1994), 33.

of Christ."[92] The *Confessio Fidei de Eucharistia*, drafted by Calvin, was co-signed by Bucer.[93] The overarching doctrinal link between Calvin and Bucer was their shared emphasis on work of the Spirit in uniting the believer to Christ.[94]

Bucer distinguished between two parallel realities in the Lord's Supper. He wrote that "there are 'duae res' (two realities), one earthly and one heavenly or spiritual."[95] Bucer understood the earthly and heavenly realities as parallel: "just as the mouth eats the bread, so the mouth of faith feeds off the body of Christ."[96] He used Augustine's definition of a sacrament to argue that the earthly reality is subordinate to the heavenly reality.[97]

Like Calvin after him, Bucer sought to set forth a mediating position between Luther's substantialist understanding of the Supper and the memorialists' symbolic view.[98] In contrast to the memorialists, Bucer affirmed that the Lord's Supper provides unique benefits to the believer that extend beyond subjective strengthening of faith: "For us it is not sufficient that he died for us on the cross. He himself must also live in us, and share with us the communion of his flesh and blood."[99] Bucer was likely concerned, as Luther was, that Zwingli's emphasis on the Supper as remembrance downplayed the current presence of Christ among believers.[100] Bucer did not, however, fully accept Luther's *unio sacramentalis,* the sacramental union between the bread of the Supper and the body of Christ. He rejected Luther's corporeal presence view, and, late in his life, modified Luther's *unio sacramentalis* to *unio pacti exhibitivi*.[101] Hazlett

---

[92] John Calvin, *Joannis Calvini Opera quae extant Omnia*, XLV, col. 4, qtd. in Van't Spijker, "Influence," 33.

[93] Van't Spijker, "Influence," 33.

[94] Ibid., 32.

[95] Hazlett, Ian, "Eucharistic Communion: Impulses and Directions in Martin Bucer's Thought," in *Martin Bucer: Reforming Church and Community*, ed. D.F. Wright (Cambridge: Cambridge University Press, 1994), 74

[96] Hazlett, "Communion," 74

[97] Ibid., 76.

[98] Ibid., 81.

[99] Martin Bucer, *Martini Buceri Opera Omnia*, qtd. in Hazlett, "Communion," 79.

[100] Hazlett, "Communion," 79. Hazlett notes that Bucer's reading of the Greek Fathers strengthened his belief in the relationship between the Christian and the ascended body of Christ.

[101] Ibid., 80.

understands "pactum" to mean "agreed means."[102] The following quote sheds some light on what Bucer means by "agreed means:" "[God] can present his benefits to anyone he wills, without any signs. However, as long as he offers them to us in specific signs, our neglect of these signs means the repudiation of his benefits. For not we ourselves, but he himself prescribes to us how we are to receive his gifts."[103] By the definition offered at the beginning of this essay, Bucer's view qualifies as a real presence view, though the connection between the sign and the thing signified is contingent on God's choice.

What precisely is the unique benefit the sacrament conveys? Bucer wrote, "In the sacrament, both Christ himself and the communion of his flesh and blood are given and received; we become his members, flesh of his flesh, bone of his bones, we remain in him and he in us."[104] The Eucharist conveys fellowship with Christ. Believers receive "the food of the new internal man, the food of eternal life, the strengthening of faith by which the just man lives, the increase of new life, the life of God in us."[105] In this passage, Bucer specifically identifies strengthened faith as one of the benefits of the Supper, though his emphasis seems to be on the communication of God's life into believers.

Conclusion

In the final analysis of the various views of the real presence, two key themes emerge. First, the history of the real presence of Christ in the Lord's Supper until Calvin seems to be a history of decreasing diversity.[106] The Fathers present a variety of views on the presence of Christ: the bodily presence view of early Antioch, the nature plus grace view of late Antioch, and the Neoplatonic view of Augustine and Tertullian.[107] None of these

---

[102] Ibid.
[103] qtd. in Hazlett, "Communion," 79.
[104] Martin Bucer, *Letter to à Lasco*, qtd. in Hazlett, "Communion," 80.
[105] Ibid., 81.
[106] The theme of decreasing diversity is the main thread of Gary Macy's *The Banquet's Wisdom*. He expresses this theme in such chapter titles as "The Origins of Diversity: The Early Church," "Diversity in Decline: The Later Middle Ages," and "Diversity Denied: The Reformation: Luther and Zwingli."
[107] These are only three among many other variations among the Fathers.

views were condemned as heretical by the early church.[108] Even the controversy between Radbertus and Ratramnus did not result in the condemnation of Ratramnus during his lifetime. When a similar controversy arose in the eleventh century, however, Berengar was condemned and forced to recant. After Aquinas, transubstantiation became the dominant position in the medieval Catholic Church.[109]

Second, the history of the real presence of Christ in the Lord's Supper until Calvin seems to be a history of a narrowing concept of what it means for Christ to be really present.[110] The worldview of the church Fathers allowed for the Lord's Supper to be both symbolic and real. In the Platonic worldview, the most real things are not those grasped with the senses but those understood with the mind. Furthermore, the Platonic worldview posits that images are not devoid of the presence of the prototype but are simply another mode of the prototype's presence.

The controversy between Radbertus and Ratramnus represents a move away from the worldview of the Fathers. Charles the Bald asked Ratramnus whether Christ is present in truth or in mystery, as if the two are necessarily opposed. The Berengarian controversy represents just how much the medievals had departed from the worldview of the Fathers. Berengar was forced to affirm that the bread and wine are "not only a sacrament but also the true body and blood of our Lord Jesus Christ, and they are physically taken up and broken in the hands of the priest and crushed by the teeth of the faithful."[111] This oath is a far cry from Augustine's denial, "Is the body of Christ consumed?...Not at all!"[112] Even the Antiochene Fathers would not have affirmed such a visceral description of believers consuming the body and blood of Christ

The second theme appears to have opened the door for the first. A worldview where the presence of the image implies the

---

[108] The Fathers did, however, often appeal to the doctrine of the Eucharist to refute heresies.

[109] The dominance of transubstantiation meant the dominance not of a real presence view over non-real presence views but of one particular understanding of the real presence over others.

[110] This important theme is highlighted by Edward Kilmartin in *The Eucharist in the West*.

[111] Berengar, *Fragments*, qtd. in Macy, *Wisdom*, 77.

[112] Augustine, *Sermon 227*, qtd. in Macy, *Wisdom*, 52.

presence of the prototype allows for various ways of stating the doctrine of the real presence of Christ. By contrast, in a worldview that has no place for image as a kind of reality, the Lord's Supper must be either figure or truth. The more the medieval church began to emphasize truth over image, the more those who emphasized image over truth were seen as enemies of sound doctrine. A philosophy that divided the image from the prototype ended up also dividing the church.

SECTION III: CALVIN'S VIEW OF THE LORD'S SUPPER

Calvin often presented his view in contrast to the what he understood to be the Zwinglians' "too narrow description" of the presence of Christ in the Supper on the one hand and "the contrary fault of excess" displayed by the Lutherans.[113] Like Luther and unlike the memorialists (whom Calvin seems to have associated with Zwingli), Calvin affirmed that Christ is present in the Supper not simply because the Supper aids believers' meditation on him. Like the memorialists and unlike Luther, Calvin denied that Christ's physical body is present on earth in the Eucharist. Calvin argued that although Christ's body is in heaven and believers are on earth, believers partake of the Supper by the power of the Holy Spirit, who "truly unites things separated in space."[114]

Calvin Rejects a Lutheran View.

Calvin rejected Luther's view because he thought it relied on an errant Christology. Luther's view, at least in Calvin's understanding, posits a local presence of Christ in the Eucharist: Christ's physical body is present on earth in the sacrament. Any

---

[113] John Calvin, *Calvin: Institutes of the Christian Religion* (Philadelphia: The Westminster Press, 1960), 4.17.7. As noted in the previous section, Zwingli did not hold to a strictly memorialist position, though some memorialists may claim Zwingli as a representative of their position. Nonetheless, when Calvin defines his view, he often uses the memorialist view, which he appears to think Zwingli held, as a foil against which he defines his view.
[114] Calvin, *Institutes*, 4.17.10.

view that asserts a local presence must explain how Christ's body can be present in more than one place at the same time. If Christ ascended to heaven, how can his body be present in the Supper? Luther explained Christ's presence in two places at once by arguing that Christ's human nature is omnipresent; therefore Christ can be both in heaven and in the Supper. Christ's human nature possesses the attribute of omnipresence by virtue of its union with his divine nature. To support his belief that Christ's human nature receives the attribute of omnipresence from his divine nature, Luther appealed to the *communicatio idiomatum* ("communication of attributes"), the doctrine that certain attributes of Christ's divinity are "communicated" to his humanity.

Calvin argued that Luther's Christology confuses Christ's two natures, divesting Christ of his full humanity. Calvin rejects Luther's appeal to the *communicatio idiomatum,* arguing that the union of Christ's human and divine natures does not imply that every attribute of divinity also belongs to Christ's humanity: "The hypostatic union of the two natures is not equivalent to a communication of the immensity of the Godhead to the flesh, since the peculiar properties of both natures are perfectly accordant with unity of person."[115] To borrow the language of the Chalcedonian definition, Calvin is concerned that Christ's human and divine natures be "united, not confused." Calvin accuses his Lutheran opponents of advocating a Eutychian Christology, the heretical Christology condemned at Chalcedon.[116] In contrast to the orthodox doctrine of the hypostatic union (Christ is one person with two distinct natures), Eutychianism teaches that Christ's humanity and divinity combined to create a different nature that was neither fully divine nor fully human. Calvin argues that his Lutheran critics commit the same error when they attribute omnipresence to Christ's humanity.

Implicit in Calvin's accusation of Eutychianism is his

---

[115] John Calvin. "Clear Explanation of Sound Doctrine Concerning the True Partaking of the Flesh and Blood of Christ in the Holy Supper, in Order to Dissipate the Mists of Tileman Heshusius," in *Calvin's Tracts Relating to the Reformation,* trans. Henry Beveridge. (Edinburgh: T&T Clark, 1860-69), 2:558.

[116] Calvin, *Institutes,* 4.17.30.

premise that an omnipresent body cannot be considered a human body. Calvin maintains that "if Christ's body existed in this state, it was a phantasm or apparition."[117] All human bodies are restricted to one location: "such is the condition of flesh that it must subsist in one definite place, with its own size and form."[118] Calvin allows no exception for Christ's physical body: "Christ's body is limited by the general characteristics common to all human bodies, and is contained in heaven (where it was once for all received) until Christ return in judgement [Acts 3:21], so we deem it utterly unlawful to draw it back under these corruptible elements or to imagine it to be present everywhere."[119] Christ's full humanity requires that his human nature be present only in one place. If his body is ascended into heaven, it cannot be present on earth in the Supper.

Calvin presents an alternative solution to the puzzle that confronts any view that affirms a partaking of Christ's flesh and blood: "How can believers partake of Christ's flesh when he is in heaven and they are on earth?" Luther solves the puzzle by arguing that Christ's flesh is omnipresent and can therefore be present on earth in the Supper. Calvin solves the puzzle by arguing believers partake of Christ's ascended flesh by the power of the Holy Spirit:

> Even though it seems unbelievable that Christ's flesh, separated from us by such great distance, penetrates to us, so that it becomes our food, let us remember how far the secret power of the Holy Spirit towers above all our senses, and how foolish it is to wish to measure his immeasurableness by our measure. What, then, our mind does not comprehend, let faith conceive: the Spirit truly unites things separated in space.[120]

Calvin is able to explain how believers can partake of Christ's flesh without Christ's body being present on earth.

---

[117] Ibid., 4.17.17.
[118] Ibid., 4.17.24.
[119] Ibid., 4.17.12.
[120] Ibid., 4.17.10.

In maintaining Christ's local absence from the Supper, Calvin is concerned not simply for Christological orthodoxy but for the glory of Christ. Calvin maintains, "We hold that there must be no local limitation, that the glorious body of Christ must not be degraded to earthly elements."[121] Calvin's view bridges the gap between heaven and earth not by bringing Christ down, but by lifting believers up.[122] Calvin appeals to the historic liturgical phrase *sursum corda* ("lift up your hearts") to argue that in the Supper, believers are raised to heaven: "it was established of old that before consecration the people should be told in a loud voice to lift up their hearts."[123]

Calvin Rejects a Memorialist View

Because of his belief that the Holy Spirit raises believers to heaven to feed on Christ, Calvin's view is often called the "spiritual presence" view. As with the terms "consubstantiation" and "memorialist," the term "spiritual presence" is easily misunderstood. Some have associated Calvin's "spiritual presence" view the memorialist view that the Lord's Supper is primarily an aid to faith. Some of Calvin's language in *The Institutes* appears to support a memorialist reading of Calvin. Calvin writes: "In this Sacrament we have such full witness of all these things that we must certainly consider them *as if* Christ here present were himself set before our eyes and touched by our hands."[124] The words "as if" make it seem as though Christ is not actually present in the Supper, but rather that the Supper is merely a witness to the benefits Christ conveys ("these things"). The presence of the benefits of union with Christ make it as though he were present even though he is not.

Calvin appears to offer support to such as interpretation when he writes:

---

[121] John Calvin, "Reply by Calvin to Cardinal Sadolet's Letter," in *Calvin's Tracts Relating to the Reformation*, trans. Henry Beveridge (Edinburgh: T&T Clark, 1860-69), 1:41.
[122] Ibid., 4.17.31.
[123] Ibid., 4.17.36.
[124] Ibid., 4.17.13. Emphasis added.

> He shows his presence in power and strength, is always among his own people, and breathes his life upon them, and lives in them, sustaining them, strengthening, quickening, keeping them unharmed, *as if* he were present in the body...In this manner, the body and blood of Christ are shown to us in the Sacrament.[125]

The language of this passage sounds almost memorialist. The Lord's Supper does not imply a special presence of Christ; Christ is "always among his own people." He sustains and strengthens them, not because he is really present, but as if he were present. Calvin's use of the language of remembrance strengthens the case for a memorialist reading of Calvin: "the Sacrament does not cause Christ to begin to be the bread of life; but when it reminds us that he was made the bread of life, which we continually eat, and which gives us a relish and savor of that bread, it causes us to feel the power of that bread."[126] Calvin's language in this passage emphasizes the subjectivity of the Lord's Supper: it "reminds" believers of Christ and causes them to "feel the power of that bread."

Elsewhere in *The Institutes*, however, Calvin vigorously denies that he holds to a purely intellectual, subjective partaking. In response to such an accusation, Calvin writes, "I leave no place for the sophistry that what I mean when I say Christ is received by faith is that he is received only by understanding and imagination."[127] Calvin rejects the view that eating Christ's flesh refers simply to the subjective action of the believer:

> For there are some who define the eating of Christ's flesh and the drinking of his blood as, in one word, nothing but to believe in Christ. But it seems to me that Christ meant to teach something more definite, and more elevated, in that noble discourse in which he commends to us the eating of his flesh. It is that we are quickened by the true partaking of him; and he

---

[125] Ibid., 4.17.18. Emphasis added.
[126] Ibid., 4.17.5.
[127] Ibid., 4.17.11.

> has therefore designated this partaking by the words "eating" and "drinking," in order that no one should think that the life that we receive from him is received by mere knowledge."[128]

For Calvin, eating Christ's flesh means not simply believing in Christ, but receiving life from him.

Not only does Calvin explicitly reject a subjective, intellectual view of the Supper, but the rest of *The Institutes* demonstrates how a "real presence" understanding of Calvin can account for the three seemingly memorialist passages discussed above. First, the presence of Christ's benefits does not exclude, but rather implies, his personal presence. Calvin writes:

> But as the blessings of Jesus Christ do not belong to us at all, unless he be previously ours, it is necessary, first of all, that he be given us in the Supper, in order that the things which we have mentioned may be truly accomplished in us. For this reason I am wont to say, that the substance of the sacraments is the Lord Jesus.[129]

Second, Christ's continued presence with his people does not exclude, but rather implies, the real presence of Christ in the Supper. Calvin explains that "the use of the Supper is not unnecessary, because we there receive Christ more fully, though already, by the faith of the gospel, he is so far ours and dwells in us."[130] Third, that the Lord's Supper is a memorial does not entail a denial of the real presence. Calvin affirms that "the Lord here not only recalls to our memory, as we have already explained, the abundance of his bounty, but, so to speak, gives it into our hand and arouses us to recognize it."[131] Calvin and the memorialists agree that the Lord's Supper is a remembrance, but only Calvin affirms that believers feed on Christ's physical

---

[128] Ibid., 4.17.5.
[129] John Calvin, "Short Treatise on the Holy Supper of Our Lord Jesus Christ," in *Calvin's Tracts Relating to the Reformation,* trans. Henry Beveridge (Edinburgh: T&T Clark, 1860-69), 2:169.
[130] Calvin, "Clear Explanation," 2:534.
[131] Calvin, *Institutes,* 4.17.37.

body (in a qualified sense).

Calvin's opponents apparently also made a less serious error and interpreted the "spiritual presence" as contrary to the bodily presence of Christ. Calvin explicitly denies that spiritual presence excludes physical presence: "I am not satisfied with those persons who, recognizing that we have some communion with Christ, when they would show what it is, make us partakers of the Spirit only, omitting mention of flesh and blood."[132] Calvin explains that the Spirit is the means, not the object, of the believers' partaking:

> They falsely boast that all we teach of spiritual eating is contrary, as they say, to true and real eating, seeing that we pay attention only to the manner, which with them is carnal, while they enclose Christ in bread. For us the manner is spiritual because the secret power of the Spirit is the bond of our union with Christ.[133]

The "spiritual presence" view does not teach that believers partake of the Spirit instead of partaking of Christ. Both Calvin and Luther affirm that Christ is the object of the believers' eating. They simply differ concerning the manner in which believers partake of Christ. For Luther, believers partake of Christ by eating his physical body which is present on earth in the Supper. For Calvin, believers partake of Christ by the Spirit.[134]

Although Calvin denies that the sacrament is merely an aid to faith, he nonetheless affirms that one of the purposes of the sacrament is the strengthening of faith:

> For seeing we are so weak that we cannot receive him with heartfelt trust, when he is presented to us by simple doctrine and preaching, the Father of mercy, disdaining not to condescend in this matter to our infirmity, has been pleased to add to his word a visible sign, by which he might represent the substance of his

---

[132] Ibid., 4.17.7
[133] Ibid., 4.17.33
[134] Keith Mathison, *Given for You: Reclaiming Calvin's Doctrine of the Lord's Supper,* (Phillipsburg, NJ: Presbyterian and Reformed, 2002), 32.

promises, to confirm and fortify us by delivering us from all doubt and uncertainty.[135]

Calvin uses the words "trust," "doubt," and "uncertainty" to refer to the subjective element of the Lord's Supper: the believer's faith. Calvin argues that by presenting Christ not only to the ears but also to the eyes, the Lord's Supper is indeed an aid to faith.

Despite his agreement with the memorialists that the Lord's Supper aids believers' faith, Calvin claims that the benefit of the Lord's Supper is not simply faith itself. Calvin writes, "For them eating is faith; for me it seems rather to follow from faith."[136] Calvin makes the same distinction in different words: "For them to eat is only to believe; I say that we eat Christ's flesh in believing, because it is made ours by faith, and that this eating is the result and effect of faith."[137] According to Calvin, the memorialist position affirms that faith is the *telos* of the Lord's Supper, whereas Calvin's position argues that faith is the means to a benefit beyond the faith itself–fellowship with Christ. Calvin affirms "that by faith we embrace Christ not as appearing from afar but as joining himself to us that he may be our head, we his members."[138] Faith is the means by which believers experience union with Christ. Calvin supports his position with the words of the church father Chrysostom:

> And Chrysostom writes the same thing in another passage: 'Christ makes us his body not by faith only but by the very thing itself.' For he means that such good is not obtained from any other source than faith; but he only wishes to exclude the possibility that anyone, when he hears faith mentioned, should conceive of it as mere imagining.[139]

Calvin affirms that faith is necessary to experience the blessing

---

[135] Calvin, "Short Treatise," 2:166.
[136] John Calvin, *Calvin: Institutes of the Christian Religion* (Philadelphia: The Westminster Press, 1960), 4.17.5.
[137] Calvin, *Institutes*, 4.17.5.
[138] Ibid., 4.17.6.
[139] Ibid., 4.17.6.

of the Lord's Supper but argues that this blessing is not faith itself but union with Christ.

Although it should be evident at this point that Calvin rejects any view that denies that believers partake of Christ's flesh, the question remains: Why does Calvin insist that believers partake of Christ's flesh? Calvin's view that believers must partake of the flesh and blood of Christ flows from his reading of John 6. Calvin reasons as follows:

> ...he himself, with his own lips, declares that his flesh is meat indeed, and his blood drink indeed. (John vi. 55.) If these words are not to go for nothing, it follows that in order to have our life in Christ our souls must feed on his body and blood as their proper food. This, then, is expressly attested in the Supper....[140]

Calvin argues that Christ's flesh and blood is believers' nourishment; therefore, believers must partake of his flesh and blood. Partaking of Christ's flesh and blood does not mean "the mixture, or transfusion, of Christ's flesh with our soul."[141] Calvin argues that "from the substance of his flesh Christ breathes life into our souls–indeed, pours his very life into us–even though Christ's flesh itself does not enter into us."[142]

Calvin identifies partaking of Jesus' flesh and blood with partaking of his humanity, of which believers must partake in order to obtain the blessings of salvation:

> "Moreover, if the reason for communicating with Jesus Christ is to have part and portion in all the graces which he purchased for us by his death, the thing requisite must be not only to be partakers of his Spirit, but also to participate in his humanity, in which he rendered all obedience to God his Father, in order to satisfy our debts."[143]

---

[140] Calvin, "Short Treatise," 2:170.
[141] Calvin, *Institutes*, 4.17.21.
[142] Ibid., 4.17.32.
[143] Calvin, "Short Treatise," 2:170.

Calvin here links partaking of Christ's humanity with partaking of the benefits of salvation. Jesus perfectly obeyed the Father as a human being. In order to gain the benefits Christ earned, believers must participate in the obedience of the man who obeyed in their place. For example, one of the benefits that flows to believers from partaking in Christ's flesh is the resurrection of the body. Calvin argues that the presence of Christ in the sacrament "not only brings an undoubted assurance of eternal life to our minds, but also assures us of the immortality of our flesh."[144] The flesh of believers "is now quickened by his immortal flesh, and in a sense partakes of his immortality."[145]

To partake of Christ's flesh and blood means to partake of Christ in his atoning work and in the benefits it brings. Calvin explains:

> It is not, therefore, the chief function of the Sacrament simply and without higher consideration to extend to us the body of Christ. Rather, it is to seal and confirm that promise by which he testifies that his flesh is food indeed and his blood is drink [John 6:56], which feeds us unto eternal life [John 6:55]. ... . And to do this, the Sacrament sends us to the cross of Christ, where that promise was indeed performed and in all respects fulfilled.[146]

Partaking of Christ's flesh and blood does not mean that the Holy Spirit infuses life into believers apart from Christ's sacrifice. Instead, the Supper is an instrument by which believers partake of the benefits Christ accomplished. Calvin maintains

> that the very powerful and almost entire force of the Sacrament lies in these words: 'which is given for you,' 'which is shed for you.' The present distribution of the body and blood of the body and blood of the Lord would not greatly benefit us unless they had once for all been given for our redemption and salvation.[147]

---

[144] Calvin, *Institutes*, 4.17.32.
[145] Ibid., 4.17.32.
[146] Ibid., 4.17.4.
[147] Calvin, *Institutes*, 4.17.3.

The Lord's Supper does not give believers a grace that is disconnected from the cross; it simply applies the benefits of the cross to believers. Calvin writes elsewhere that "the Supper is an attestation that, having been made partakers of the death and passion of Jesus Christ, we have everything that is useful and salutary to us."[148] The Supper itself does not make believers partakers; it attests to the partaking believers already have.

The language of sealing, confirmation, and attestation may sound rather memorialist. Calvin might seem to be arguing that the Supper merely reminds believers of the work Christ accomplished on the cross. On the contrary, Calvin maintains that the only way believers partake of the benefits of Christ is by partaking of Christ himself, as quoted above: "But as the blessings of Jesus Christ do not belong to us at all, unless he be previously ours, it is necessary, first of all, that he be given us in the Supper, in order that the things which we have mentioned may be truly accomplished in us."[149] The pattern of the Lord's Supper mirrors the pattern of salvation. When believers come to faith, they are united with Christ and therefore receive the benefits that flow from union with him. Similarly, in the Supper, believers partake of Christ and therefore receive the blessings that flow from him. The Supper is therefore both a reminder and a microcosm of union with Christ. The Supper not only symbolizes union with Christ; it is in itself an experience of that union.

Calvin closely identifies the presence of Christ in the Supper with the presence of Christ with believers at all times. Calvin writes that "fellowship with Christ is the result of the gospel no less than of the Supper" and that the believer's union with Christ is a "perpetual union."[150] If Christ is always present in believers, why should they partake of the Lord's Supper? Calvin argues that "the use of the Supper is not unnecessary, because we there receive Christ more fully, though already, by the faith of the gospel, he is so far ours and dwells in us."[151] Believers already have Christ, but the Supper allows believers to partake of him more fully. Calvin supports this argument by claiming

---

[148] Calvin, "Short Treatise," 2:168.
[149] Ibid., 2:169.
[150] Calvin, "Clear Explanation," 2:520.
[151] Ibid., 2:534.

that "the communion of Christ is conferred upon us in different degrees, not merely in the Supper, but independently of it."[152] The claim that believers obtain fellowship with Christ by faith is consistent with the claim that believers also grow in that fellowship through means such as the Lord's Supper.

The partaking of Christ's flesh and blood by believers does not imply the partaking of his flesh by unbelievers. Calvin distinguishes between the offering of Christ's body and the receiving of it: "it is one thing to be offered, another to be received."[153] Calvin uses the analogy of rain on a rock to explain this distinction: "just as rain falling upon a hard rock flows off because no entrance opens into the stone, the wicked by their hardness so repel God's grace that it does not reach them."[154] Calvin explains the unworthy partaking in terms of the Spirit, faith, and the word. Calvin's belief that the Holy Spirit unites believers to Christ in the Supper helps explain how a believer can partake of Christ's flesh while an unbeliever cannot: "Christ's flesh itself in the mystery of the Supper is a thing no less spiritual than our eternal salvation. From this we infer that all those who are devoid of Christ's Spirit can no more eat Christ's flesh than drink wine that has no taste."[155] If Christ is present in the Supper by the Spirit, then those devoid of the Spirit do not partake of Christ. They remain as far from Christ's flesh as heaven is from earth.

Calvin states his point not merely in terms of the Spirit but also in terms of faith and the word. Whether a person receives the gift offered in the Supper depends on whether that person has faith. Referencing Augustine, Calvin asserts that "men bear away from this Sacrament no more than they gather with the vessel of faith."[156] Calvin can also explain the unworthy partaking in terms of the absence of the word: "the bread is a sacrament only to those persons to whom the word is directed."[157]

---

[152] Ibid., 2:535.
[153] Calvin, *Institutes*, 4.17.33.
[154] Ibid., 4.17.33.
[155] Ibid., 4.17.33.
[156] Calvin, *Institutes*, 4.17.33.
[157] Ibid., 4.17.5.

Unbelievers do not simply fail to receive the sacrament; rather, "it is turned into a deadly poison for all those whose faith it does not nourish and strengthen, and whom it does not arouse to thanksgiving and to love."[158] The imagery of deadly poison does not imply that unbelievers actually partake of the sacrament. Making explicit reference to Paul's warning to the one who "eats the bread or drinks the cup in an unworthy manner,"[159] Calvin argues that "they are not condemned because they have eaten, but only for having profaned the mystery by trampling underfoot the pledge of sacred union with God, which they ought reverently to have received."[160]

Calvin's Sacramentology

Calvin's rejection of Luther and memorialism depends not only on his Christology but also on his sacramentology. For Calvin, a sign is distinct from yet inextricably linked to what it signifies. Calvin explains the two poles of his sacramental theology: "I indeed admit that the breaking of the bread is a symbol; it is not the thing itself. But, having admitted this, we shall nevertheless duly infer that by the showing of the symbol the thing itself is also shown."[161] Calvin thus distances himself from the Lutherans on the one hand and from the memorialists on the other. In the *unio sacramentalis,* Luther identifies the sign (the elements) with the thing signified (the body of Christ). The memorialists, on the other hand, separates the sign from the thing signified, making the sign merely an intellectual aid. Calvin distances himself from both positions: "To distinguish, in order to guard against confounding them, is not only good and reasonable, but altogether necessary; but to divide them, so as to make the one exist without the other, is absurd."[162] In regard to the nature of sacraments, Calvin urges that "the godly ought by all means to keep this rule: whenever they see symbols appointed by the Lord, to think and be persuaded that the truth of the thing signified is surely

---

[158] Ibid., 4.17.40.
[159] 1 Cor. 11:27
[160] Calvin, *Institutes,* 4.17.33.
[161] Ibid., 4.17.10.
[162] Calvin, "Short Treatise," 2:171.

present there."¹⁶³ To "assert that an empty symbol is set forth," (as Calvin imagines the memorialists to be doing), "would be to call God a deceiver."¹⁶⁴

Calvin seems to argue not simply that sign and reality are joined not merely as simultaneous events but as means and end. B.A. Gerrish distinguishes Calvin from the view that sign and signified are joined merely in time, a view Gerrish labels the "occasionalist" view of Charles Hodge.¹⁶⁵ Gerrish instead identifies Calvin with a position he calls "symbolic instrumentalism," the belief that the sacrament is an instrument by which God accomplishes what the sign signifies.¹⁶⁶

Gerrish's position makes the most sense of Calvin's language. Calvin himself uses the language of instrumentality: "This name and title of body and blood is given to them because they are as it were instruments by which the Lord distributes them to us."¹⁶⁷ Calvin argues that what is signified by the sacrament cannot be divorced from the sign: "It is not a bare figure but is combined with the reality and substance. It is with good reason then that the bread is called the body, since it not only represents but also presents it to us."¹⁶⁸ Calvin uses similar language elsewhere, "It not only symbolizes the thing that it has been consecrated to represent as a bare and empty token, but also truly exhibits it."¹⁶⁹ By contrast, "Humanly devised symbols" are "images of things absent rather than marks of things present."¹⁷⁰ But "those things ordained by God...have the reality joined with them."¹⁷¹ In each of these examples, Calvin seems to link the sign itself with the reality, not simply in time, but in its essence. The sign itself is the means by which the partaker experiences what the sign signifies.

The close link between sign and reality, however, does not make the word irrelevant. Calvin maintains that "whatever

---

[163] Calvin, *Institutes*, 4.17.10.
[164] Ibid.
[165] B. A. Gerrish, *The Old Protestantism and the New* (Chicago: University of Chicago Press, 1982), 167.
[166] Gerrish, *Protestantism*, 167.
[167] Calvin, "Short Treatise," 2:171.
[168] Ibid., 2:172.
[169] Calvin, *Institutes*, 4.17.10.
[170] Ibid., 4.17.21
[171] Ibid.

benefit may come to us from the Supper requires the Word."[172] The Word must accompany the sacraments because "The principal thing recommended by our Lord is to celebrate the ordinance with true understanding."[173] Calvin rages against the Roman church, which "wanted to have the whole force of the consecration depend upon the intention of the priest, as if it did not matter at all to the people, to whom the mystery ought most of all to have been explained."[174] For the Lord's Supper to be rightly practiced the congregation must understand what is happening. This understanding comes through the preaching of the Word. Calvin follows Augustine in identifying the sacrament itself as a *verbum visibile,* a visible word.[175] Word and sacrament work together to proclaim the same message.

Calvin's sacramentology allows him to explain the words "This is my body" as "metonymy."[176] In this figure of speech, "the name of the visible sign is...given to the thing signified" and vice versa.[177] In light of Calvin's view of the sacraments, it makes sense to give the name of the thing signified to the visible sign. In interpreting a passage in which Calvin claims that "The ark of the covenant is distinctly called the Lord of hosts," Calvin writes that "the name of God is transferred to a symbol because of its inseparable connection with the thing and reality."[178] Calvin asserts that "this is a general rule in regard to all the sacraments"[179]

Calvin argues that metonymy is necessary to understand many Old Testament texts. Calvin argues that according to the logic of his opponents who take the phrase "This is my body" literally, "as the Scripture distinctly attributes to God feet, hands, eyes, and ears, a throne, and a footstool, it follows that he is corporeal."[180] Applying a strictly literal hermeneutic to all of Scripture leads to absurdity. Calvin argues that metonymy is

---

[172] Ibid., 4.17.39.
[173] Calvin, "Short Treatise," 2:190.
[174] Calvin, *Institutes,* 4.17.39.
[175] Gerrish, *Protestantism,* 110.
[176] Calvin, *Institutes,* 4.17.21.
[177] Ibid.
[178] Calvin, "Clear Explanation," 2:508.
[179] Ibid.
[180] Ibid.

"a figure of speech commonly used when mysteries are under discussion."[181] As examples, Calvin cites "such expressions as 'circumcision is a covenant' [Gen. 17:13], 'the lamb is the passover' [Ex. 12:11], 'the sacrifices of the law are expiations' [Lev. 17:11], and finally, 'the rock from which water flowed in the desert' [Ex. 17:6], 'was Christ' [1 Cor. 10:4]."[182] By presenting these examples, Calvin establishes continuity between the sacramental language of the Old Covenant and the sacramental language of the New Testament. Just as the Old Testament mysteries were metonymies, so the New Testament mystery of the Lord's Supper is a metonymy.

Calvin contrasts his view of the words of institution with the views of his opponents. He argues that the Roman Catholics interpret *est* ("is") as "'to be converted into something else.'"[183] Some of his Lutheran opponents interpret "This is my body" as "the body is with the bread."[184] Other Lutheran critics (particularly Joachim Westphal) "do not hesitate to assert that, properly speaking, the bread is the body, and in this way truly prove themselves literalists."[185]

Conclusion

Calvin's view can be helpfully summarized by an overview of what he says the presence of Christ is not. After articulating his belief that Holy Spirit raises believers to heaven to feed on Christ, Calvin admits, "if anyone should ask me how this takes place, I shall not be ashamed to confess that it is a secret too lofty for either my mind to comprehend or my words to declare...I embrace without controversy the truth of God in which I may safely rest."[186] Calvin is not interested in parsing out the precise details of how believers feed on Christ. In his section heading entitled, "How is the presence of Christ in the Lord's Supper to be thought of?" Calvin articulates

---

[181] Calvin, *Institutes*, 4.17.21.
[182] Ibid.
[183] Ibid., 4.17.20.
[184] Ibid.
[185] Ibid.
[186] Ibid.,4.17.32.

> two limitations...(1) Let nothing be withdrawn from Christ's heavenly glory–as happens when he is brought under the corruptible elements of this world, or bound to any earthly creatures. (2) Let nothing inappropriate to human nature be ascribed to his body, as happens when it is said either to be infinite or to be put in a number of places at once.[187]

Calvin rejects any explanation of Christ's presence that diminishes his glory or de-humanizes his body, explanations he would ascribe to his Lutheran opponents.

> But when these absurdities have been set aside, I freely accept whatever can be made to express the true and substantial partaking of the body and blood of the Lord...and so to express it that they may be understood not to receive it solely by imagination or understanding of mind, but to enjoy the thing itself as nourishment of eternal life.[188]

Here Calvin distinguishes himself from his memorialist opponents, who he believes understand the Supper as something to be received only by the imagination or intellect. But Calvin leaves much ground open between the two positions. Thus, in the broadest sense, a Calvinist view of the Lord's Supper is any view that affirms a true partaking of Christ's flesh while denying a local presence of Christ's flesh.

SECTION IV: CALVIN AND REAL PRESENCE

In his *Last Admonition* to his Lutheran opponent Joachim Westphal, Calvin makes a claim about the kind of presence implied by his view of the Lord's Supper:

> I do not simply teach that Christ dwells in us by his Spirit, but that he raises us to himself as to transfuse

---

[187] Ibid., 4.17.19.
[188] Ibid., 4.17.19.

the vivifying vigour of his flesh into us. Does not this assert a species of presence, viz. that our souls draw life from the flesh of Christ, although, in regard to space, it is far distant from us?[189]

In the first section of this thesis, I offered a taxonomy of historical perspectives on the presence of Christ in the Supper. In the second, I explicated Calvin's view of the Lord's Supper. In this third section, I will seek to explain why Calvin's view of the Lord's Supper should be considered a real presence view. In doing so, I will be offering a way of parsing philosophically what Calvin here expresses intuitively: that the transfusion of the vigor of Christ's flesh into believers supports the claim that Christ is really present in the Lord's Supper.

Arguing that Calvin's view of the Lord's Supper is a real presence view requires offering an understanding of real that is neither reducible to memorialism nor indistinguishable from substantialism. For Calvin's view to be a real presence view, Christ must be present in a way that does not simply reduce to his being present at all times in all places. At the same time, in order for Calvin's view to avoid collapsing into a substantialist view, Christ must be present in a way that can be articulated without resorting to substance metaphysics. Both the Lutheran and Roman Catholic views of the Eucharist are concerned with the substantial nature of the elements because they view the elements as the locus of Christ's presence. Lutheran and Roman Catholic views require identifying both the time and the location of Christ's presence. Calvin's while, while specifying that Christ is uniquely present during the Lord's Supper, does not require locating where Christ meets his people.

Meeting is Presence

Because Calvin refuses to specify where the encounter between Christ and his people takes place, his view must be articulated in light of an ontology that prioritizes events over

---

[189] qtd. in Joseph Tylenda, "Calvin and Christ's Presence in the Supper—True or Real," (Scottish Journal of Theology 27, no. 1 (February 1974), 73.

substances in order for it to be considered a real presence view. In an event ontology,[190] the reality of presence is sufficiently established by temporal proximity, regardless of spatial distance. In Robert Farrar Capon's book, *The Supper of the Lamb*, an event ontology emerges from the way the author describes a "meeting" between a human being and an onion.[191] Capon encourages his readers to place an onion in front of them and meditate on its being:

> You will note, to begin with, that the onion is a *thing*, a being, just as you are. Savor that for a moment. The two of you sit here in mutual confrontation. Together with the knife, board, table, and chair, you are the constituents of a *place* in the highest sense of the word. This is a *Session*, a meeting, a society of things.... You have, you see, already discovered something: The uniqueness, the *placiness*, of place derives not from
>
> abstractions like *location*, but from confrontations like man-onion. Erring theologians have strayed to their graves without learning what you have come upon. They have insisted, for example, that heaven is no place because it could not be defined in terms of spatial co-ordinates. They have written off man's eternal habitation as a "state of mind." But look what your onion has done for you: It has given you back the possibility of heaven as a place without encumbering you with the irrelevancy of location.[192]

Capon defines place as a confrontation of beings. What is most fundamental to place is not location; Capon specifically says

---

[190] A technical definition of event ontology is beyond the scope of this thesis. I am simply using something like an event ontology to explain how Calvin's view of the Lord's Supper can be considered a real presence view.

[191] Capon is not making a point about the Lord's Supper in the following passage. Nonetheless, the ontology that arises from this passage can be used to explain how Calvin's view of the Lord's Supper can be considered a real presence view.

[192] Robert Farrar Capon, *The Supper of the Lamb: A Culinary Reflection* (New York: Random House, 2002), 11. Emphasis original.

place need not "be defined in terms of spatial co-ordinates."[193] If place is a confrontation of beings, and place is not defined by spatial co-ordinates, then a confrontation of beings is not defined by spatial co-ordinates. Capon's definition of place leaves open the possibility that real meeting, real encounter, or real presence might occur without being encumbered by the irrelevancy of location. Capon continues as follows: "Location is accidental to [a place's] deepest meaning. What really matters is not where we are, but who—what real beings—are with us."[194] Capon reiterates his fundamental point: location (i.e spatial coordinates) is not essential to place (i.e. a meeting of things). For Capon, *with* matters more than *where*.

Capon's point about the priority of meeting, or as I am suggesting, events, can perhaps be best understood by analogy to music. When someone listening to a piece of music becomes wrapped up in it, that person can lose a sense of space. To ask the question, "Where is the music?" is to ask an irrelevant question. This is not to say that music does not take place within space; sound waves still strike the human ear even when no one is thinking about them. Nonetheless, the temporal encounter is sufficient to undergird the judgement that a real meeting has taken place, regardless of whether one can identify where that encounter has happened.

The New Testament itself appears to offer support for this way of thinking about events or meetings. Paul writes to the Corinthians, "For as often as you eat this bread and drink the cup, you proclaim the Lord's death until he comes."[195] In this passage, Paul uses the word "often," which is a temporal term. In doing so, Paul identifies the proclamation of Christ in the Lord's Supper not with a particular place, but with a particular time. Paul does not speak here, as he does elsewhere, of the participation in Christ's body and blood. Nonetheless, he identifies a particular event, the proclaiming of the Lord's death, with a particular time. The participation of Christ's body and blood could also be identified with a particular time: as often you eat this bread and drink the cup, Christ communes with

---

[193] Capon, *Supper*, 11.
[194] Ibid., 12.
[195] 1 Corinthians 11:26 (ESV).

his people. Such an ontology could leave room for a presence defined not by space but only by time.

The encounter with the onion, the analogy of music, and the teaching of Paul each explain a way of thinking about real meeting or real presence that is agnostic about spatial location. In Capon, a meeting occurs even if its location cannot be specified. Listeners know that music has occurred even if they cannot specify where the music happened. And in 1 Corinthians 11, Paul bounds the proclamation of the Lord's death by time rather than by place. Each of these examples suggests that Christ can really meet his people in the Supper even if they cannot specify where he meets them.

Eating Is Meeting

Calvin asserts that Christ does indeed meet his people in the Supper, and he remains agnostic about where this meeting takes place. Distinguishing Calvin's view from memorialism and substantialism requires answering two questions. First, who is present in the meeting? Second, what is the nature of the encounter?

The following chart contains three summary quotes from Calvin describing who is present in the Lord's Supper and what happens in the encounter.

The above passages demonstrate that, in Calvin's view, believers encounter the body of Christ in the Supper. The word "partaking" suggests that the encounter between the communicant and Christ is as objective as the physical encounter between the communicant and the elements. Calvin makes this parallel explicit in another passage: "our souls are as much refreshed by partaking of Christ's flesh as bodies are by the bread they eat."[196] As the nourishment from the bread is real so the nourishment from Christ is real. Furthermore, just as physical nourishment implies the presence of physical bread, so also the nourishment of the soul implies the presence of Christ. Like the wind, the presence of Christ can be inferred from its effects.

Calvin's use of the word "partaking" highlights the difference

---

[196] Calvin, *Institutes*, 4.17.6

between a memorialistic and Calvinistic understanding of the event of the Lord's Supper. In both a memorialistic and a Calvinistic view, an objective encounter takes place. In the memorialistic view, the communicant encounters the physical elements. In the Calvinistic view, the communicant encounters and partakes of Christ by encountering and partaking of the elements. According to the memorialist, a meeting takes place on only one level[197]; according to the Calvinist, a meeting takes place on two levels. According to the memorialist, the believer encounters only bread and wine; according to the Calvinist, the believer encounters both the physical elements and Christ himself.

Calvin explicitly distinguishes between faith and partaking, as illustrated in the chart below.

This chart demonstrates that in Calvin's view, what happens in the Lord's Supper is more than a mere strengthening of believers' faith; it is communion with Christ himself. Calvin

---

[197] In a certain sense, even a memorialist view asserts an encounter on two levels: Christ is present with the gathered church in worship. But this presence is not unique to the celebration of the Lord's Supper.

Calvin's Language	What is Present?	What Happens?
"[I]n the Supper there is a true partaking of the flesh and blood"	Christ's flesh and blood	Partaking
"We deny not that the flesh and blood of Christ are communicated in the Supper"	Christ's flesh and blood	Communication
"[T]he bread which we break is truly the communion of the body of Christ"	Christ's body	Communication

does not simply distinguish faith from partaking; he also describes the relationship between the two. Calvin explains that partaking is not faith but rather follows from faith. In other words, faith is not partaking but is a necessary condition for partaking. Calvin offers a helpful analogy to explain how faith is a necessary condition for partaking, "[M]en bear away from this Sacrament no more than they gather with the vessel of faith."[198] The purpose of a vessel is to be filled with something. Similarly, the purpose of faith is to receive something, namely, Christ; faith is nothing without an object of faith. The relationship between faith and sacramental partaking is therefore not a relationship of exact identity but of receptivity and gift. Faith receives the gift of Christ given in the sacrament.

At this point, a substantialist might offer the following objection: if the benefits of the sacrament are limited to those who have faith, the presence of Christ in the Supper is not truly objective. If it were, anyone who eats the bread and drinks the cup would receive the benefits of the Supper. To answer this objection, it is important to distinguish between two kinds of encounters with Christ. In Calvin's view, both the one who has faith and the one who does not have faith encounter Christ in the Lord's Supper. The believer's encounter with Christ is a blessing, but the unbeliever's encounter with Christ is a curse. Calvin writes that the bread of the Supper "is turned into a deadly poison for all those whose faith it does not nourish and strengthen, and whom it does not arouse to thanksgiving and to love."[199] Calvin seems to be following the teaching of Paul in 1 Corinthians 11:29: "For anyone who eats and drinks without discerning the body eats and drinks judgment on himself." The presence of Christ in the Supper, though not spatially defined is nonetheless objective. This objective presence is made manifest not only in the blessing received by those who have faith, but in the curse received by those who do not have faith.

That the gift offered in the Lord's Supper is Christ himself can be seen by its effects. The following chart lists a range of terms that Calvin uses to describe the benefit that flows from partaking of Christ.

---

[198] Calvin, *Institutes*, 4.17.33.
[199] Ibid., 4.17.40

Calvin's Language	The Supper Is...	The Supper is Not...
"I leave no place for the sophistry that what I mean when I say Christ is received by faith is that he is received only by understanding and imagination. For the promises offer him not for us to halt in the appearance and bare knowledge alone, but to enjoy true participation in him."	True participation	Mere understanding or imagination; appearance and bare knowledge
"I freely accept whatever can be made to express the true and substantial partaking of the body and blood of the Lord...and so to express it that they may be understood not to receive it solely by imagination or understanding of mind, but to enjoy the thing itself as nourishment of eternal life."	Partaking of the body and blood	Mere imagination or understanding

Calvin's Language	The Supper Is...	The Supper is Not...
"For there are some who define the eating of Christ's flesh and the drinking of his blood as, in one word, nothing but to believe in Christ. But it seems to me that Christ meant to teach something more definite, and more elevated, in that noble discourse in which he commends to us the eating of his flesh. It is that we are quickened by the true partaking of him; and he has therefore designated this partaking by the words "eating" and "drinking," in order that no one should think that the life that we receive from him is received by mere knowledge."	More definite; more elevated; true partaking of Christ	Nothing but to believe; mere knowledge

Calvin's Language	The Supper Is...	The Supper is Not...
"And Chrysostom writes the same thing in another passage: 'Christ makes us his body not by faith only but by the very thing itself.' For he means that such good is not obtained from any other source than faith; but he only wishes to exclude the possibility that anyone, when he hears faith mentioned, should conceive of it as mere imagining."	The very thing itself; a result of faith	Faith only; mere imagining

Calvin's Language	The Supper Is...	The Supper is Not...
"[F]or them eating is faith; for me it seems rather to follow from faith."	A result of faith	Mere faith
"Moreover, I am not satisfied with those persons who, recognizing that we have some communion with Christ, when they would show what it is, make us partakers of the Spirit only, omitting mention of flesh and blood."	Communion with Christ	Partaking of the Spirit only
"I now pass over those who would have the Supper only a mark of outward profession"	N/A	A mark of outward profession

Calvin links the benefit listed here, stated variously as life, vivifying/quickening, and spiritual food, with the person of Christ himself. It is the flesh of Christ that gives believers life.

Given Calvin's understanding of the metaphysics of salvation it could not be otherwise. Calvin believes that the benefits of Christ are inextricably linked to the person of Christ. Calvin writes, "[W]e are taught from the Scriptures that Christ was from the beginning that life-giving Word of the Father [John 1:1], the spring and source of life, from which all things have always received their capacity to live."[200] Calvin explains how

---

[200] Ibid., 4.17.8.

this life which was with the Father was made manifest to human beings: "The same John afterward adds that life was manifested only when, having taken our flesh, the Son of God gave himself for our eyes to see and our hands to touch [1 John 1:2]."[201] Calvin explains that the life-giving power of Christ's flesh is not an inherent power:

> [T]he flesh of Christ does not of itself have a power so great as to quicken us, for in its first condition it was subject to mortality, and now, endowed with immortality, it does not live through itself. Nevertheless, since it is pervaded with fullness of life to be transmitted to us, it is rightly called 'life-giving.'[202]

As Scriptural evidence for his belief in the derivative, life-giving power of Christ's flesh, Calvin quotes John 5:26: "As the Father has life in himself, so he has granted the Son also to have life in himself [John 5:26, cf. Vg.]."[203] Unsurprisingly, Calvin also appeals to John 6 as evidence "that his flesh is truly food, and his body truly drink [John 6:55; cf. ch. 6:56, Vg.]."[204] In addition to these four Johannine texts, Calvin argues for Christ's life-giving flesh from Paul's language of Christ as the head of the body in Ephesians 1:23, 4:15-16, and 5:30, and 1 Corinthians 6:15.[205]

Calvin argues not only that Christ possesses life in himself, but also that believers must participate in Christ in order to receive this life. Calvin writes that "because man (estranged from God through sin and having lost participation in life) saw death threatening from every side, he had to be received into communion of the Word in order to receive hope of immortality."[206] Believers receive life by means of communion with the life-giving Word. Calvin quotes the words of Christ in John 6 to make this point:

> 'I am,' he says, 'the bread of life come down from heaven. And the bread which I shall give is my flesh, which I shall give for the life of the world' [John 6:48, 51; cf.

---

[201] Ibid.
[202] Ibid., 4.17.9.
[203] Ibid.
[204] Ibid., 4.17.8.
[205] Ibid., 4.17.9.
[206] Ibid., 4.17.8.

Life	Vivifying/Quickening	Food
Believers "enjoy the thing itself as nourishment of *eternal life*"	Christ "renders that flesh in which he fulfilled our righteousness *vivifying* to us,"	"Christ's flesh... becomes our food"
Believers "are truly made partakers of Christ, so that...he instills *life* into our souls from his flesh,"	Christ "raises us to himself as to transfuse the *vivifying vigour* of his flesh into us,"	"our souls are as much refreshed by partaking of Christ's flesh as bodies are by the bread they *eat*"
"our souls obtain *spiritual life* from his substance"	Believers "are *quickened* by the true partaking of him,"	
since [Christ's flesh] is pervaded with fullness of life to be transmitted to us, it is rightly called 'life-giving.'		
"whoever has partaken of his flesh and blood may at the same time enjoy *participation in life*."		
"Christ pours his *life* into us"		

> ch. 6:51-52, Vg.]. By these words he teaches not only that he is life since he is the eternal Word of God, who came down from heaven to us, but also that by coming down he poured that power upon the flesh which he took in order that from it participation in life might flow to us.[207]

Christ, who is life, came to earth to communicate life to believers. Calvin compares participating in life to drinking from a fountain:

> Water is sometimes drunk from a spring, sometimes drawn, sometimes led by channels to water the fields, yet it does not flow forth from itself for so many uses, but from the very source, which by unceasing flow supplies and serves it. In like manner, the flesh of Christ is like a rich and inexhaustible fountain that pours into us the
>
> life springing forth from the Godhead into itself. Now who does not see that communion of Christ's flesh and blood is necessary for all who aspire to heavenly life?[208]

This passage explains the sequence of how the life of God comes to believers. Christ's flesh, by virtue of its divinity, possesses in itself the very life of the Trinity. By communion with the flesh and blood of Christ, believers can therefore participate in the divine life.

Perhaps the best way to explain Calvin's view in more familiar theological terms is to speak of the Lord's Supper as a deepening of the believer's union with Christ. Calvin writes, "This is the purpose of the gospel, that Christ should become ours, and we should be engrafted into his body."[209] In discussing union with Christ, it is helpful to distinguish between two related aspects of union with Christ: legal union and vital/organic/mystical union. Legal union is the union by which the sins of believers

---

[207] Ibid., 4.17.9.
[208] Ibid.
[209] qtd. in Dirk Jacobus Smit, *Calvin on the Real Presence of Christ in the Lord's Supper*, (Lutheran Forum 46, no. 1 (2012) 41.

are imputed to Christ and his righteousness is imputed to believers. Christ is the substitute for his people. Though legal union receives most of the attention in evangelical circles, no less important is vital union, the union by which Christ nourishes believers with his very life. Legal union corresponds to justification; vital union corresponds to sanctification.

Against the backdrop of Calvin's understanding of the metaphysics of salvation, Calvin's view of the presence of Christ can be more clearly understood. For Calvin, wherever the life-giving power of Christ is, Christ himself also is. Calvin makes it clear that the life-giving power of Christ is present in the Lord's Supper to nourish believers. Therefore, Christ himself is present in the Lord's Supper. The encounter between Christ and his church in the Lord's Supper is one in which believers are engrafted more deeply into Christ.

It should be clear by now that the presence of Christ in the Lord's Supper that Calvin describes is more than a mere metaphor for faith. What is less clear is how the presence of Christ in the Lord's Supper is different from the presence of Christ with believers all the time. Union with Christ is a continual reality that is not limited to the Lord's Supper. So what makes the presence of Christ in the Lord's Supper different from the presence of Christ with believers all the time?

The difference between the presence of Christ in the Eucharist and the presence of Christ to believers at all times is like the difference between the kinds of union that exist between a husband and a wife. In marriage, there is both a legal union and a vital union. The legal union is a static, unchanging reality. No matter the ups and downs of the relationship between husband and wife, the legal union remains intact. The vital union, however, can be experienced in varying degrees. Some seasons of a marriage will be better than others. This need not be thought of merely in terms of seasons. Even throughout the course of a day, there will be times when the husband and wife will be in the same place and times when they will not be. When they are physically apart, the husband and wife are united in one sense and separated in another. Similarly, believers are definitively united with Christ at the moment of conversion; Christ will never divorce them or let them finally fall away. The union between Christ and his bride is eternally secure. Though

Christ and his bride are definitively united and he is always present with her, Christ manifests his presence in unique ways, through such means as the word and the sacraments.

In *The Old Protestantism and the New*, B.A. Gerrish distinguishes between three different perspectives on how Christ is present according to Calvin. From the perspective of the believer, Christ is present by faith. From the perspective of God, Christ is present by the Holy Spirit. From the perspective of the means of grace, Christ is present in the Word. For Calvin, the sacrament is a subspecies of the Word; Calvin follows Augustine's definition of sacrament as visible word.[210] The presence of Christ by faith is a continuous (or at least potentially continuous) event: a believer can look to Christ in faith at any moment to experience that kind of union with Christ. The presence of the Holy Spirit is also a continuous event. Although believers can grieve the Holy Spirit, the Holy Spirit does not finally leave any true believer. The presence of Christ from the perspective of external means, however, is not continuous, but is bounded. The presence of Christ in preaching is bounded by the sermon. Similarly, the presence of Christ in the Lord's Supper is bounded by the celebration of the Supper. The content of the presence in all three modes is Christ, but this does not mean that the three modes are not distinct. The content is the same; the method is different.

Eating Is Presence

In conclusion, a real meeting can take place, even if its physical location cannot be specified. Calvin argues that the meeting between Christ and believers is a real meeting, even while remaining agnostic about where it takes place. Like music, Christ is present even if he cannot be located. When Calvin describes believers partaking of Christ, he is not speaking metaphorically. Although faith is necessary for believers to partake of Christ, faith and partaking are not identical. Faith is rather the necessary condition for a beneficial encounter with Christ, who is offered in the Supper to all who will receive

---

[210] Gerrish, *Protestantism*, 109.

him. Like rustling leaves that reveal the presence of the wind, the benefit of the Supper—divine life— reveals the presence of Christ. Although Christ is always united with his people, this union can be seen through different angles: faith, the Holy Spirit, and external means. As Christ is present at all times, but also uniquely in the preaching of the Word, so Christ is present at times, but also uniquely in the Lord's Supper.

If Calvin himself were here, however, I suspect he would rather be eating the Supper than debating it. Commenting on Ephesians 5, Calvin writes,

> But Paul graced with a still more glorious title that intimate fellowship in which we are joined with his flesh when he said, 'We are members of his body, of his bones and of his flesh' [Eph. 5:30]. Finally, to witness to this thing greater than all words, he ends his discourse with an exclamation: 'This,' he says, 'is a great mystery' [Eph. 5:32]. It would be extreme madness to recognize no communion of believers with the flesh and blood of the Lord, which the apostle declares to be so great that he prefers to marvel at rather than to explain it.[211]

When confronted with our mystical union with Christ, I suspect that Calvin, like Paul, would rather marvel at it than explain it.

SECTION V: CONCLUSION

Calvin's view of the real presence of Christ in the Lord's Supper should remind Reformed believers of their roots. In the years since the Reformation, the Reformed tradition has drifted away from the robust sacramentology of John Calvin. The story of this journey is embodied in the conflict between two men: John Williamson Nevin (1803-86) and Charles Hodge (1797-1878).[212] Raised in a Presbyterian home of the old Reformed

---

[211] Calvin, *Institutes*, 4.17.9.
[212] For the following discussion of Nevin and Hodge, see Riggs, *Reformed Tradition*, 130-134. On pages 134-139, Riggs also discusses a conflict between the twentieth-century theologians Karl Barth and Donald M. Baillie that highlights the contrast in the Reformed tradition between memorialism and nonmetabolic real presence.

variety, Nevin experienced a personal "revival" while a Union College in New York, a revival he would later lament as overly introspective. Nevin realized how his revival experience had shaped him, and he embraced a theology that comforted to believers with the living, objective presence of Jesus Christ. In 1846, Nevin published *The Mystical True Presence: A Vindication of the Reformed or Calvinistic Doctrine of the Holy Eucharist*.

Nevin's study met with disapproval from fellow Reformed theologian Charles Hodge, who distinguished between two different understandings of what it means to receive Christ's flesh and blood:

> All the Reformed answered, that by receiving the body and blood of Christ, is meant receiving their virtue or efficacy. Some of them said it was their virtue as broken and shed, i.e., their sacrificial virtue; others said, it was a mysterious, supernatural efficacy flowing from the glorified body of Christ in heaven; and that this last idea, therefore, is to be taken into the account, in determining the nature of the union between Christ and his people.[213]

Though Hodge said that "fairest answer" is "neither to the exclusion of the other," he asserted that "the higher authority is certainly due to the doctrine of the sacrificial efficacy first mentioned."[214]

Nevin disagreed. The sacrificial efficacy of Christ's death, he asserted, could not be separated from vital union with his person: "The life of Christ is the true and real basis of his sacrifice, and so the natural and necessary medium of communion with it for the remission of sins."[215]

---

[213] qtd. in Riggs, *Reformed Tradition*, 133. [Original Source: Charles Hodge, review of *The Mystical Presence: A Vindication of the Reformed or Calvinistic Doctrine of the Holy Eucharist*, by Rev. John W. Nevin, D.D., *Princeton Review* 20, no. 2 (1848): 229]

[214] qtd. in Riggs, *Reformed Tradition*, 133. [Original Source: Hodge, *Mystical Presence*: 251]

[215] qtd. in Riggs, *Reformed Tradition: An Essay on the Mystical True Presence*. (Louisville: Westminster John Knox, 2015), 133. [Original source: De Bie and Littlejohn, eds., *Mystical Presence*, 241, 258-92, 292-314 (291-92, 315-59, 359-401)]

The foregoing passages suggest that Hodge and Nevin represent contrasting views not only of the Lord's Supper but also of union with Christ. The view of union with Christ that emerges from Hodge's quotation is primarily an external or nominal reality, a legal exchange. For Nevin, by contrast, union with Christ is internal or realistic; Christ's legal substitution for the believer is predicated upon a vital, organic, or mystical union with Christ's person.

Reformed Christians of both memorialist and substantialist persuasions ought to know of this debate. Reformed Christians of a memorialist persuasion ought to know that they are (if my reading of Calvin is correct) departing from the oldest and most venerable stream of their own tradition. They need not agree with Calvin, but they should recognize where he and they part company. And they should have solid biblical and theological grounds for departing from the most prominent theologian of their tradition. Reformed Christians drawn to more overtly sacramental traditions should know of this debate. They should know that the Reformed churches they reject for holding a deficient view of the sacraments are churches who hold a view that differs from Calvin's. They should know of the resources within their own tradition for a nonmetabolic real presence understanding of the Lord's Supper. They need not agree that Calvin provides a sufficiently robust view of the sacraments, but they should not leave the Reformed tradition thinking it allows for only a memorialist view of the Supper.

Reformed Christians already affirming the real presence should take heart that they stand with the most prominent theologian of the Reformed tradition. If memorialists within the Reformed tradition claim that a real presence view is merely Lutheran or Roman Catholic theology in disguise, Reformed Christians affirming a real presence will have an answer. The ability to distinguish a Reformed understanding of the Lord's Supper from a Luther or Roman Catholic view could also help such Reformed believers to refine their own views of the Lord's Supper. Some Reformed Christians, in seeking to affirm the real presence, may inadvertently adopt substantialist language and thinking, simply because they know no other way of regarding the real presence. For such Christians, I hope this thesis provides alternative ways of speaking and thinking about the Lord's Supper that affirm a real presence while remaining faithful to the Reformed tradition.

Calvin's view of the Lord's Supper impacts the way Reformed Christian should think not only about their own tradition but about its relationship to other traditions.[216] Calvin's view of the Lord's Supper stands in the Augustinian tradition of the nonmetabolic real presence view. It affirms a real presence of Christ in the Supper, but is agnostic about where it takes place. The nonmetabolic real presence view has had its adherents since the time of the church fathers. The historical pedigree of Calvin's view makes it a potential aid to ecumenical dialogue. If some of the Fathers had a view similar to Calvin's view, then Calvin's view could in the future become more acceptable to non-Reformed branches of the Christian tradition. Ecumenical movements often rely on finding a source that many (if not all) traditions can claim as their own. The Fathers are just such a source. Since they stand at the fountainhead of all theological discourse after the Scriptures, every tradition worth the name can claim the Fathers as their own, as the Reformers themselves often did.

Assessing the strength of such an ecumenical movement or guessing what shape it might take is beyond the scope of this paper. Perhaps the divisions highlighted in the Reformation are too deep to be healed. But if any Reformation-era view of the Lord's Supper can claim a historical pedigree, it is Calvin's view. The memorialist view finds no support among the Fathers, except perhaps in Origen or late Tertullian. Though the Lutheran view affirms the real presence, it possesses a more tenuous link to the Church Fathers. Perhaps the Roman Catholic view could claim an ancestor in the more metabolic thinkers of the early and medieval church, but it is primarily a late medieval doctrine articulated in response to the rise of Aristotelian philosophy. Of all the views present in the Reformation, Calvin's possesses the strongest claim to continuity with the broader tradition. Such continuity makes it a potential rallying point for ecumenical dialogue.

Though exploring Calvin's view has helped me to answer

---

[216] Smit, *Real Presence*, 43.

some questions, it has left others unanswered. Although exploring Calvin's view has strengthened my understanding of the sacramental relationship between Christ and the believer, it has done little to shape my view of the relationship between God and nature. As a result of this project, I can better see how the Supper is "charged with the grandeur of God," but not how "the world is charged" with his grandeur.[217] Calvin's view has helped me to see an enchanted event (the Eucharist) and an enchanted relationship (Christ and his church) but not an enchanted universe.

This project has also failed to give me confidence in any particular view of the Lord's Supper. Although I have spent the past two years writing about Calvin's view of the Lord's Supper, I have not become fully persuaded for or against it. Much of my energy has gone into the exegetical task of figuring out what Calvin meant. I have devoted most of my evaluative work to answering the question, "Is Calvin's view of the Lord's Supper a real presence view?" rather than the question, "Is Calvin's view of the Lord's Supper the truest one?" It may seem hard to believe that such an important question could be pushed into the background, but such has been my experience with this project. Having completed my thesis, I would like to step back and contemplate the more important question, "Which view of the Lord's Supper is the truest one?"

Despite its deficiencies in some respects, this thesis has helped me think about one of the most important issues of all—the nature of the gospel. Calvin wrote that "the purpose of the gospel" is "that Christ should become ours, and that we should be engrafted into his body."[218] The purpose of the gospel, according to Calvin, is union with Christ, marriage between Christ and his church. The bride becomes her beloved's, and her beloved becomes hers.

Union with Christ is not a mere moral union.[219] Believers are not merely united with Christ in the sense that they have a

---

[217] Hopkins, "God's Grandeur," 66.
[218] qtd. in Smit, *Real Presence*, 41.
[219] John W. Nevin, *The Mystical Presence and Other Writings on the Eucharist*, ed. by Bard Thompson and George H. Bricker, Lancaster Series on the Mercersburg Theology, vol. 4 (Philadelphia: United Church Press, 1966), 55.

certain sympathy with him, as in friendship. Believers' union with Christ does not consist merely in believing the right things about Jesus or doing the right things; it consists in union with the person of Christ himself. Union with Christ is not something believers do; it is something they are. It is not a state they achieve; it is a gift they receive.

Union with Christ is not mere legal union.[220] Christ indeed represents believers before the Father, having taken their sin upon himself and given them his righteousness. But this legal representation presupposes a union with the person of Christ himself,[221] a union that cannot be reduced to its legal implications. Believers receive the benefits of Christ's work because they are united to Christ himself. They are not united merely with the Holy Spirit or the divinity of Christ, but with the whole Christ in his full divinity and humanity.

Calvin's doctrine of union with Christ should impact the way believers regard fellowship with Christ. According to Calvin, fellowship with Christ cannot be reduced to thinking really hard about Jesus or to his legal representation of believers. Communion with Christ is not limited to those first-century disciples who saw, heard, and touched him. Nor is it limited to the day when Christ returns and dwells forever with his people. Though the Supper looks backward to the cross ("Do this in remembrance of me"[222]) and forward to the Second Coming ("I will not eat of this fruit of the vine until the kingdom of God comes"[223]), it also both symbolizes and embodies Christ's presence with believers now in this age.

Given that Calvin's view of the Lord's Supper shows that a Reformed view of the real presence is possible, opens up possibilities for ecumenical dialogue, and sheds light on a sacramental understanding of the relationship between Christ and the believer, this project has accomplished much of what I had hoped it would accomplish. I can now adopt a view of the Lord's Supper that is neither memorialist nor Lutheran/Catholic and can encourage others to do the same. To my friends who are considering leaving the Reformed tradition

---

[220] Nevin, *Mystical Presence*, 57.
[221] Ibid.
[222] Lk. 22:19.
[223] 1 Corinthians 11:26.

in light of apparent deficiencies in Reformed sacramental theology, I can offer the robust sacramental resources of the Reformed tradition. To my friends who belong to other theological traditions, I can more clearly recognize both the similarities and the differences between our views of the Lord's Supper. I had hoped to find a view of the Lord's Supper that would place me within the broader river of real presence views without cutting me off from the stream of Reformed theology. Calvin's continuity with tradition suggests that this aim has succeeded.

Most importantly, this project has demonstrated how the doctrine of the Lord's Supper shapes and is shaped by one's larger understanding of the gospel. Calvin's view of the Lord's Supper has shaped the way I think, not only about the Supper but also about fellowship with Christ. Calvin's doctrine of union with Christ has provided an understanding of fellowship with Christ that remedies the deficiencies I see in memorialist thinking, not only in regard to the Lord's Supper, but in regard to the Christian life as a whole. For Calvin, salvation is not only about a present faith that looks backward to the work of Christ and forward to his return; it is also about the presence of Christ here and now.

IN SEARCH OF MARKAN INTENTION: A CALL TO CONTINUE THE CONVERSATION ABOUT THE LONGER ENDING OF MARK

Brandon Harper

INTRODUCTION

With much of modern New Testament text-critical scholarship conceding that Mark's gospel definitively concludes with 16:8, is the time for debating Markan intention past? The great advancements in textual criticism over the last few centuries have led the vast majority of scholars to one of two conclusions. The first is that the "abrupt ending" (AE) at 16:8 is indeed the true ending of the narrative and that it was Mark's intent. The second is that, even if 16:8 was not the intended conclusion, the true ending has been lost or destroyed, and textual critics do not possess the means to re-discover it. These conclusions are contrary to what was long held to be the canonical ending of Mark. Namely, the Church traditionally affirmed the so-called "Longer Ending" (LE), which includes 16:9–20. Due to certain external discoveries and linguistic concerns, primarily regarding Markan authorship, the LE has found much disfavor, and it has since been relegated as inauthentic to the canon.

As such, it has become quite popular to affirm the closure of the conversation. Most of the prominent textual scholars who have weighed in on this issue have deemed the LE as clearly non-Markan and have thus rejected its place in the New Testament. Keith Elliott considers the internal evidence alone against the Markan authorship of the LE as sufficiently conclusive, so much so that he remarks, "It is self-deceiving to pretend that the linguistic questions are still 'open.'"[1] He dogmatically concludes "language, style, and theological content brand it [the LE] as non-Markan."[2] Bruce Metzger, too,

---

[1] J. K. Elliott, "The Last Twelve Verses of Mark: Original or Not?" in *Perspectives on the Ending of Mark: 4 Views* (Nashville, TN: B&H Academic, 2008), 82.
[2] Ibid., 40.

affirms that study of the linguistic qualities of the LE naturally entails its exclusion from the Markan account.[3] James Kelhoffer, likewise, in his near-exhaustive discourse on the properties of the LE, candidly brands the LE as "Markan forgery," that it was a 2nd century work composed by an otherwise unknown scribe who was well familiar with Mark's style.[4] N. T. Wright laments that any desire for or pursuit of a different ending than the AE has been contemporarily construed as "literary or theological naivety."[5]

The purpose of this excursus, though it may embrace this naïve aspiration, is to keep the conversation going, despite attempts to shut it down. While indeed much contemporary thought on the matter lends favorability to the AE, there remains reason to let the conversation continue. The rejection of the LE, though popular, is not universal. Prominent New Testament scholars such as Nicholas Lunn, David Black, Maurice Robinson, and N. T. Wright have all weighed in, each calling for the preservation of the LE. Even if the LE is to be judged as most likely non-Markan, these thinkers and others have maintained that there is enough gray in the matter, enough of a bounty of complexifying factors, to warrant ongoing investigation. Thus, the goal here is a modest yet crucial one: to show that though there is sufficient evidence for suspicion of the LE, there is not sufficient evidence for the removal of the LE.

The question at hand, then, is primarily threefold. Firstly, just how conclusive is the textual evidence regarding the LE's Markan or non-Markan nature? Secondly, in light of the first consideration, can the LE be considered as authoritatively instructive for the modern church? Lastly, what does the LE have to teach 21st-century believers, both in terms of linguistic studies narrowly and the Christian life broadly?

This treatise does not endeavor to prove the canonicity of

---

[3] Bruce Metzger, *The Text of the New Testament: Its Transmission, Corruption, and Restoration* (New York and Oxford: Oxford University Press, 1968), 227.
[4] James A. Kelhoffer, *Miracle and Mission: The Authentication of Missionaries and Their Message in the Longer Ending of Mark*. Wissenschaftliche Untersuchungen Zum Neuen Testament. Reihe 2, 112. (Tübingen: Mohr Siebeck, 2000).
[5] N. T. Wright, *The Resurrection of the Son of God* (Minneapolis, MN: Fortress Press, 2003), 619.

the LE, which essentially would come down to empirically demonstrating Markan authorship, as such goes beyond the scope of this analysis; rather, this is meant as a brief overview of the LE's academic treatment, with attention given to both external and internal considerations, unto showing that Markan authorship should not as of yet be wholly discredited in New Testament textual criticism. Though favor here is given to the authenticity of the LE, the debate still remains largely inconclusive. However, there is enough valuable material in the LE to warrant further study of its authenticity.

Thus, the final portion of this work offers a verse-by-verse analysis of the LE in the hopes that, even if it is ultimately excluded from the canon, Christians may yet learn more through it regarding the resurrection appearances of Jesus and the livelihood of early Christianity. That portion of the analysis focuses on how well the LE thematically and literarily coincides with the preceding pericope (16:1-8), how it furthers the overall message of Mark's gospel, and its role in the story of the New Testament. Because the modern consensus favors the AE, not much exposition has been done on the LE. If there is any reason to believe that authenticity is possible, as the first two sections aim to suggest, then further exposition of the text by Christian scholars is still worthwhile. The LE has not been authoritatively or universally ruled out as non-canonical; it still appears in the vast majority of Bible translations, even if bracketed off.

This means that there are those who, whether it be due to lack of awareness or conscious persistence that the LE should remain, will continue to preach the text. So long as Bible translations continue to include the text of the LE, whether bracketed off or not, Christians who do not know of the significance of textual concerns will continue to read this passage of Scripture as authoritative. Thus, even if the LE is popularly marked as inauthentic and non-canonical, it is still the responsibility of Christian scholars to offer gateways to preaching it well through commentary. Though there are portions of the LE that may make some nervous, such as Jesus' prediction of snake-handling and poison-drinking, no content of the LE is doctrinally opposed to the rest of Mark, and thus there need not be any fear of its exposition.

EVALUATION OF THE LE'S EXTERNAL TEXTUAL SUPPORT

We have first to consider the external evidence of the matter. Specifically, this part of the analysis focuses on the numerical presence of the LE in the MSS, the antiquity of the MSS that include or omit the LE, and the diversity of text-types which include or omit the LE. However, it is worth asking first why it would have been omitted in the first place if the early scribes and church leaders considered such a lengthy passage as the LE to be original. One response is to rely upon the possibility that the real ending was lost or destroyed, but this is mainly speculative, and so it is still necessary to think through scribal tendencies. Is it more likely that the scribe would find the AE odd and, under the intention of "fixing" the text, make the addition of the LE? Or is it more likely that the scribe, determining the LE to be out of place, would erase the entirety of the passage? Regarding this conundrum, Bruce Metzger concludes that a scribe likely "knew a form of Mark which ended abruptly with verse 8 and [he] wished to provide a more appropriate conclusion,"[6] thus supporting the likelihood of the former possibility. Wallace agrees, seeing the sheer diversity of different endings past verse 8 as an indication that Mark intended the AE and supposing all of the other possibilities to have come from scribes trying to improve what they saw as a damaged or lost text.[7]

The Possible Endings of Mark

Tentatively, there are five primary possibilities for how Mark's gospel may end insofar as they appear in any MSS. Phillip Comfort lists these possibilities as the following (footnoted for these are abbreviated lists of their external support as noted by

---

[6] Metzger, *Text of the New Testament*, 227.
[7] Daniel Wallace, "Mark 16:8 as the Conclusion to the Second Gospel," in *Per spectives on the Ending of Mark: 4 Views*, ed. David Alan Black (Nashville, TN: B&H Academic, 2008), 24.

the 28th edition of the Nestle-Aland Greek New Testament):[8] (1) the "abrupt ending" (AE) at 16:8,[9] (2) the "shorter ending" that adds a small text after verse 8,[10] (3) the longer ending that goes to 16:20,[11] (4) the longer ending with a short addition known as the Freer Logion,[12] and (5) both the shorter ending and the longer ending together.[13] There is some terminological confusion among these possible endings. For example, the shorter ending (2), is not the ending at v. 8 (1), which is confusingly enough the shortest ending. For the purposes of this analysis, since (2) has minimal textual support and is generally rejected as canonically verifiable, it will be treated as secondary, and the ending at verse 8 will exclusive be referred to as the "abrupt ending" (AE). Likewise, though options (4) and (5) are both longer than option (3), the title of "Longer Ending" (LE) will be reserved for option (3), as it is the more textually supported variant.

Introducing the Synoptic Problem: Which Gospel Came First?

A brief discussion of the historicity of the Gospels is in order, as it relates to the acceptance or rejection of the LE. Namely, this has to do with the consideration of whether Mark was written before or after Matthew and Luke, otherwise known as the Synoptic Problem. On one hand, if Mark wrote first, then we may safely assume that there would be nothing problematic with the AE and its seemingly uncharacteristic narrative drop-off. This hypothesis, Markan priority, would mean that Mark was setting a literary standard rather than

---

[8] Philip Comfort, *A Commentary on the Manuscripts and Text of the New Testament* (Grand Rapids: Kregel, 2015), 197–98.

[9] ℵ B 304 syr^s cop^{saMS} arm geo^{MSS} MSS$^{according\ to\ Eusebius}$ MSS$^{according\ to\ Jerome}$ MSS$^{according\ to\ Severus}$

[10] itk (The shorter ending reads, "And all that had been commanded them they told briefly to those with Peter. And afterward Jesus himself sent out through them, from the east and as far as the west, the holy and imperishable proclamation of eternal salvation. Amen.")

[11] A C D Θ f^{13} 33 Maj MSS$^{according\ to\ Eusebius}$ MSS$^{according\ to\ Jerome}$ MSS$^{according\ to\ Severus}$ Irenaeus, Apostolic Constitutions, Epiphanius, Severian, Nestorius, Ambrose, Augustine.

[12] W MSS$^{according\ to\ Jerome}$

[13] L Ψ 083 099 274^{mg} 579 syr^{hmg} cop^{sa,boMSS}

following one; thus, this theory grants plenty of logical room for Mark having a different kind of ending than the other gospel writers. It also would serve to explain some of the parallels that readers may notice between it and Matthew and Luke. Markan priority, with few exceptions, has remained the common view of modern text-critical scholarship. Thus, scholars like Daniel Wallace and Keith Elliott have no problem with the possibility that Mark could end intentionally at verse 8.

However, if Mark's account came later on, then it would indeed be odd for him to have broken away from the conclusive style set forth by Matthew and Luke. This has less to do with sheer stylistic consistency than it does with content, namely the content of Christ's resurrection appearances, the great commission, and the ascension, all of which are present in the former gospels. If Mark already had access to Matthew or Luke, why would he insist on excluding such a prominent element of their conclusions?

The older assumption regarding priority gave the edge to the Matthean hypothesis, the idea that Matthew was indeed the first gospel written, partially reflected in its placement as the first book of the New Testament. Breckenridge cites Farmer's concise yet near-comprehensive list of criteria for that edge: "[Mark's] lack of an independent chronology, the obvious interdependence of Matthew and Luke, plus external evidence and logical historical development all seemed to declare both the dependent and subsequent nature of Mark as well as the priority of Matthew."[14]

In the 20th century, however, the consensus among text-critical scholarship shifted to the endorsement of Markan priority. In spite of this, Farmer still defended extensively the favorability of Matthew's precedence, and he relied heavily on this source-critical presupposition to vindicate the LE. He believed the popularizing of Markan priority to be the fruit of a drastic shift in the methodological framework of critical scholarship, namely that era's "intellectual climate."[15] An ecclesial-scholastic claim from Thomas Huxley, a significant

---

[14] James Breckenridge, "Evangelical Implications of Matthean Priority," *Journal of the Evangelical Theological Society* 26 (1983): 117–21.

[15] William Farmer, *The Synoptic Problem: A Critical Analysis* (Dillsboro, NC: Western North Carolina Press, 1976), 178.

thinker of the 19th century, summarizes well that climate: "The Christianity of the Churches stands or falls by the results of the purely scientific investigations of these questions."[16] Farmer saw that there was a correlation between the progressing preeminence of scientific study in all scholarly realms and the ever-increasing willingness to let go of the traditionally accepted solution to the Synoptic problem.

Farmer, though by no means assuming his conclusion was inarguably correct, believed that the Gospels were written in the order of Matthew, Luke, Mark, and finally John.[17] Why, then, would the canon authorities eventually place Mark in between Matthew and Luke? Black contrives that this was due to an understanding of Mark's purpose to be a synthesis of Matthew and Luke devised by Peter in response to a cultural demand for his own account of Jesus' life.[18]

The LE's Presence Across the MSS

It should not be ignored that the LE has a significant amount of external support, namely appearances in roughly 95 percent of MSS across all text-types, and textual scholars have gone back and forth as to whether the external evidence generally favors the LE or AE. The oldest available extant uncials, Sinaiticus (א) and Vaticanus (B) may lack the LE, but this does not necessarily mean that the LE is left wanting for external support. Lunn provides the following table containing a near-comprehensive list of the vast external support for the LE.[19] Each entry in this table represents a specific MS which includes the LE.

As evident from this collection, the external support for the LE of Mark is widespread. This is both a numerical claim as well as a geographical one. Another strong point in the

---

[16] Thomas Huxley, *Science and the Christian Tradition: Essays* (London: Macmillan: 1894), 270.
[17] Farmer, *Synoptic Problem*, 200.
[18] David Alan Black, "Mark 16:9–20 as Markan Supplement," in *Perspectives on the Ending of Mark: 4 Views*, ed. David Alan Black (Nashville, TN: B&H Academic, 2008), 188.
[19] Nicholas Lunn, *The Original Ending of Mark: A New Case for the Authenticity of Mark 16:9–20* (Eugene, OR: Pickwick Publications, 2014), 25.

favor of the LE's authenticity is that the text can be found in a multitude of different regions and across all major text-types.

(a) *Uncials:* A C D E F G H K M N S U V X W Γ Δ Θ Λ Π Σ Φ Ψ Ω.
(b) *Minuscules:* 28 33 89 115 126 157 164 174 180 230 262 278 338 348 371 399 411 461 468 496 504 561 548 565 597 607 652 700 892 1006 1009 1010 1071 1076 1079 1097 1120 1143 1166 1172 1203 1225 1241 1243 1292 1340 1342 1357 1378 1392 1421 1458 *Lect,* et al.
(c) *Versions:* Diatessaron, Old Latin (most), Curetonian Syriac, Peshitta, Harklean Syriac, Palestinian Syrica, Gothic, Vulgate, Arabic, Old Church Slavonic. Well attested in Coptic, Armenian, Ethiopic, Georgian.
(c) *Fathers: Justin,* Tatian, Irenaeus, Hippolytus, Marinus, Didymus, Aphrahat, Cassian, Nestorius, Chrysologus, Ambrose, Augustine, Patrick, Leo, et al.*
* This list of church fathers given, it should be noted, is also merely representative. In the next chapter this shall be added to signifcantly.

Sinaiticus and Vaticanus

The AE tends to be esteemed because it has the oldest support in codices Sinaiticus and Vaticanus, both mid-fourth century Alexandrian uncials.[20] There have been to date no discoveries of papyri (the most ancient form of external codices to be found in textual criticism) containing the ending of Mark, so Sinaiticus and Vaticanus are of great repute in the determination of Mark's ending. Discovered in the 19th century, most textual critics maintain that these are of the most importance in the discussion of Markan authorship and authenticity, and thus build the case of omission greatly on the grounding of these MSS. Elliott notes that the witness of Sinaiticus and Vaticanus "has meant that nearly all English translations since 1881 . . . do not have the last twelve verses of Mark."[21] Though Elliott overstates his case a bit, since most translations do contain the

---

[20] Lunn, *Original Ending of Mark,* 25.
[21] J. K. Elliott and Ian Moir, *Manuscripts and Text of the New Testament: An Introduction for English Readers* (Edinburgh: T&T Clark, 1995), 39.

LE (they are just bracketed off as suspect), the viability of these MSS cannot be overstated. Their scribal origin has been given rich affirmation by modern scholarship, with Elliott describing them as "splendidly produced and evidently prepared as *deluxe* editions."[22]

However, these uncials, invaluable though they may be, are not without their own complexifying factors. There is sufficient evidence for reasonable doubt as to whether or not they verify the LE's non-Markan status. Vaticanus, particularly, contains a large blank portion following v. 8 that could presumably have been saved for the LE to be written in.[23] As documentation was incredibly expensive at the time of its writing, it is highly unlikely that such a large portion of the document would have remained empty, with no scribal notes or commentary. A few possibilities could explain this phenomenon. As previously stated, it is possible that this section of Vaticanus could have been reserved for the LE intentionally, but was ultimately left blank due to some unforeseen external circumstance preventing the scribe from finishing.

Secondly, the space could have been deliberately left blank so as to show a familiarity with the LE but an uncertainty of its authenticity. This option would entail that there were indeed copies of the LE circulating prominently before the writing of Vaticanus. Such a phenomenon does not empirically prove a Markan timeline, though, because, as Kelhoffer lays out, there would have been plenty of time in the 2nd century to begin wide circulation of the text. Even so, it does narrow the scope of the timeline to the mid-late 1st century (if Mark was the author) or the early 2nd (given that Iranaeus makes mention of the LE).

Or, finally, the space could have been left blank to make a declarative statement in favor of omitting the text. Of these options, the most likely seems to be the second, in which the scribe was aware but suspicious of the LE, not unlike modern critics. Even Westcott and Hort affirm the likelihood that the scribe would have known of the existence of a different ending than what he had written, and thus left a space for it in the

---

[22] Elliott, "Last Twelve Verses," 82.
[23] Lunn, *Original Ending of Mark*, 28.

case that it needed to be added later.[24] The point here is to say that this particular manuscript, one that is so readily cited in favor of omission, suggests a plausibility of the LE.

Sinaiticus, likewise, contains its own particularity in the form of "cancel-leaves," leaves that were "sewn in containing a corrected form of the text."[25] These were necessarily added because of damage that happened to the original copy of Sinaiticus. Immediately, then, we have evidence that the portion of this manuscript that had the ending sections of Mark (including 16:1-8) was at some point ruined. Also, Sinaiticus' conclusion of Mark has a form of double-ornamentation unique to this gospel. While various decorative styles are common in the tradition of MSS, the ornamentation present in Sinaiticus is, to use a technical term, overkill. Lunn suggests that this overt ornamentation was a deliberate attempt "to tacitly express the view that this [the AE] was, in the opinion of the scribe at least, the correct ending of the book."[26] In spite of the viewpoint expressed by the scribe, if they were incensed to draw so much attention to this ending, it follows that the LE was already in broad enough circulation to have been familiar to the scribes of that era, further illustrating the ancient nature of the LE.

Other External Sources

Though the respective ages of Sinaiticus and Vaticanus may be a crucial factor, it is not as if they are incomparably more ancient than all MSS which do contain the LE. There are MSS that are only slightly younger than Vaticanus and Sinaiticus; namely, Codices Alexandrinus (dated around 400 A.D.) and Ephraemi Rescriptus (dated early 5th century) follow closely behind and include the LE.[27]

Of course, the external considerations, though most primarily concerned with majuscules, do not stop there. Other early biblical sources, such as translations into other languages ("versions") as well as patristic writings, help in the evaluation

---

[24] B. F. Westcott and F. J. A. Hort, *The New Testament in the Original Greek: Introduction and Appendix* (New York: Harper, 1882), 29.
[25] Lunn, *Original Ending of Mark*, 28.
[26] Ibid., 33.
[27] Ibid., 25.

of textual validity, at least in terms of more accurately dating a text's origin. After all, Markan authorship lives or dies by the authentication of its historical origin. If the LE was written in the early 2nd century, as advocates of omission attest, then Markan authorship is of course disproven. Fortunately for advocates of the LE's authenticity, though the LE loses the battle in the earliest uncial MSS, it wins in the arena of versions and patristics.

With regard to patristic validity, Lunn points out that Justin, Tatian, and Iranaeus decisively valued the LE as canon long before any of the "negative" patristic evidence came to be.[28] Saint Augustine also showed knowledge of the LE, comparing the Markan and Lukan accounts of the Emmaus road experience[29] as well as including 16:16 in his discussion of resurrection from the dead.[30] That said, other prominent early Christian writers like Origen and Clement show no direct knowledge of the LE.[31] In fact, Eusebius claimed directly that the LE, at least as we know it now, was absent from the majority of the manuscripts which he had access to.[32] Jerome likewise affirmed this noticeable lack of vv. 9–20.[33] Elliott notes that Mark's account "was not popular in the second century,"[34] thus it is not surprising that the citation evidence of Mark (much less its ending in particular) is lacking. To make an argument for omission on this basis, however, is to argue from silence.

Diversity of MSS Containing the LE

We can see, then, that the LE does have a numeric advantage, both in terms of age and textual appearances. Additionally, diversity of MSS lends itself to the vindication of the LE. When considering external evidence, critics have found there to be four main textual "families" or "text-types": Byzantine, Western,

---

[28] Ibid., 26.
[29] Augustine, Edmund Hill, John E Rotelle, and Augustinian Heritage Institute, *Sermons (230-272b) on the Liturgical Seasons* (New Rochelle, NY: New City Press, 1993), 61.
[30] Augustine, *Sermons (230-272b)*, 34–37.
[31] Wallace, "Mark 16:8 as the Conclusion," 20.
[32] Comfort, *Commentary on the Manuscripts*, 159.
[33] Ibid.
[34] Elliott, "Last Twelve Verses," 87.

Caesarean, and Alexandrian. These categorizations refer to the different geographical regions that encompass the majority of known New Testament manuscripts. While all of the families are not treated with equal prominence, if a text can be shown to appear across all four, it bodes well for the authenticity of that text. As it happens, the LE does appear across all four of these text-types; this cannot be said of the AE, which is more "localized."[35]

Scribal Uncertainty Regarding the LE

Advocates of the AE maintain that though the LE has such a notably widespread presence, many of the MSS contain scholium (marginal inscriptions) or *obeli* (brackets around the text) that render the LE suspect.[36] While it is possible that later readers added these marks to deliberately achieve such an effect, this phenomenon along with the presence of spacious gaps on the pages suggest that scribes were at least aware of both types of endings, even if they did not know which one was to be taken as authentic to the gospel.

With regard to the scribal notations, there are several caveats to keep in mind before attributing them to be testimony for omission. Lunn highlights that in many of these instances (which are ultimately in the late minority of MSS which contain the LE), they are in reference to the secondary "intermediate/ shorter ending" which had been inserted between the SE and the LE.[37] This means that many of the *scholia* were not made with the intention of discounting the LE, but the intermediate text that only a minimal amount of MSS possessed. Further, the vast majority of the *scholia* do not explicitly suggest that the LE is unoriginal; rather, they merely address the differentiation within the manuscript tradition. For example, many read like the following: ἔν τισι τῶν ἀντιγράφων ἕως ὧδε πληροῦται ὁ εὐαγγελιστής· ἐν πολλοῖς δὲ καὶ ταῦτα φέρεται ("In some of the copies the Evangelist is completed to this point. But in many

---

[35] Lunn, *Original Ending of Mark*, 26.
[36] Comfort, *Commentary on the Manuscripts*, 158.
[37] Lunn, *Original Ending of Mark*, 35.

these [verses] are also present").[38]

Another interesting example appears in this form: ἐντεῦθεν ἕως τοῦ τέλους ἔν τισι τῶν ἀντιγράφων οὐ κεῖται, ἐν δὲ τοῖς ἀρχαίοις πάντα ἀπαράλειπτα κεῖται ("From here to the end does not occur in some of the copies, but in the ancient copies it all occurs in full").[39] This latter example even more clearly suggests inclusion of the LE with its reference to "ancient copies," thus contradicting the idea that all instances of *scholia* added to the textual suspicion of the LE. This leads Lunn, as well as this writer, to conclude that many of the arguments negating the LE on the basis of scribal suspicion are "grossly overstated, if not completely misinterpreted." [40]

EVALUATION OF THE LE'S INTERNAL TEXTUAL SUPPORT

With the observation that the external evidence is heavily divided, though sufficient to raise suspicion as to the LE's originality, the next step is to explore the findings of internal evidence. When it comes to these internal considerations, scholars have in mind factors such as lexical, stylistic, and thematic consistency. That is, when looking at the internal qualities of any given text, the general question at the heart of the investigation pertains to how well these qualities correspond with the authorial tendencies established elsewhere in the work.

When it comes to New Testament textual criticism, internal methodologies are limited in their authority because they are dependent upon having enough source material to establish authorial styles. Given that Mark's gospel is ultimately a short account and the only work available to us that was written by him, critics have had great difficulty in clearly establishing Markan technique. Beyond that, investigation of

---

[38] Ibid., 36.
[39] Ibid.
[40] Ibid.

phenomena such as shifts in style, tone, and vocabulary are not in themselves reason enough to signify variant authorship. On a general level, humans cannot be expected to always write in the same way without deviation. Any writer, while having particular designs to which he may frequently return, is prone to exhibiting new vocabulary or varied styles depending on his subject-matter. This means that claims regarding the LE based on internal evidence can only carry so much weight in the overall discussion; thus, external evidence tends to be favored, as there are more consistent and objective standards by which it may be judged. Even so, to completely ignore the linguistic features of the LE does not do justice to the process as a whole. With this in mind, we may still retain that the ruling of internal evidence, secondary though it may be, is greatly divided in textual scholarship, and there are just as many ways in which the internal evidence vindicates the LE as there are ways that it renders the LE suspect.

Concerns Regarding the LE's Lexicon

One common critique of the LE's authenticity pertains to its lexicon, the focus of which is given typically to 17 particular words that are supposedly unique to this pericope.[41] The words included in this list of 17 have fluctuated across the writings of different scholars.[42] The words that stand most notably outside of typical Markan vocabulary are the following: θεομαι (vv. 11, 14), απιστεω/απιστια (vv. 11, 14, 16), ετερος, υστερον, καν, and αναλαμβανω.[43] In addition to this, there are particular word orders and combinations present in the LE that are elsewhere absent: τοις μετ' αυτου γενομενοις (v. 10), επιθησουσιν επι followed by an accusative noun (v. 18), μεν ουν (v. 19), ο κυριος (vv. 19-20), and the genitive absolute construction at the finale (v. 20).[44] Some of these terms will be addressed specifically in the

---

[41] Ibid., 119.
[42] For example, Elliott incorporates more strict parameters in his determination of the Markan nature of certain words and phrases, whereas other scholars, like Metzger, are a little more open.
[43] Elliott, "Last Twelve Verses," 88.
[44] Ibid., 88–89.

textual analysis to follow, but for now it is sufficient to say that these lexical variants should not be taken as empirical evidence against the LE. As any other writer, Mark exhibits throughout the work an aptitude for diverse vocabulary. In fact, Lunn's analysis shows that most sections of Mark's gospel incorporate words not found elsewhere in the narrative. If anything, the lexical variety in the LE is a testimony for the LE rather than against it.

Concerns Regarding the LE's Style

In addition to the lexical concerns, the stylistic consistency within the LE has itself been a matter of dispute. One of the benefits of such a long variant is that it grants room for critics to more thoroughly analyze the intrinsic style of the text in a way that smaller variants do not allow. Authorial style shows itself much more clearly in a lengthy pericope, yet France notes that "the style of the Longer Ending as a whole . . . is such a mixture of elements from other sources."[45] That said, there are authorial tropes that textual critics may justifiably discern from the text. For example, Greenlee highlights a small but significant stylistic detail: "In Mark 16:9 the first day of the week is called πρωτη . . . and in all other instances of this phrase in the NT the word used is a form of μια."[46] This presence of uncharacteristic language in combination with content seemingly parallel with other works in the N.T., presumably including Acts, has reinforced the consensus that the work was written and added to Mark's gospel after the first century.[47] If this is true, then Markan authorship becomes impossible.

Another issue of concern is the sheer literary awkwardness of the transition (if the LE was to be taken as original) between v. 8 and v. 9. This is namely evident in the abrupt change in subject from the women to Christ. This and the seemingly unnecessary description of Mary of Magdalene in v. 9 (after she

---

[45] France, *The Gospel of Mark*, 687.
[46] J. Harold Greenlee, *Introduction to New Testament Textual Criticism* (Peabody, MS: Hendrickson Publishers, 1995), 114.
[47] Evans, *Word Biblical Commentary: Mark 8:27-16:20*, 547.

had already been introduced in the beginning of the chapter)[48] leads Metzger to conclude that the LE is internally incongruent with pericope ending at v. 8.[49] France takes the point further to suggest that the continuation of v. 9 actually "contradicts" the closing of v. 8.[50] Hort even claims that the LE constitutes an entirely different literacy device, calling it "a summary or epitome of events after the Resurrection, covering in a few lines a considerable period" as opposed to an extension of the narrative.[51]

Concerns Regarding the LE's Theology

There are other considerations of content that the critic must take into account regarding the LE, most notably regarding Jesus' commissioning of signs that are presumably nowhere else in the Gospels, certainly not in the other accounts of Jesus' final commission. This question has less to do with the overall viability of these signs in the apostolic church than it does with the uniqueness of these predictions compared to the other Synoptics. In fact, Greenlee cites these predictions as a potential cause (though not solely sufficient) for the scribal omission/inclusion of the LE.[52] Also, Longman and Garland note that the severity of Christ's rebuke does not cleanly align with the rest of the Gospel.[53]

---

[48] F. J. A. Hort, *Expository and Exegetical Studies* (Minneapolis, MN: Klock & Klock Christian Publishers, 1980), 199.
[49] Metzger, *Textual Commentary*, 104.
[50] France, *The Gospel of Mark*, 687.
[51] Hort, *Expository and Exegetical Studies*, 199.
[52] J. Harold Greenlee, *The Text of the New Testament: From Manuscript to Modern Edition* (Peabody, MS: Hendrickson Publishers, 2008), 77.
[53] Tremper Longman III and David Garland, *The Expositor's Bible Commentary: Matthew & Mark* (Grand Rapids, MI: Zondervan, 2010), 988.

CONTEMPORARY CASES FOR INCLUSION OF THE LE

General Concerns Regarding the Abrupt Ending

When making a case for the widely accepted AE, one of the most immediate concerns that arise is the literary strangeness of its abrupt and pessimistic finale. As advocates of the LE may attest, there is an inconsistency between such an ending and the opening statement of the Gospel, which connotes an uplifting tone: "The beginning of the gospel of Jesus Christ, the Son of God."[54] With such a strong introduction, it does appear odd that Mark would employ such a non-chiasmic ending.

While such an ending does appear at odds with the style of the introduction, it is not necessarily uncharacteristic when compared to other passages in Mark. There are many parts of this Gospel that can come off to the reader as unexpected or strange. Strauss cites several of these peculiar instances: Jesus gets angry with someone seeking to be healed (1:41–43), Jesus has trouble healing (6:5 and 8:23–24), Jesus speaks in parables so that no one can understand (4:10–12), and Jesus curses a fig tree for not bearing fruit in (11:12–14).[55] The case made from these citations supposes that if Mark could employ strange literary style and content within the body of the text, then he could likewise end on a strange note, namely one of confusion rather than elation. Additionally, a case can certainly be made that the strong beginning *does* mirror the SE in that both may be considered abrupt, even though the tone itself appears different.

Though plenty of defenses have been offered for an intentional ending with εφοβουντο γαρ,[56] it is hardly arguable that such an ending could be considered "normal." This claim pertains not only to the scope of the New Testament, but also,

---

[54] Mark 1:1.
[55] Strauss, *Exegetical Commentary*, 722.
[56] cf. Wallace, "Mark 16:8 as the Conclustion."

as Metzger points out, "the vast range of Greek literary works."[57] Particularly with reference to the syntactic oddity of ending a pericope (much less an entire book), with γαρ, Metzger concludes that the AE "does not represent what Mark intended to stand at the end of his Gospel."[58] Metzger is here tipping his hat towards a popular conclusion, contra Wallace, that the truest ending of Mark's gospel was lost. This may help shed light on the reason for such a variety of possible endings, namely that scribes (potentially even Mark himself if David Black, who will be discussed below, is right) wanted to supply endings that corresponded most closely with the original conclusion.

Nicholas Lunn: The Unity of the LE with the Rest of Mark

Perhaps one of the greatest helps in Lunn's work is his evaluation of literary styles and themes throughout Mark. Here will be highlighted just a few of the key ideas. Ancient writers made use of a great number of particular literary devices that aided in defining their individual styles. The New Testament writers were no different in this way. One crucial literary device that appears across the Scriptures is *inclusio*. Lunn summarizes the various ways in which *inclusio* manifests:

> While the discourse function of the inclusio is always that of closure, the precise nature of the repetition involved can vary. Sometimes it is a mere echoing of terms found at the beginning of the text. On other occasions, however, the terms might relate by way of comparison or contrast. In other instances there might be an intensification, where the related terms or themes possess a greater significance at the conclusion than at the beginning.[59]

Inclusio, then, is not limited to one element of the narrative,

---

[57] Metzger, *Text of the New Testament*, 228.
[58] Ibid.
[59] Lunn, *Original Ending of Mark*, 210.

as it can be grammatical as easily as it can be thematic. Lunn goes on to suggest that *inclusio* shows up prominently throughout Mark, and thus should be expected to occur in the conclusion of the book.[60]

Thus, the question becomes which ending more appropriately adheres to the chiasmic expectation of Mark's introduction and conclusion. Both thematic and syntactic/lexical *inclusio* is demonstrable between the introduction (1:1-12) and the LE. Lunn lists the most notable examples: (1) the editorial usage of κυριος (1:3, 16:19-20), (2) the presence of βαπτιζω proceeding from preaching discourse (1:5, 16:16), (3) the appearance of κηρύσσειν τὸ εὐαγγέλιον (1:14, 16:15), (4) the relationship between preaching and belief (1:15, 16:16), and (5) the casting out of demons, εκβαλλω (1:12, 16:9).[61] These examples show a lexical congruence as well as thematic consistency between the beginning and end of Mark in a way that is not as obviously present when assuming the AE (while there are certainly connections, they are not as substantially persuasive).

With regard to the odd relationship between vv. 1-8 and the LE, Lunn suggests that a similar parallelism is at work.[62] There are three pertinent parallels that stand out: the presence of Mary Magdalene on the Sabbath (vv. 1, 9-11), an authoritative exhortation (vv. 5-7, 14-18), and an activity in response to that speech (vv. 8, 19-20). Further, the LE exhibits the same kind of overall logical patterns of parallelism present in the whole of the book.[63] This potential parallelism may help to smooth out the seemingly strange relationship between these texts. At any rate, however, even if the presence of parallelism is rejected, a textual case should not be built in favor of omission merely on the basis of transitional awkwardness.

These points of literary comparison are only the beginning. Lunn eventually cites six total literary devices that show up prominently in the LE as well as throughout Mark.[64] Were it left up to the speculation of one possible literary device, the

---

[60] Lunn, *Original Ending of Mark*, 212.
[61] Ibid., 210.
[62] Ibid., 220.
[63] Ibid., 240.
[64] Ibid.

conversation would not traverse very far; however, Lunn shows that close observation of the text reveals enough similarities at least to keep the running questions regarding Mark open. The substantial literary and thematic unity of the LE with the rest of Mark leads Lunn to ultimately conclude,

> "... in the matter of fear giving way to faith, the place given to the proclamation of the gospel, with respect to Elijah typology, and above all with regard

> to the more pervasive motif of the exodus/new exodus. Taken together . . . these stand as strong indicators that affirm the common authorship of 16:9–20 and 1:1—16:9."[65]

David Alan Black: The LE as Markan Supplement David Black has offered a case for the canonicity of the LE that attempts to reconcile the authorial suspicions with the unity in the text. He has referred to this reconciliation as "Markan Supplement."[66] The idea is that Mark was indeed the writer of the LE, even though the LE was not written immediately after he wrote 16:1–8. His case relies upon the original purpose for the transmission of the Markan gospel, which he suggests was initially a 5-part discourse crafted by Peter. Black assumes that Peter would have had access to Matthew's gospel prior to orchestrating the writing of Mark, and he wished to synthesize the gospel account (primarily with attention to Matthew, though Black also holds that Peter knew of Luke's account) into essentially a series of lectures. The text, Black says, "was not intended to supersede either Matthew or Luke."[67] Black lists the 5 sections as the following: (1) 1:2–3:19, (2) 3:20–6:13, (3) 6:14–10:1, (4) 10:2–13:37, and (5) 14:1–16:8.[68] Black ultimately concludes that Mark was the author of the LE, but that it was a later addition to the text itself:

---

[65] Lunn, *Original Ending of Mark*, 272.
[66] Black, *Markan Supplement*, 103.
[67] Ibid., 119.
[68] Ibid., 118.

"The most plausible explanation is that after Mark had satisfied the immediate demand of those who wanted copies of the five discourses, which ended at Mark 16:8, the matter rested there until after the martyrdom of Peter and Mark's decision to go off to establish the church of Alexandria (AD 67–69). As an act of piety to the memory of Peter, Mark then decided to publish an edition of the text that would include the necessary sequel to the passion and death of the Master."[69]

It is the lateness of the LE's addition that, according to Black, has resulted in the long tradition of divided positions towards its authenticity.

Concerning the possibility that Mark would have added the LE himself later on after the initial writing, one possibility for stylistic reconciliation is that Mark took a narrative from the oral tradition, fit it to his style, and incorporated it at the end. Elliott rejects this supposition vehemently: "[The LE] is an inferior piece of writing, plodding and grey, compared with Marks racy, simple, and colloquial writing elsewhere. If he did find such a passage already in existence, he certainly did not refashion it in his own style."[70] Elliott does allude, though, to the chance that this ending could have originated from a conglomerate of "other Easter stories."[71] Moreover, Hort suggests a high likelihood that the LE is in some way linked to another external passage on the basis that the subject of verse nine is an implied Ιησους.[72] As no remnants of such stories with exact parallels of the LE have yet been found, this suggestion is purely speculative, albeit sensible.

N. T. Wright: The LE as Revelatory Finality

N. T. Wright has weighed in on the discussion of Mark's ending, not because he is by a trade a textual critic per se, but rather he does so as a part of his extensive work on the

---

[69] Ibid., 120.
[70] Elliott, "Original or Not?," 91.
[71] Elliott and Moir, *Manuscripts and the Text*, 41.
[72] Hort, *Expository and Exegetical Studies*, 199.

resurrection of Christ. Of course, one of the great concerns involved in embracing the AE as canon is the subsequent sacrifice of a Markan resurrection narrative. Put simply, the AE as canon means that Mark ends *unhappily*. For the majority of scholars, while this is noteworthy, it does not provide any robust grounding for critiquing the AE. They see Mark as a "grown-up piece of writing, not a naïve happy-ever-after book."[73] As Wright acknowledges, the level of intentionality among scholars to relinquish a Markan resurrection narrative is uncertain, but the general omission is nonetheless manifold.

Wright has attributed much of the skepticism regarding the LE as a kind of postmodern expectation that has been projected onto a text. His suspicion applies well to the popular notion that Mark intended to end at verse 8 so as to offer the reader a provocation: "What will you do in response to these things?" Wright rejects this possibility as an unlikely attempt to assign reader-response methodology onto a literary tradition that would have been void of such a style. Reflecting on Mark's ending, he says,

> "I tried for some years to believe that Mark was really a postmodernist who would deliberately leave his gospel with a dark and puzzling ending, but I have for some time now given up the attempt. Grammatically, the gospel could have ended with 'for they were afraid'; structurally, it could not have ended without the story of the risen, vindicated Jesus."[74]

For Wright, the omission of the resurrection is no small matter, as he sees the whole of Mark's gospel as a kind of apocalyptic book, "designed to unveil the truth about who Jesus is through a series of revelatory moments."[75] With so many sections of Mark, especially particular parables, granting focus to the identity of Christ and the inevitability of His victorious work (namely rising from the dead), one may justifiably expect

---

[73] Wright, *Resurrection*, 619.
[74] N. T. Wright, "Early Traditions and the Origin of Christianity," *Sewanee Theological Review*, vol. 41 (1997), 136.
[75] Wright, *Resurrection*, 620.

that Mark's conclusion would reflect this theme. Specifically, there are several instances in the account where situations steeped in pain, suffering, fear, etc. (not unlike the "fear and trembling" in the AE) are followed and fulfilled by an uplifting revelation. This pattern constitutes a Markan theme that would rightly be expected to persist in his conclusion.

Though an exhaustive listing of these thematic moments cannot happen here, a few examples are nonetheless in order. First, as Wright points to, one of the most notable instances of this occurs in the climactic Petrine confession in 8:29 that ushers in the second half of Mark's gospel.[76] After Peter's admission of Jesus as the Messiah, Christ begins to instruct them regarding the need for His suffering and death and thus their own. It is not for nothing that shortly after these cryptic instructions, Jesus takes the inner circle up to witness His marvelous transfiguration. This sequence of events follows the pattern of a fear- or confusion-inducing realization proceeded by a spectacular, revelatory *event*, one that is seen.

Another example that more directly parallels the situation in the conclusion is found in 5:33, where a fearful woman touched the hem of Jesus' garment and was healed of her affliction. The "fear and trembling" with which she initially approaches him does not remain in her departure, as he affirms her, saying, "your faith has saved you."[77] Immediately following this comes Jesus' exhortation to Jairus, whose daughter had fallen asleep, "Do not be afraid; only believe."[78]

Wright associates this literary theme of fear-to-revelation with a theological one that is present in the story: "the point of fear, throughout Mark, is that it should be overcome by faith."[79] If that is true, and it seems to be given that so many instances of fear in the gospel are indeed turned in on themselves within the context of a Christological appearance, then why would Mark have intended to suddenly forsake that theme in his conclusion?

Another outworking theme of this fear-to-faith paradigm

---

[76] Ibid., 621.
[77] Mark 5:33-34.
[78] Mark 5:36.
[79] Wright, *Resurrection*, 621.

involves the movement from silence to declaration. Throughout the narrative, subsequent to these marvelous events, Jesus instructs his audiences to say nothing until after the event of the resurrection. This cycle of silence exists in multiple locations, and so one may point to this trend in order to suggest that the women's fear, trembling, and subsequent silence (at least in so far as what is explicitly recorded in the AE) coincides with the rest of the silent responses. However, the fundamental flaw with any such supposition is that the "fear and trembling" of the AE occurs *after* the resurrection had already taken place. It is not a terrible interpretive leap to maintain that it was then time for the silence to be broken. Would this not have motivated Mark to write, among all possible different endings, one which included human declaration of the event? This is where the reader-response hypothesis of Strauss and others, the idea that Mark left the ending unfulfilled so as to ask "What will *you* do in response?" falters, for the story was consistently building up specifically to the proclamation of the gospel by those who had seen the events.

All of this points to a serious suspicion of whether Mark could have intended the AE. Wright admits the possibility that Mark meant to write a longer ending, but either died before he could finish it or some other phenomenon stood in the way of its completion.[80] However, he maintains that the more likely option is that Mark did finish it, and either the LE is that writing or the original was indeed lost. Even if the hypothesis of its loss holds merit, though, scholars may still surmise a general sense of what such an ending contained, namely the resurrection appearances. As such, being that the LE does contain an outline of such material, discrediting its helpfulness in finalizing the Markan message would be a mistake.

If the AE is to be taken as the preferred text, then the critic is tasked with addressing why this gospel account, unlike any of the others, ends without a post-resurrection appearance of Christ to the disciples. Advocates of the LE place great stress on the importance of this narratival element in the characterization of a Gospel. Greenlee, though, suggests that

---

[80] Ibid., 623.

this expectation for such an appearance is unreliable, for it exists only as a result of a kind of reading bias. He explains, "The words and forms in [the LE] are so different . . . that a student who had read Mark . . . but had not read any of the rest of the New Testament in Greek would find himself in unfamiliar material."[81]

Final Remarks on the Evidence

Though the evidence shown above suggests strongly that a definitive authentication of any given ending for Mark is improbable, what does seem evident is the dubiety of the AE as Markan intention. What is left, then, is the decision between the "lost ending" hypothesis and the acceptance of the LE. Should the LE be rejected as original, then based on the impressions of the external and internal investigations, a working claim is thus: Mark wrote an epilogue to his gospel, which would have included the resurrection appearances of Christ, the commissioning of the disciples, and the ascension. This original conclusion may have gotten circulated, but at some point in the process was damaged or destroyed. It did, however, circulate enough for first- and second-century scribes to be well aware of a longer version. This awareness would have allowed them essentially replicate Mark's original ending, with LE deemed as the truest version of the original. Under such a view, though the LE might be considered unoriginal, biblical scholars need not necessarily take it as *inauthentic*, insofar as it does preserve Markan intention, thematically at least if not syntactically.

SECTIONAL EXPOSITION OF THE LE'S CONTENT

With this study thus concluding that the LE thoroughly preserves the gist of Mark's original ending, it remains to exposit certain key portions of the text. This portion of the analysis is not exhaustive; it deals only with certain key features of

---

[81] J. Harold Greenlee, *Scribes, Scrolls, and Scripture: A Student's Guide to New Testament Textual Criticism* (Grand Rapids, MI: Eerdmans, 1985), 91.

the pericope. It gives special attention to the LE's finalization of the Markan theme of moving out of disbelief and fear into belief and obedience.

Jesus' Appearance to Mary (16:9–11)

The final series of events in Mark's gospel, as relayed by the LE, begins with an affirmation of the resurrection. The author uses the perfective-active αναστας, which seems to be acting temporally given the immediately proceeding clause specifying the Sabbath. This resurrection verb is used frequently in Mark (16 times outside of the LE), usually with reference to rising from the dead. With only a few exceptions, Mark tends to use the perfective active form of ανιστημι; the exceptions appear in 10:34 and 12:25, both of which refer to resurrection from the dead (the former referring to Christ and the latter referring to the bodily resurrection of others), but use the future, imperfective indicative rather than the perfective participle. Kelhoffer assumes αναστας to be a non-Markan word, but its regular presence in his account (sixteen appearances outside of the LE) leaves that assumption suspect.[82]

Mark does make use of the other prominent New Testament term for resurrection, εγειρω, throughout His account. While the two words do appear in similar contexts, there is a significant contrast between their semantic tones. According to BDAG, ανιστημι generally refers to the act of rising up, whether specifically with regards to resurrection from the dead or from a simple bodily rising of any kind, whereas εγειρω implies something more along the lines of causation to rise.[83] A clarifying example of this is found in 9:27, where εγειρω and ανιστημι are used together.[84] So the usage of ανιστημι in the LE may place emphasis on Christ's agency in rising from the dead contra the usage of ἠγέρθη in verse 6. Regardless, the variant lexical

---

[82] Kelhoffer, *Miracle and Mission*, 179.
[83] Frederick Danker, *A Greek-English Lexicon of the New Testament and other Early Christian Literature* (Chicago and London: University of Chicago Press, 2000), 272.
[84] ὁ δὲ Ἰησοῦς κρατήσας τῆς χειρὸς αὐτοῦ ἤγειρεν αὐτόν, καὶ ἀνέστη. "But Jesus took him by the hand and lifted him up, and he arose."

description of the resurrection need not amount to disunity between the pericopes.

What is the logical flow, if one exists, involved in the changing of focused cast from the women to Jesus (embedded in αναστας)? Levinsohn's discussion on back reference and global VIP may shed some light on the intention of the LE's author in transitioning to the new pericope after verse 8. Jesus, being the global VIP of the gospels, has a change in role between the circumstances of vv. 1-8 and 9-20, specifically from being a background figure in the former to being the active agent in the latter. This does constitute a boundary break following Levinsohn's qualifications: "In summary, a change in participant cast or roles provides supporting evidence for a boundary if it affects the global VIP."[85]

What about the *chronological* relationship between v. 8 and v. 9? The opening participle in the LE has often been translated as "now when he rose" or "having risen" in the attempt to preserve the perfective aspect of the αναστας. These translations leave the temporal progression a tad vague. Is the writer incorporating a flashback-like technique so as point the reader back to the time of 16:1? Alternatively, is the writer attempting a direct chronological progression, so that the events of the LE follow directly after those of vv. 1-8? It is the impression of this writer that both are essentially happening. Namely, the LE writer is directly drawing the reader's mind back to the same circumstance of vv. 1-8 in the sense that the Resurrection contextualizes both pericopes.

The writer of the LE, while maintaining the overall timeline of "early morning on the first day of the week," employs a slightly different phrasing compared to 16:2. There, the author uses the phrase λίαν πρωΐ τῇ μιᾷ τῶν σαββάτων, whereas in the LE, it is abbreviated to πρωῒ πρώτῃ σαββάτου. Aside from the preservation of πρωΐ, a word of Mark's appearing six total times in his Gospel, the phrases have some noticeable differences, including a strengthening adverb λιαν in the first, different terms for "first," and a difference in number in reference to the Sabbath or week.

---

[85] Stephen Levinsohn, *Discourse Features of New Testament Greek* (Dallas, TX: SIL International, 2000), 278.

Next comes a reintroduction of one of the main figures from vv. 1–8, Mary Magdalene. Some critics find it odd that, were the LE to be taken as original to Mark, he would have reintroduced her in this manner, namely that he would not have used a pronoun (since she was already an "active" character in the narrative and did not need to be renamed) and that he would identify her with the seemingly out of place detail of Christ's ridding her of demons. Why might the author of the LE have included such a detail? Does it add anything significant to the pericope or the chapter?

The only other place where Mary Magdalene is referred to in the same way is in Luke 8:2, wherein she and two other women who accompanied the disciples are given favorable introductions. Specifically, Mary had been freed of demons (arguably insinuating her faith), Joanna was a faithful manager of her household, and Susanna was generous to the disciples according to her means. There, the identification served to show forth the worthiness of the women in the presence of the disciples. A similar thing may be happening in the LE in that the writer may be giving a nod to the worthiness of Mary Magdalene to be the first person before whom Christ appears. The detail then would be a means of answering a possible patriarchal objection: "Why would Jesus appear first to a *woman?*" By including the detail of Mary's freedom from demonic activity, the writer is reminding the reader of Mary's faith, a fully satisfactory qualification for this privilege, especially given the theme of the male disciples' unbelief. If such is the case, then the inclusion of this detail is at least vindicated with regard to its internal congruity, and at best, it suggests an authorial plausibility of its placement in v. 9 rather than the opening of the chapter.

The worthiness of Mary progresses into her proclamation of Christ's resurrection to the disciples – an apostolic action. Critics note that the use of πορευομαι here is problematic, for two reasons in particular: (1) it is used 3 times in the LE, whereas it only appears in one other location in Mark (9:30), and (2) there is no consistency in the syntactical form. With regard to the first concern, we ought only give a limited amount of authority to particular authorial word usage, for there is a literary sense in which it is not wholly improbable that any given writer, Mark included, could use vocabulary in one portion that is variant to the rest of the work. While this detail should not be ignored entirely, claims of inauthenticity based on unexpected word choice are feeble. Specifically, with the multiple foci upon motion and appearance in this pericope, why would Mark not utilize one of the stronger N.T. words for coming and going.

Her proclamation τοῖς μετ' αὐτοῦ γενομένοις fulfills the directive of the angel in v. 8, preserving the chronological progression of the chapter as a whole. There are two attested variants in uncials that add extra identification of the disciples, one including μαθητης, but both lack any range of support. Their existence, though, does imply that though the phrase used here to address the disciples is odd, its referent remains fairly clear. Further, while the construction here is unique, it does have similarities with a construction that appears early in Mark's writing: ἵνα ὦσιν μετ' αὐτοῦ (in order that they might be with him).[86]

The use of κακεινοι is not exclusive to the LE, appearing 3 other times in the Gospel (though the first is in the uncompounded form). Jesus uses the phrase in 4:20 in providing a qualitative distinction between the seed sown in good soil and those that were not. In chapter 12, Christ again uses the phrase, twice this time, to distinguish between similar but distinct characters, namely the different servants involved in the parable. The word appears once more two verses later in the LE, wherein it refers to the two Emmaus disciples returning to the others. In each of these cases, characters of similar traits are placed in narrative contrast with the usage of this particular phrase, and the same seems to be the case here. Specifically, it refers to the other disciples who had been with Jesus alongside the women. Here, the commonality between the two distinguished characters are their participation in Christ's journeys. Thus, though this phrase is slightly rare in the N.T. and scarce in Mark, its usage in the LE is consistent with the rest of the account.

The consecutive usage of πενθεω and κλαιω does appear in two

---

[86] Mark 3:14.

other N.T. passages,[87] but is otherwise unique. The imperfective aspect shows that the disciples were already weeping and mourning at the time that Mary relayed the news to them. Even in the midst of their mourning, where such good news as what Mary had was so needed, the disciples would not believe her testimony. There are a variety of possibilities as to why they disbelieved. For one, they could have rejected her message on account that she was a woman; this may well have discredited her testimony amidst a group of first-century Jewish men. Another possibility is that their mourning was too great for them to so easily accept that Christ had risen. At any rate, their disbelief does follow along with the general trajectory of the gospel as a whole, building up to that conclusive moment when they would finally believe.

Jesus' Appearance to the Disciples on Emmaus Road (16:12–13)

Verse 12 ushers in the next section of the LE, one that closely parallels the first. Here, though, the author mentions that Jesus has come to them εν ετερα μορφη (with a different form), a phrase unique to this passage. In fact, the only other place in the NT where μορφη is used is in Philippians, where Paul dichotomizes Jesus' divine "form" and His human "form."[88] We may surmise that Christ's different form here likely refers to his glorified body. The writer does not, however, elaborate on how the disciples came to recognize Him, whereas in Luke's narrative, their eyes are opened after inviting Jesus to stay and dine with them.

While many scholars see this portion of the LE as evidence of the author's access to other canonical texts (in this case, Luke), Robinson suspects the opposite to be the case. If the author of the LE was putting together a summary of other gospel writings and early Christian tradtions, Robinson suggests that the author would have included *more* detail, or at least more precise detail, in this instance. He says, "A summary compiler

---

[87] Luke 6:25 and James 4:9.
[88] Phil 2:6–7.

of pre-existing narrative would closely follow the sources, even if abridging; additional unverifiable material would *not* be created or included."[89] In this case, the additional information would be Jesus' different μορφη, contra Luke's description: οἱ δὲ ὀφθαλμοὶ αὐτῶν ἐκρατοῦντο τοῦ μὴ ἐπιγνῶναι αὐτόν (but their eyes were being held back from him, to not recognize him).[90] Of course, it may be that Jesus' different μορφη was the means by which their eyes were restricted, so that the summarizing effect remains, but this seems unconvincing.

This section of the text concludes like the first, with a responsive disbelief after a claim to have seen Christ. This time, however, given that the declaration comes from two of the called disciples, one might expect that the others would be more prone to accepting their tale. The rejection of τοις λοιποις means now that the whole of the group has at one point chosen disbelief, as we may likely infer that the Emmaus disciples were among those who initially rejected Mary's claim. Slowly but surely, the narrative is yet building up to a climactic moment of belief.

Jesus' Commissioning of the Eleven (16:14–18)

With verse 14 begins a section of the LE that noticeably differs from the two preceding scenes. It differs from them in a few key ways: the length of the pericope, the amount of detail given, actual dialog instead of second-hand reference to conversation, and the end result of the events. One possibility for the abbreviated nature of the prior sections, as Kelhoffer notes, could be the building of suspense for the climactic portion of the narrative, namely Jesus' last appearance.[91] The opening exhortation of the LE's account of Jesus' commission has great similarity to those of other gospels, especially Matthew: πορευθέντες οὖν μαθητεύσατε πάντα τὰ ἔθνη (therefore go, teaching all nations).[92] How significant is it that the author employs two different words to describe the disciples' target audience?

---

[89] Robinson, *Four Perspectives*, 72.
[90] Luke 24:16.
[91] Kelhoffer, *Miracle and Mission*, 180.
[92] Matt 28:19.

First is κοσμον, a term which tends to refer the systematic whole of the created order, and then κτισις, which implies individual products of creative acts. There does seem to be a kind of parallelism between the two exhortations, and such is captured in the two separate but similar words. Ultimately, reading any kind of significant distinctness of audience based on the two words may be an exaggerative exegesis, but perhaps what can be fairly garnered is a universality of audience. That is, the complementary usage of κοσμον and κτισις further the point that the disciples have a responsibility to declare their faith to all kinds of people.

Wallace suggests that the perfective participles are acting imperfectively so as to function as "generic utterances."[93] He further notes the strangeness of combining the perfective πιστευσας with the promise of σωθήσεται, whereas in the majority of the New Testament, that pairing tends to utilize the imperfective πιστευων.[94]

The participial phrases ought to be taken as *conditional* participles, thus appropriately rendered "If one has believed and was baptized..." Wallace understands these two participles to be working as distinct pieces of the overall conditional phrase. Namely, he explains the relationship in the following way:

> "One might be cause, the other might be ground or evidence. If that is the case here, 'If you believe' is the cause and the fulfillment of the apodosis depends on it; 'and are baptized' is the evidence of belief and the apodosis does not depend on it for fulfillment. This would explain the following sentence: 'The one who does not believe shall be condemned.'"[95]

This reading supports the theological idea of supplemental baptism, which is crucial in defining the soteriological relationship between baptism and belief. Calvin highlights that it ought not be thought of as a kind of percentage game,

---

[93] Wallace, *Beyond the Basics*, 615.
[94] Ibid., 621.
[95] Ibid., 688.

where belief makes up a certain portion of salvation whilst baptism makes up the rest. Rather, he says, "we must hold that [baptism] is not required as *absolutely necessary* to salvation ... for it is not added to faith, as if it were the half of the cause of our salvation, but as a testimony."[96] Thus, this part of the LE need not seem theologically at odds with the broader NT teaching of baptism's relationship with salvation.

As far as the specific nature of πιστευω, Augustine notes that the kind of believing which Christ here refers to is not the kind that may be attributed to entities such as demons, who have a knowledge-belief that results in their trembling before him.[97] Augustine's reason for this distinction has to do with narrowing Christ's focus to those who express *authentic faith* and receive the true baptism of repentance by the Spirit.[98]

For vv. 17–18, Wallace treats the subjects of εκβαλουσιν, λαλησουσιν, and αρουσιν as categorical plurals, which "focus more on the action than the actor."[99] Thus, taking this section of the LE as saying that all believers will have the capacity to do these things misses the intended meaning. Rather than saying that all believers *can* do these things, Christ is more likely predicting that someone *would*, even if only once, accomplish such feats. This is to understand the text primarily as a specific *prediction* rather than a general *promise*.[100]

There is no clear biblical example of poison-drinking, and the only clear instance of snake-handling in the rest of the canon is found in Acts 28, where Paul is bitten by a snake, which the Greeks take to be a sign of his impiety, yet he suffers no harm and casts the serpent back into a flame. In Luke, though, Christ gives authority to the disciples to πατεῖν ἐπάνω ὄφεων (tread upon serpents).[101] A case could be made as well that John's account gives a nod to this idea, given his reference to Moses: Μωυσῆς ὕψωσεν τὸν ὄφιν ἐν τῇ ἐρήμῳ (Moses lifted up the serpent in the wilderness).[102]

This notion that Christians could have such authority

---

[96] Jean Calvin and William Pringle, *Commentary on a Harmony of the Evangelists, Matthew, Mark, and Luke* (Grand Rapids: Baker, 1989).
[97] Augustine, *Sermons*, 255.
[98] Ibid.
[99] Wallace, *Beyond the Basics*, 404.
[100] Ibid., 405.
[101] Luke 10:19.
[102] John 3:14.

over snakes is in itself an inverse of the consequences of unbelief. Paul refers to this specifically with regard to those who unfaithfully tested Jesus: ὑπὸ τῶν ὄφεων ἀπώλλυντο (they were being destroyed by serpents).[103] Further, and perhaps most importantly, one of the climactic moments in the New Testament's narrative is an instance of eschatological snake-handling: καὶ ἐκράτησεν τὸν δράκοντα, ὁ ὄφις ὁ ἀρχαῖος . . . καὶ ἔδησεν αὐτὸν χίλια ἔτη (and he seized the dragon, the ancient serpent . . . and he bound it for a thousand years).[104] It can thus be seen that this prediction of snake-handling is not necessarily at odds with how we perceive the Christian life. Particularly, if this is indeed a prediction rather than a promise, it may well be an *eschatological* prediction, one to eventually be truly fulfilled by the Faithful One.

Furthermore, there is also a creational element of the promise that harkens back to the cursing of the serpent in the Garden. There, God foretells that the seed of woman, namely Christ himself, will crush the serpent's head. At the very outset of the redemptive story, then, the Christian tradition maintains that the true Son of God (with the eventual interpretive expansion to all believers, the sons of God) would ultimately be given total authority over the workings of the serpent. Thus, the point of the snake-handling prediction seems to be allegorical rather than literal, even though there have certainly been mystical examples of real snake-handling. Nonetheless, Jesus' inclusion of it in this commission should primarily be construed as an assurance of the authority over evil which all believers possess in Christ. We may likewise expect the same principle to be at work with his reference to drinking deadly things.

Jesus' Ascension and the Disciples' Faith (16:19–20)

Scholars often dialog about the presence or absence of the resurrection in Mark's conclusion, but in addition to the commissioning of the disciples, there is another crucial Gospel element that the LE records: the ascension. The ascension is no trifle punctuation to the narrative of Christ; rather, it is indeed

---

[103] 1 Cor 10:9.
[104] Rev 20:2.

essential, for Christ himself makes clear elsewhere that if He does not go, then the Spirit cannot come.[105] Thus, if the LE is to be omitted, then we are left with a gospel account that lacks the resurrection appearance, commission, and ascension.

Wallace understands λαλησαι to be functioning as an "infinitive of antecedent time [occurring] before the action of the controlling verb."[106] Thus, preserving the accusative meaning of μετα το, the phrase is best rendered as "*after* he spoke," with the controlling verb being ἀνελήμφθη. The phrase εκ δεξιων is strange for two reasons: (1) the prepositional component seems awkward, and (2) the number of the noun is plural, an oddity given the specificity of δεξιος as it refers to the right hand. We may address the second conundrum by embracing a metaphorical reading of the word, one that would bring to mind rightness as opposed to wrongness rather than as opposed to left-ness. The idea, then, would be that in the ascension, Jesus' placement is by the *righteous* hand of God. While such an odd phrase might initially raise a question of the LE's suspicion, Lunn points out, "it is noteworthy that in this case the unusual form is located within 16:1-8, while the more usual ἐκ δεξιῶν is found in the disputed ending (16:19)."[107] Indeed, as far as Mark's writing goes, the phrase appears in this form five other times in the whole account. Lunn's allusion to vv. 1-8 is pertinent, as that is the *only* deviant form of the term δεξιος in the whole of Mark's gospel. Such a point further illustrates that any given pericope of Mark is prone to contain its own textual oddity.

At long last, as far as the narrative goes, the disciples believed. The LE, having such a focus on their initial disbelief, concludes with their faithful response, which comes only after this final commissioning and Jesus' subsequent ascension. They go on to fulfill both of Christ's earlier imperatives to go and proclaim to the whole of the world. This ending not only satisfies the systemic unbelief that occurs earlier in the pericope; it also reverses the fear and silence of v. 8. This, of course, is a wondrous picture of the reality of faith in all believers.

---

[105] John 16:7.
[106] Wallace, *Beyond the Basics*, 594.
[107] Lunn, *Original Ending*, 130.

CONCLUSION

As a general principle, it is not good practice to build a system of theology on any singular text, especially one under dispute. Luckily, though the LE may have some rich insights into the post-resurrection appearances of Christ, it does not contain any problematic or totally unique doctrines. In this sense, its remaining in the canon of Scripture is not dramatically necessary for the survival of any particular Christian commitment. That said, the LE, if taken as authentic, does serve to fulfill the thematic direction of the rest of Mark, and it provides a harmony with the other Synoptics. To call it suspect is a fair assessment, but as of yet, any definitive claims have come down to speculative decisions. That does not mean that the speculations should cease; rather, as has been the aim of this treatise, the discourse must continue. With the means of textual criticism continuing in technological advancement, it is always possible that a new piece of evidence or a new perspective will solidify a position, but until such a discovery happens, there is no reason to erase the LE from the Biblical narrative.

THE CENTRALITY OF ADOPTION FOR JOHN CALVIN

Josh Leamon

CALVIN AND ADOPTION

"The time is ripe, therefore, for us to cast another glance at John Calvin who has influenced the life of the world to such an extent."[1] The Doctor—Martyn Lloyd-Jones—spoke this sentence about Calvin. In this modern era, Calvin and the Calvinist-Reformed Tradition has seen a resurgence. Now, a decade since the 500th anniversary of the birth of John Calvin, his writings, thoughts, and ideas are now being considered more than ever. Over this past decade, more books have been published, conferences have been attended, and addresses have been given about the life and works of John Calvin.[2]

A doctrine not often highlighted in the whole of Christian tradition has come under recent attention. Notable works by David Garner, Scott Lidgett, Julie Canlis, S. B. Ferguson, John Murray, and J. I. Packer have given attention and significance to the doctrine of adoption. How did the doctrine of adoption surface in the thinking of these authors? I argue that in part they were influenced by Calvin himself. B. B. Warfield, among others, concluded that God's fatherhood is more pervasive in Calvin's piety even than God's sovereignty.[3]

Calvin expressed his understanding of adoption with several terms: The Fatherhood of God, union with Christ, the sonship of the believer, and the doctrine of participation. For Calvin, he does not treat adoption as a separate *locus*, or place, in the *Institutes*. Rather he "weaves the doctrine [of adoption] throughout the tapestry of God's marvelous work

---

[1] D. Martyn Lloyd-Jones, *Knowing the Times: Addresses Delivered on Various Occasions*, 32.

[2] Michael Dewalt and Maarten Kuivenhoven, "Calvin's Practical View of Adoption: Its Privileges and Duties," *Puritan Reformed Theological Journal* (2009): 3-4.

[3] Michael Horton, *Calvin on the Christian Life: Glorifying and Enjoying God Forever* (Wheaton: Crossway, 2014), 108.

in the salvation of sinners."[4] Calvin also thinks about adoption as a privilege for believers. Adoption has been described by J. I. Packer as the highest privilege that the gospel offers: higher even than justification.[5] Whether or not Calvin would have said it as Packer did, it is clear that adoption is a central doctrine in the writings of Calvin.

"For who are we, that God should honor us by taking us into his own house?"[6] Calvin clearly presents adoption as a great privilege and reality of the believer. He also presents adoption in several places throughout the *Institutes*. Therefore, adoption is vital to understand salvation and must be considered carefully and thoughtfully. What is the Christian life if not adoption, or to put it another way, what is salvation for? This paper realizes Calvin's understanding of adoption both in its nature and purpose by asking the question: How is the doctrine of adoption central both in Calvin's *ordo salutis* and his overall theological framework? Calvin considered highly the grace and blessing of adoption which is significant in rightly understanding the believer's relationship with their God.

CALVIN'S UNDERSTANDING OF THE NATURE OF ADOPTION

Trinitarian Adoption

Adoption, for Calvin, is a work of the Trinity. A statement so grand requires us to unpack several things. Thinking of Romans 8:15 and Galatians 4:6, Calvin presents a stunning truth about the adoptive work of the Father, the Son, and the Spirit. Concerning adoption, God the Spirit is a witness to us of the free benevolence of God the Father and God the Son. He reveals to us the nature of God which we will come to see is good, gracious, and loving. God the Father embraces us in

---

[4] Dewalt and Kuivenhoven, 5.
[5] J. I. Packer, *Knowing God* (London: Hodder & Stoughton, 2013), 206.
[6] Dewalt and Kuivenhoven, 15.

his beloved Son in order to become a Father to us. He makes a way for us to come to him as our Heavenly Father. God the Son came *for* us to bring the hope of salvation and came *to* us to become our Mediator. The three members of the Trinity are all working for our adoption through their specific roles. Before we are able to understand how God adopts people into his family, we must first consider what has been revealed by God himself.

As theologians have considered the nature of our Trinitarian God, Calvin contributes by showing how God has fellowship within himself. God can only have fellowship within Himself if indeed there are distinct persons within the Trinity. Following Gregory of Nazianzus, Cyril of Alexandria, and Epiphanius, he rejects the causal subordinationism.[7] John of Damascus says it this way,

> But if we say that the Father is the origin of the Son, and greater than the Son, we do not suggest any precedence in time or superiority in nature of the Father over the Son (for through his agency He made the ages) or superiority in any other respect save causation. And we mean by this that the Son is begotten of the Father
>
> and not the Father of the Son, and that the Father naturally is the cause of the Son: just as we say in the same way not that the fire proceedeth from light, but rather light from fire.[8]

Calvin affirms the full deity and *autotheos*, or aseity, of Christ [and by implication the Spirit].[9] This means that the members of the Trinity are equal in their being, power, and essence, but also distinct in their person, role, and activity. God the Father has a personal relationship as Father to God the Son as Son. Thus within the Trinity, there are personal relationships because there are three distinct persons.

---

[7] Douglas Kelly, "The True and Triune God: Calvin's Doctrine of the Holy Trinity," in *A Theological Guide to Calvin's Institutes* (Phillipsburg, NJ: P&R, 2015), 84.

[8] Ibid., 83.

[9] Ibid., 86.

Calvin shows that the distinction lies in the order of revelatory and redeeming activity in which Father is first, Son is second, and Spirit is third.[10] In the order of which God revealed himself to man, the Father is first. From the Father, the Son proceeds, and from the Father and the Son, the Spirit proceeds. The order is significant because they are one in essence which means each member is equal in importance, and they function together for one purpose: adoption. For Calvin, adoption is a Trinitarian work with each member of the Trinity having a specific role.

The first person of the Trinity is the believer's Father who is the agent of adoption. Calvin often describes the Father's providence and kindness. He looks to Psalm 107 which contains multiple examples of the Father exercising his providential kindness for his people. In these examples, Calvin concludes that what may often be observed as chance occurrence is actually proof of heavenly providence, *especially* of fatherly kindness.[11] The Father is in control and within his control, he exercises his kindness.

If God the Father were to only exercise control and kindness towards his people by means of physical needs, then we could conclude the righteousness and graciousness of His nature. But God in his Fatherhood within the Trinity extends a Fatherhood towards his people. He invites the believer who has been made right in Christ to participate in the fellowship of the Trinity. God in the depths of his kindness declares those in Christ *sons* and *daughters!* In 1 John 3:1, Calvin draws out the implications of the word "bestowed." The foundation of adoption is the love of God, and this love has been bestowed, as a gift, towards us. Calvin says, "He [the author John] means that it is from mere bounty and benevolence that God makes us his children; for whence comes to us such a dignity, except from the love of God?"[12] Thus, in his love for us God the Father bestows that love to us that we should be called children of God.[13]

---

[10] Ibid., 87.
[11] Jean Calvin, *Institutes of the Christian Religion* (Philadelphia: Westminster Press, 1960), 1:5:8.
[12] *Comm.* on 1 John 3:1.
[13] 1 John 3:1.

The next question follows. How is this love bestowed to us? The answer to that question is found in the second person of the Trinity— God the Son. For Calvin, the bestowal of God's love did not begin after we were reconciled to Him in Christ but began before the world was created. Augustine describes this love as "incomprehensible and unchangeable."[14] This means that God's love is constant and unconditional. From before our birth, God loved us with such a love that would bring about salvation and adoption. Jesus— God the Son—is the Mediator between us and God the Father.

God loves us by sending his Son to us to secure our salvation and adoption. Because God loved us before we were even created, his love is not based upon our merit or works. God loves us out of his own free choice. Adoption then is a privilege rather than an achievement. "Bestowal" has implications of being a gift. This is why adoption can be seen as a gift given by God to people undeserving of it. Therefore adoption is a privilege that happens through Christ.

> In his commentary of John 1:12 Calvin says, Christ exhibited an astonishing instance of his grace in conferring this honour on such persons, so that they began, all at once, to be sons of God; and the greatness of this privilege is justly extolled by the Evangelist, as also by Paul, when he ascribes it to God, who is rich in mercy, for his great love with which he loved us, (Eph. 2:4.)[15]

Because Calvin so closely connected adoption to the work of Christ's saving act, adoption becomes redemptive in nature. Christ in making sinners right before a holy God also makes them right to be called sons of God.

A final question follows. How can we receive the love bestowed to us? Calvin answers stunningly, "Hence, too, we infer that we are one with the Son of God; not because he

---

[14] David W. Hall and Peter A. Lillback, *A Theological Guide to Calvin's Institutes* (Phillipsburg, NJ: P&R, 2015), 229.
[15] *Comm.* on John 1:12

conveys his substance to us, but because, by the power of his Spirit, he imparts to us his life and all the blessings which he has received from the Father."[16] The *principal work*, as Calvin says, of God the Spirit is faith.[17] Looking to 2 Thessalonians 2:13, Calvin explains the role of the Spirit as the inner teacher who seals in our minds and hearts the promise of salvation which otherwise would have only struck the air or beat upon our ears.[18] God the Spirit supplies the faith by which to trust Christ and be united with him.

Throughout his *Institutes* and commentaries, Calvin presents the privilege of adoption as a Trinitarian work. Each member of the Trinity works towards this end of adoption within their own respective roles. The Father is the Initiator and Author of adoption as the believer's Heavenly Father. The Son is the promised Messiah and Mediator who descends to us as Jesus to be the incarnate bestowment of God's bounty and benevolence of adoption. And the Spirit is the giver of faith to trust and respond to Christ's sacrifice and God's gracious adoption. The work of adoption is fundamentally Trinitarian in Calvin's theology which has deeper implications of the covenantal, redemptive, and gracious nature of adoption.

Covenantal Adoption

The Trinity is firstly important to understand Calvin's view of adoption. Another foundational belief that undergirds Calvin's adoption is the idea of covenant. This Trinitarian God relates and has a relationship with his people through covenants. Covenants are always initiated and sustained by God himself and not his people. During the Reformation, covenant theology became more refined in its systematic formulation. Covenant theology recognizes three types of covenants: (1) *a covenant of works*, (2) *a covenant of grace*, (3) *and a covenant of redemption*.

Calvin's covenant theology has been described as *extensive*

---

[16] *Comm.* John 17:21.
[17] Calvin, *Institutes*, 3:1:4.
[18] Ibid.

but *incomplete*.[19] It could be viewed as being limited to the covenant of grace only, therefore excluding the covenant of works. It is important to note that the full development of covenant theology did not happen until the seventeenth century which was expressed in the Westminster Confession (1647) in chapter VIII. Calvin did not anticipate a covenant of works standing beside a covenant of grace which is why it seems he only gives attention to the covenant of grace and the covenant of redemption. Adoption happens within the context of covenant. Therefore, we must understand covenant in order to properly understand adoption.

Calvin begins chapter ten in book two of his *Institutes* in this way, "Now we can clearly see from what has already been said that all men adopted by God into the company of his people since the beginning of the world were covenanted to him by the same law and by the bond of the same doctrine as obtains among us."[20] Notice the connection between adoption and covenant. All men adopted by God were also covenanted by him.

Covered throughout the *Institutes*, Calvin develops his understanding of the covenants, specifically how they relate with adoption, as follows. Tending to see all the covenants as fundamentally gracious in nature, Peter Lillback makes a stunning point, "Because the covenant is the 'source and spring of salvation'[21] and the 'hope of salvation is founded on the covenant'[22] the covenant is inseparable from Christ."[23] Calvin observes that salvation is found in the covenant because the covenant ultimately rests on Christ himself. The bigger point

---

[19] Peter Lillback, "Calvin's Interpretation of the History of Salvation: The Continuity and Discontinuity of the Covenants," in *A Theological Guide to Calvin's Institutes: Essays and Analysis*, 178. Many scholars have juxtaposed Calvin's theological system with Covenant Theology proper. Three main conflicts arise. The first conflict is that Calvin's view of grace seems to be opposed to the Melanchthonian law/gospel distinction developed in the covenant of works. The second conflict is that Calvin's view of predestination is incompatible with the conditional nature of covenant in the Rhineland Reformers. The third main conflict is that Calvin's theology is again incompatible with the medieval scholastic covenant theology, especially concerning federalism.
[20] Calvin, *Institutes*, 2.10.1.
[21] *Calvin's Commentaries* on Ps. 67:2 (5.3.3).
[22] *Calvin's Commentaries* on Zech. 12:1 (15.5:340).
[23] Lillback, "Calvin's Interpretation of the History of Salvation," 202-203.

Calvin is making is that in searching through the covenants, one will inevitably find Christ as the foundation. Therefore the point is strengthened, our adoption through Christ happens in the covenants established by God.

The covenant made with the patriarchs found in the Old Testament is so similar to the New Covenant in essence and substance that the two are actually one in the same.[24] Calvin sees continuity through the Old and New Testament which means there is a consistent and unified history of salvation. Salvation though appearing different in the Old Testament is nevertheless by grace alone through faith alone in Christ alone. Does Scripture sufficiently support this claim? Calvin uses the following passages of Scripture to support his understanding. Paul, as he introduces himself in his letter to the Romans, says, "Paul, a servant of Christ Jesus, called to be an apostle, set apart *for the gospel of God*, which he *promised beforehand through his prophets* in the holy Scriptures (emphasis added)." Later in his letter, "But now the righteousness of God has been manifested apart from the law, *although the Law and Prophets bear witness to it*—the righteousness of God through faith in Jesus Christ for all who believe (emphasis added)." Elsewhere Scripture gives support of the continuity of the Testaments: Luke 1:54-55,72-73, John 8:56, 1 Corinthians 10:1-6,11, and Hebrews 13:8.[25]

The patriarchs participated in the same inheritance and hope for salvation by the grace of the same Mediator.[26] It has always been the work of Christ which has brought salvation and adoption as Christ has been the fulfillment of the covenantal promise. God in his covenantal dealings with his people promises hope of salvation and hope of entering into his family. Calvin says,

> We ought to esteem Abraham as one equal to a hundred thousand if we consider his faith, which is set before us as the best model of believing; to be children of God, we must be reckoned as members of his tribe [Gen. 12:3].

---

[24] Calvin, *Institutes*, 2.10.1.
[25] Calvin, *Institutes*, 2.10.3,4,5.
[26] Ibid., 2.10.1.

Redemptive Adoption

"For, even then in receiving free adoption as sons those who were enemies, he showed himself to be their Redeemer."[27] The fellowship within the Trinity has been extended towards those redeemed in Christ. Faith is, for Calvin, union with Christ. Adoption, as seen so far, is a unified work of the Trinity in which each member has a distinct and specific role concerning the work of adoption. Adoption is also covenantal in nature in that the covenanted people of God are the ones who are adopted into the family of God. Adoption is thirdly redemptive in nature.

Trinitarian and covenantal elements previously discussed will continue to be weaved together with the redemptive aspect of adoption. Julie Canlis has published a brilliant work on Calvin's theology of ascent and ascension. In her chapter titled "The Spirit: The Eucharistic Ascent," Canlis gives notice of adoption in the theology of Calvin. She argues adoption to be the doctrine overlooked by the Reformed tradition as one of Calvin's most significant doctrines.[28] What a bold claim! Canlis goes on to argue that ascent, for Calvin, is the orientation of the Christian life and the means by which we go. In a letter written by Calvin, he says, "Christ, for this reason, is said to send the Spirit from his Father (John 16:7) to raise us, by degrees, up to the Father."[29] She says here that "ascent does not go far enough; it describes the *telos* of humanity—communion—but not the type." Adoption then is the type or substance by which we understand the purpose of ascent.

Ascent means nothing if we have not descended first from God. The fall of humanity through the sin of Adam caused us to descend from our relationship with the Father. Calvin himself says so, "In this ruin of mankind no one now experiences God either as Father or as Author of salvation, or favorable in any way until Christ the Mediator comes forward to reconcile him

---

[27] Ibid., 1.10.1.
[28] Julie Canlis, *Calvin's Ladder: A Spiritual Theology of Ascent and Ascension* (Grand Rapids, MI: Eerdmans, 2010), 131.
[29] Ibid.

to us."[30] Our descension from the Father ruined by sin leaves humanity disconnected from the Father, that is until Christ reconciles him to us. Adoption, then, could be understood as ascension into the triune community.

As Calvin thinks about the glorious reality of addressing God as "Our Father" in prayer, he poses an illustration. What better advocate to plead his cause than to his own father? Is there another who could better act as an intermediary to recover the lost favor? Is there a more genuine humility and brokenness than a son imploring of his father's mercy? What of the Father of all mercy, the God of all comfort (2 Cor. 1:3)?[31] Calvin draws a stunning insight from Paul in Romans 8:3. Paul sees Christ as the bond whereby God may be found to us in fatherly faithfulness.[32] Therefore, God has made a way through Christ for us to *participate* in the family of God by way of adoption.

Participate was a carefully chosen word because it has rich meaning in Calvin's thought. The idea of participation began to develop in the thought of Plato who understood that things "participate" in the eternal for their very existence.[33] I mention Plato only because he is one of the early figures who began to develop a robust understanding of the concept of participation. Thinking back to the idea of ascent and descent, I want to push the idea of human ascent a little further. God taking on full humanity descended from the heavenly place to come and dwell on earth. The God-man—Jesus Christ—was crucified, died, was resurrection, ascended, and is now seated at the right hand of the Father. Christ ascended so as to lead us back to the Father. "Thus, for Calvin, the only appropriate human ascent is a matter of participating in Christ."[34] We participate in Christ in that we are united with him. All of these ideas: the Fatherhood of God, the Sonship of Christ, union or participation with Christ, ascent, and covenant, and redemption are all woven together as a marvelous tapestry of the glorious work of adoption.

---

[30] Calvin, *Institutes*, 1.2.1.
[31] Calvin, *Institutes*, 3.20.37.
[32] Ibid., 3.2.32.
[33] Canlis, *Calvin's Ladder*, 3.
[34] Ibid.

Gracious Adoption

Calvin often speaks of "double grace." Double or twofold grace is justification and sanctification. In Calvin's mind, he assumes both have to be true of the believer. There is not a believer who is justified only; there is also no believer who is being sanctified without first being justified. Calvin holds hand-in-hand justification and sanctification. Justification as a grace of God and not the merit of man stood in opposition to the Catholic Church's doctrine of justification. Since justification happens because of God, Calvin realizes that it is grace.

Grace in justification begins with the giving of Christ to us from the Father. Calvin says,

> By partaking of him, we principally receive a *double grace:* namely, that being *reconciled* to God through Christ's blamelessness, we may have in heaven instead of a Judge a *gracious Father;* and secondly, that sanctified by Christ's spirit we may cultivate blamelessness and purity of life.

Notice several elements we have already considered: "partaking" which is participation, "double grace" within the covenant of grace, and "a gracious Father" being the central agent of adoption. In our fallen state which was separated from God the Father because of our sin, Christ was given to us by the Father for our redemption. Redemption is accomplished in the work of justification. Justification is thus the hinge on which religion turns.[35] Adoption is so intimately linked with Calvin's double grace that it is important to consider further the nature of justification and sanctification as they relate to adoption.

Calvin can say that if the believer does not correctly understand what his relationship with God is, then he will not have the foundation of salvation nor the ability to build piety towards God.[36] Justification highlights two aspects of God's nature: his righteousness and judgment. Where sin is, there also is the wrath of God. Of course, we can speak to

---

[35] Calvin, *Institutes*, 3.11.1.
[36] Ibid.

the abundant grace that God would withhold his wrath for a period of time because we are not struck dead upon our first sinning. He must, however, deal ultimately with sin through his judgment. The other aspect of God is his righteousness. Only righteous men can be accepted by God. We need to speak with extreme clarity here. God only accepts righteous men though there is not one who is righteous.[37] How does he accept anyone? The answer is by his grace he has sent his Son to impute to us his own righteousness and take away our sin. Through faith in Christ as the substitutionary atonement for our sins, we are imputed with his righteousness in the sight of the Father; we are accepted by God through entering into his favor as righteous men.[38] Therefore we earned no right before God that he would do this on our behalf; it was not of our own merit or privilege. It was, as Paul says, "Even as he chose us for adoption to himself as sons through Jesus Christ, according to the purpose of his will, to the praise of his *glorious grace*, with which he has blessed us in the Beloved."[39] God's act of choice was not based upon foreknowledge of any kind, as Calvin adamantly opposes.[40]

This particular idea of foreknowledge,[41] which is often posed against Calvin's view of election, pushes against the grain of grace as a gift from God to us. If this view of foreknowledge pushes against the grain, then it would also have implications for the certainty of adoption. We must then be clear of the Scriptural teaching concerning the nature of grace and how it relates to election or foreknowledge. Calvin puts it this way,

> We shall never be clearly persuaded, as we ought to be, that our salvation flows from the wellspring of God's free mercy until we come to know his eternal election, which illumines God's grace by this contrast: that he does not indiscriminately adopt all into the hope of salvation but gives to some what he denies to others.[42]

---

[37] Romans 3:10–12.
[38] Calvin, *Institutes*, 3.11.1.
[39] Ephesians 1:4–6.
[40] Calvin, *Institutes*, 3.22.1.
[41] Foreknowledge in the sense that God looks forward to those worthy that he decides to save and adopt.
[42] Calvin, Institutes, 3.22.1.

Calvin argues the origin or source of salvation is God himself. God's grace is actually heightened when election is properly understood. For it would have been just of him to leave all people in their sin and to exercise his wrath and judgment towards us. But God, as he magnifies his own glory and seeks our good, has planned to adopt those who believe and trust in Christ.

Election in the mind of the modern thinker seems unspeakably unfair.[43] Modern thought has been influenced by individualism, reductionism, and fundamentalism. Therefore, we need to understand Reformation thought. The doctrine of predestination is a catholic doctrine.[44] "Predestination was one of the central issues in medieval theology."[45] Augustine, Thomas of Aquinas, Bonaventure, Heiko Oberman, Thomas Bradwardine, Gregory of Rimini, Marsilius von Inghen, Johann von Staupitz, and John Wycliffe not only argued predestination but double predestination.[46] These theologians were the forerunners to Calvin's understanding of predestination.

Francois Wendel notes, "It is true enough that Calvin attributed great importance to predestination in both its forms—election and reprobation—and that he never shared the point of view of Melanchthon, who thought it a subject hardly suitable for discussion."[47] Wendel argues that Calvin's understanding of predestination grew in accordance with his ecclesiology and pastoral preoccupations rather than being the main foundation of his theology.

Adoption is a comforting but difficult doctrine. It is comforting to the believer that they have been brought into the family of God to share in the inheritance of Christ in fellowship with God himself. Why are not all men adopted into his family?

---

[43] In this next section, I use the words "Election" and "Predestination" interchangeably.

[44] R. Stott Clark, "Election and Predestination: The Sovereign Expressions of God," in *A Theological Guide to Calvin's Institutes: Essays and Analysis*, 91. R. C. Sproul wrote an article in which he briefly summarized the history of the doctrine of double predestination. He summarizes it as God sovereignly decreeing both election and reprobation. He concludes this article quoting the Reformed Confession (1536), "Our salvation is from God, but from ourselves there is nothing but sin and damnation."

[45] Ibid., 91.

[46] Ibid., 92.

[47] Francois Wendel, *Calvin: Origins and Development of His Religious Thought* (Grand Rapids, MI: Baker, 2002), 264.

This question is dangerous because we are not to assume a lack of goodness in God's plan. Election is essential to adoption. Election must not become a cold and heartless doctrine but rather one that is glorious and always seen in relation to the love of God.

Turning towards the *Institutes* specifically, Calvin presents his chapter titled, "Eternal Election by which God has Predestined Some to Salvation, Others to Destruction." Calvin pastorally presents and warns of two dangers of approaching this doctrine: curiosity and anxious silence. Calvin warns against the two extremes of becoming curious to the point of arrogance or ignorance and becoming silent due to anxiousness and a lack of confidence. This doctrine then is something we can neither avoid nor take lightly. We should then approach election as "penetrating the sacred precincts of divine wisdom."[48]

"As Scripture, then, clearly shows, we say that God once established by his eternal and unchangeable plan those whom he long before determined once for all to receive into salvation, and those whom, on the other hand, he would devote to destruction."[49] God has chosen for some to be saved and thus adopted based solely on his gracious choice.

Returning to double grace, sanctification is also intimately connected to adoption. Richard Gaffin notes a common phrase within Calvin's theology: distinct but not separate.[50] Sanctification is distinctly different from justification but cannot be separated in any way. Francois Wendel summarizes Calvin's thought on sanctification, "Mortification of the old man, and participation in the new life."[51] Adoption is the reality of the believer in which they practice these two things. They participate in the death of Christ though putting sin to death, and they participate in the resurrection of Christ by being revivified in a newness of life.[52]

The gracious nature of adoption is seen in the free choice of God by which he does not base his choice off our merit but

---

[48] Calvin, *Institutes*, 3.21.1.
[49] Ibid., 3.21.6.
[50] Richard Gaffin, "Justification and Union With Christ," in *A Theological Guide to Calvin's Institutes: Essays and Analysis*, 255.
[51] Wendel, *Calvin*, 242.
[52] Calvin, *Institutes*, 3.3.9.

for his own good pleasures. Adoption then for the believer is humbling to the highest degree to which we cannot but help to cherish adoption as the highest privilege. The believer is left with no room to boast in anything but Christ himself. The twofold grace is intimately connected to adoption, thus making adoption another kind of grace.

ARGUING THE CENTRALITY OF ADOPTION FOR CALVIN

At this point, we have only begun to probe the depths of the riches of adoption in Calvin. This paper does not attempt to present a comprehensive theology of adoption in Calvin. However, this paper observes the key insights of adoption in Calvin and secondary sources with the intention of showing adoption's centrality for Calvin. The core of Christian faith is the gospel.

> Paul states that the truth of the gospel must supercede anything that we may devise ... he is showing us that we ought to know the substance of the doctrine which is brought to us in the name of God, so that our faith can be fully grounded upon it. Then we will not be tossed about with every wind, nor will we wander about aimlessly, changing our opinions a hundred times a day; we will persist in this doctrine until the end. This, in brief, is what we must remember."[53]

I want to argue the centrality of adoption in Calvin's understanding of the gospel. In order to accomplish this, I will consider four central elements of the gospel as presented in 1 Corinthians 15— death, burial, resurrection, and appearances.

Adoption and the Cross

God the Son is the one for whom all things were created and through whom all things were made. The Son of God became

---

[53] *Calvin's Series:* Sermons on Galatians.

the Son of Man, and that which was his by nature is ours by grace.⁵⁴ Jesus died on the cross for our salvation.⁵⁵ The cross was a Roman method of execution meant for the worst of criminals. How could God use something as evil as the cross to bring about good? This is surely what the disciples had in mind when Jesus prophesied his death, yet he realized it was a necessary part of God's plan of redemption.

The cross is the place of the wonderful exchange. "Who could have [restored us to God]... had he not taken what was ours as to impart what was his to us?"⁵⁶ Calvin says later in the *Institutes* that in becoming the Son of man with us, he has made us sons of God with him.⁵⁷ The wonderful exchange is that on the cross Christ bears the full penalty of our sin. Christ satisfies the full wrath of God towards our sin. He knew no sin which is Calvin's words means "that he was entirely exempt from sin, but was *made* sin for us."⁵⁸ The righteousness or blamelessness of Christ is imputed to us so that we are rendered righteous in the sight of God. For this is the wonderful exchange of the cross.

Our access to the Father in prayer is a way "opened to us by the blood of Christ, [that] we may rejoice fully and openly that we are the children of God."⁵⁹ Adoption is central to the cross because we understand for what end Christ died. Michael Horton says, "Even justification is important not as an end in itself, but because it secures that filial relationship that the Godhead willed from all eternity."⁶⁰ Christ has saved us to secure us as sons of the Heavenly Father.

Further, Galatians 2:20 offers insights into our connection to the cross and crucifixion of Christ. Calvin gives an illustration of a twig connected to the root when he discusses our secret energy as we are engrafted into the death of Christ. We are

---

[54] Calvin, *Institutes*, 2.12.2.
[55] 1 Cor. 1:18, Eph. 2:16, Php. 2:8, Col. 1:20 Col. 2:14, Heb. 12:2 are only a few passages that explicitly mention the cross of Christ.
[56] Calvin, *Institutes*, 2.12.2.
[57] Ibid., 4.17.2.
[58] *Comm.* on 2 Corinthians 5:21.
[59] Nigel Westhead, "Adoption in the Thought of John Calvin," *Scottish Bulletin of Evangelical Theology* 13, no. 2 (1995): 105.
[60] Michael Horton, *Calvin on the Christian Life: Glorifying and Enjoying God Forever* (Wheaton: Crossway, 2014), 108.

connected to Christ through his Spirit which has been given to us. Through his Spirit, we are united with Christ in his death so as to experience victory over the dominion of sin. For adoption is to be grafted into a family you once did not belong. Through adoption, we are brought into such belongingness. Therefore our union with Christ through the cross grafts us into the family of God once for all.

Adoption and the Tomb

"That Christ died for our sins in accordance with the Scriptures, that he was *buried.*"[61] Upon first thought, one might ask what connection is there between adoption and the tomb? In the tomb for three days, Christ's physical body lay lifeless, and his soul descended into hell. Calvin accepts the phrase "descended into hell" while rejecting certain interpretations of it. In Thomas Aquinas' *Summa*, he speaks of certain saints under a penalty whereby they were excluded from the life of glory for a time. Calvin firmly rejects this notion that Christ died to free saints from a limbo and escorted them to paradise.[62] Rather Christ descended into hell to experience spiritual torment on our behalf. Christ not only suffered on the cross but also in hell. Adoption then came at an infinitely costly price.

Christ bore upon himself the full wrath of God towards sin. He also experienced separation from the Father. The cost of our adoption was the life of the only righteous One. This costly price says something deeper about the love of Christ that he would willingly die for us. The love of Christ heightens our appreciation for adoption as a grace and privilege.

As our love of God is heightened through our appreciation for adoption, our hatred of sin should be proportionally heightened as well. With the metaphor of the tomb in mind, Calvin speaks of mortification in this way, "Furthermore, when
he is touched by any sense of the judgment of God (for the one straightway follows the other) he then lies stricken and overthrown; humbled and cast down he trembles; he becomes

---

[61] *Comm.* on 1 Corinthians 15:3.
[62] Calvin, *Institutes*, 2.16.9.

discouraged and despairs."[63] Mortification is the appropriate response towards sin and is an evidential fruit for the believer. True hatred of sin shows the work of Christ being brought about by his Spirit. All who are adopted into the family of God must rightly understand mortification. For it was the judgment of God that caused Christ to descend to hell for us, and it is the work of his Spirit that brings about the power and desire to put sin to death in our own hearts.

Adoption and Ascension

The joyful celebration of Easter is due to the glorious reality of Christ resurrecting from the dead. Through his resurrection, we experience the victory over sin and death as Christ does. Paul can say, "And if Christ has not been raised, then our preaching is in vain and your faith is in vain."[64] We have discussed participating with Christ in his death, and we will now consider participating with Christ in his resurrection. Calvin says, "If we share in his resurrection, through it we are raised up into newness of life to correspond with the righteousness of God."[65]
Sharing in the resurrection means we are spiritually raised up into newness of life—a life of righteousness.

Resurrection is new life. For the believer, this is a glorious reality. The climax of our newfound life in Christ is to one day be in his presence, that is, to ascend to him. Thus, I group together resurrection and ascension in this section.[66] Both resurrection and ascension relate and inform our understanding of adoption. Resurrection is then followed by Christ ascending back to the right hand of the Father which as we have seen has the implication of us ascending to the Father with Christ.

Ascension then is the movement of our adoption towards God. How does this ascension happen? I argue with Canlis that for Calvin, the Spirit is first called the Spirit of adoption in that he reminds us of our new relationship that is now an

---

[63] Ibid., 3.3.3.
[64] *Comm.* on 1 Corinthians 15:14.
[65] Calvin, *Institutes*, 3.3.9.
[66] Resurrection and ascension are distinct without being separate. For the sake and argument of this paper, I put resurrection as leading towards ascension.

ontological reality.⁶⁷ Our ascension happens by way of the Spirit residing within us and bringing us to the place Christ is. The Spirit leads us towards God and persuades our hearts that we are children of God.⁶⁸

Thus, our identity as an individual and as a community is fundamentally shaped by the reality of the Spirit of God dwelling with us. For Calvin, the category of adoption reminds the church that its primary profession is to be sons and daughters.⁶⁹ More than just our role or responsibility but our primary profession is to simply be God's adopted child. Sanctification then becomes living more deeply into this identity as children. Prayer begins to flow as an outpouring of our hearts to our Father. Freedom is given to us rather than fear of earning our right as sons.⁷⁰ Therefore in the Christian life, we are left in deeper adoration of our adoption and empowered by his love to love him more.

Ascension and participation become more than helpful metaphors of articulating our relationship with God and help serve as our identity in Christ as an individual. Again the idea of distinct without separation helps us understand that our individual identity is not lost in Christ but remains distinct. Our identity is distinct and so intimately linked with Christ that it can never be separated. "If, then, we are through him united to God, we may be assured of the immutable and unfailing kindness of God towards us."⁷¹

Adoption and Appearances

The final aspect of the gospel account in 1 Corinthians 15 is the appearances. Jesus appeared to Peter, the disciples, a crowd of 500, James, and then to all the apostles. What is the significance of the appearances, and how does it relate to adoption? Several reasons have been given as to why Paul mentioned the 500— to confirm the tradition's veracity, to establish continuity in the

---

[67] Canlis, *Calvin's Ladder*, 149.
[68] Calvin, *Institutes*, 3.13.4.
[69] Canlis, *Calvin's Ladder*, 149.
[70] Ibid., 150.
[71] *Comm.* on Romans 8:38.

message he passed on and how it went back to the beginning, to show the apostles' unity on the resurrection and ascension of Christ. It is clear that Christ appeared to many for their own faith and encouragement. As the Lord appeared to many and was seen by them, they had more faith and credibility in their testimony. Christ is his appearances brought comfort of his resurrection and encouraged them in their faith. Adoption, in a sense, is a kind of living testimony such as Jesus' appearances. Adoption as the appearances should be visible as well as serving to establish the credibility of our testimony.

The appearances of Jesus gives us some orientation of our testimony towards others. Adoption is not necessarily a visible or physical thing but is an inward spiritual reality for the believer that is manifested in the thoughts, desires, and the will of the believer. Therefore, our spiritual adoption should inform and affect our outward Christian life. "We have been adopted for this reason: to reverence him as our Father."[72] Calvin also speaks in his commentary on 2 Corinthians 6:18 that we do a mighty injury to God if we call him "Father" yet continuing defiling ourselves with idols. In this warning towards our high calling, Calvin reminds us not to excuse ourselves from personal holiness and purity. It would be a most despicable thing to even use our privilege of adoption as the reason to become lazy in our efforts of sanctification. Our adoption should be the reality by which we pursue holiness for the sake of being close with God all the more.

Calvin helps to connect this spiritual reality of adoption to the day-to-day life of believers by exhorting all who are sons and daughters of God to be ready and able to share everything with one another. For since Christ has shared with us his glorious inheritance through union with him, we, therefore, should be eager to share all we have with one another.[73] Adoption does indeed impact our relationships with other believers, and it also impacts our relationships with unbelievers.

As a mark of adoption, Calvin sees the characteristics of charitability and forgiveness impacting and informing our

---

[72] Calvin, *Institutes*, 3.17.6.
[73] Calvin, *Institutes*, 3.20.36.

relationships with unbelievers as well. "The Lord excludes from the number of his children those persons who being eager for revenge and slow to forgive, and practice persistent enmity and foment against others the very indignation that they pray to be averted from themselves."[74] Calvin does not view lightly the actions and attitudes of those who profess to be children of God. This stern critique should not be a cause of worry or anxiousness. Rather it should be a reminder of the grace we have been given in Christ and how our bond to Christ transforms our hearts to become more Christ like. The Father supplies to us the means by which we are to be transformed. His Spirit enables us through prayer and the Scripture to mortify the deeds of the body and walk in newness of life.

Therefore, Calvin's teachings on the Christian life serve to bring together all that he has taught concerning adoption and to apply it in practice with our relationship with God, believers, and unbelievers. The grace and privilege of adoption reckons us as sons and daughters of the Father and causes us to view all of life in relation to our adoption. Calvin would be the first to say that adoption does not stop at the cognitive level but works into the depths of our heart which produces good fruit that marks true adoption. The great hope of adoption is put this way, "The kingdom of Heaven is not servants' wages but sons' inheritance...which only they who have been adopted as sons by the Lord shall enjoy, and that for no other reason than this adoption."[75]

CONCLUSION

Calvin offers this prayer as we address God as our Father, "O Father, who dost abound with great devotion toward thy children, and with great readiness to forgive, we thy children call upon thee and make our prayer, assured and clearly persuaded that thou bearest toward us only the affection of a father, although we are unworthy of such a father." Adoption

---

[74] Ibid., 3.20.45.
[75] Ibid., 3.18.2.

is the highest privilege for the believer. For Calvin specifically in his *Institutes*, he weaves adoption throughout the tapestry of God's marvelous work in the salvation of sinners. Adoption undergirds Calvin's understanding of salvation as he relates it to justification, sanctification, and the whole of the Christian life. While Calvin often covers specific doctrines at one place in the Institutes, the doctrine of adoption is interwoven with several other doctrines throughout his work. The depth of Calvin's understanding and appreciation for adoption is seen in his understanding of the Fatherhood of God, the Sonship of Christ, our union in Christ, and our participation with Christ. Therefore, adoption should be admired greatly, understood carefully, and appreciated to the highest degree.

AN EVALUATION OF DIVINE LOVE IN THOMAS AQUINAS AND MARTIN LUTHER

Briley Ray

INTRODUCTION

God is love (1 John 4:8).[1] At the mention of this truth, warm feelings may arise, or a sense of comfort. What a great thing it is for God to love! Yet, what does this statement truly mean? The doctrine of God's love has perplexed many in church history. Two theologians in particular, Thomas Aquinas and Martin Luther, speak extensively on the love of God. While they speak similarly at times, their positions could not be farther from each other. Thus, this paper will first explore the differences and similarities in the doctrine of divine love between Thomas Aquinas and Martin Luther. Then I will evaluate their positions and offer concluding thoughts.

Thomas writes about the love of God from a philosophical perspective and holds that the essence of God's love lies in his will and goodness. Divine love, for Thomas, is any good that God wills to something. Luther, on the other hand, looks solely to the Scriptures and finds God's love displayed chiefly on the cross. His position points to what God has revealed in God the Son. Even though both perspectives begin with different philosophical and theological presuppositions, their positions can be combined to form a view that looks *at* God's love from the bird's eye view and looks *along* his love from the human perspective. In this manner, both the biblical and philosophical perspectives found in Thomas and Luther contribute to a wholistic view of God's love.

Section two begins a preliminary discussion of divine love in Augustine's thought. Both Thomas and Luther incorporate

---

[1] All Scripture citations, unless otherwise indicated, come from the English Standard Version.

different aspects of Augustine's thought into their own. Augustine writes about the love of God from two different perspectives in his works "Tractate on John 110" and *De Trinitate*. His tractate focuses on the concept of God's love from John 17:23b from a philosophical perspective, whereas *De Trinitate* centers on God's most loving action, namely, the cross. Thus, section two seeks to draw elements from Augustine that exist in both Thomas and Luther.

Section three deals with Thomas's doctrine of God's love from the *Summa Theologica*. He develops this doctrine from logical reasoning concerning the nature of God's essence and his will. This section attempts to capture the cardinal points of Thomas's reasoning from the simple form of love found in creatures and God to the highest form of love found in God, that is, friendship. Lastly, it also seeks to identify the elements of Augustine's thought within Thomas's theological framework.

Section four pursues the insights of Martin Luther throughout a various number of his works but focuses particularly on the *Heidelberg Disputation*. Recent Lutheran scholarship draws attention to the relatively unexplored doctrine of divine love in Luther's theology. Therefore, this section attempts to point out that Luther is a theologian of love and how he finds God's love primarily in the Son of God dying for sinners.

Section five is an evaluation of Thomas and Luther's positions. Each thinker's view is examined and critiqued for biblical and philosophical accuracy. This evaluation also includes various practical and theoretical implications for each thinker's line of thought. Then, this section aims to combine their sound and cogent philosophical principles and Biblcal exegesis to form a comprehensive picture of God's love.

Lastly, section six concludes the paper with a short summary of each thinker's major points, as well as the evaluation of each position. Basically, this seeks to wrap up the centuries old debate of what constitutes God's love. Here, the reader will encounter the paper's synthesis of their positions and any final thoughts.

THE MISSIONAL LOVE OF GOD IN AUGUSTINE

One difficulty in assessing the theological framework of God's love in Augustine's writing originates from the sheer volume of works he produced. A prolific writer, Augustine composed around five million words; yet, for the purpose of this research, its scope focuses on his "Tractate on John 110" and *De Trinitate*. Thomas Aquinas follows Augustine's conclusions in his tractate quoting his work in article three of question twenty in the *Summa*.[2] Also, Luther's reasoning on the love of God relates to several themes in *De Trinitate*. Thus, it is necessary to examine Augustine in order to understand both Thomas and Luther.

Tractate on John: 110

Augustine spends his lectures on John expositing the gospel text and deals with the question of God's love in John 17:23b, which says, "so that the world may know that you sent me and loved them even as you loved me." This text addresses Jesus's "high priestly prayer." Here, Augustine tackles the dichotomy of God's love and hatred, and the (in)equality of God's love.

The Dichotomy of God's Love and Hate

First, Augustine explains what it means for Christ to say that God has loved "them" (believers in Christ) as he has loved Christ. He asserts that God the Father loves Christians because he has loved the Son. God must love the members of Christ, for he loves the Son, which includes loving his body. Yet, he does not love the body of Christ in the same manner he loves the Son. Instead, he loves the Son as himself since he shares equality in the Godhead.

After the Son's incarnation, God loves the God-man because the Word becomes flesh. Thus, the "flesh of the Word" is "dear

---

[2] Thomas Aquinas, *Summa Theologica*, trans. Fathers of the English Dominican Province (Notre Dame, IN: Ava Maria Press, 1981), 1.20.3. From this pointforward, the *Summa Theologica* will be abbreviated *ST*.

to him."[3] Given that God loves the Son incarnate, he also dearly loves the members of his Son. For Augustine, this extends to eternity past through predestination of the saints. Augustine believes that God predestined those who will become members of the Son. Therefore, he says that on account of predestination, God loves the members of Christ before they exist.[4] This strong predestinarian love flows from God's intra-trinitarian love and Jesus's incarnation.

Following God's immutable love for members of the Son, Augustine begins explaining the love of God in accordance with his hatred. He declares that God's love exists for predestined saints while they remain at enmity with God. God's love does not begin once reconciliation takes place. It exists even as God's hatred resides upon a sinner.[5] Therefore, Augustine strives to join two opposing concepts.

He undertakes this by writing of why God hates the wicked. He utters, "He hated us, in so far as we were not what He Himself had made." He also says that God hates vice and everything abhorrent to his providence.[6] God does not create evil according to Augustine's understanding of divine hatred. In this way, what God hates is not his original creation.

Yet, this does not insinuate that God lacks hatred for the wicked. Augustine's remarks about the hatred of God suggests God hates the wicked because they have deviated from the *telos* of what God intended for them. Fundamentally, God hates them because of what they have done. Insofar as they exist, God loves them; insofar as they commit iniquity, God hates them. God did not create the evil he hates in them. Thus, God can hate them for what they do, but love them because he created them.[7]

---

[3] Augustine, "Tractate on John 110 (John 17:21–23)," New Advent, accessed November 12, 2018, http://www.newadvent.org/fathers/1701110.htm, 5.
[4] Ibid.
[5] Ibid.
[6] Ibid.
[7] Ibid.

Concerning the Equality of God's Love

Augustine continues his exposition by proposing an inequality of God's love. Augustine suggests that God loves Christians more than any other created thing; but even more so, he has greater love for Christ than all creation. Knowing that God loves sinners insofar as they exist and he hates sinners insofar as they commit transgression, God loves members of the Son more than anything else he created. Members of the Son are reconciled by the death of the Son; thus, this removes the hatred of God from the body of Christ.

Members of Christ are recipients of his "beneficence through healing."[8] Therefore, even though God loves all things because they exist, Augustine may proclaim, "who can worthily describe how much He loves the members of His Only-begotten?"[9] Christians receive a greater affection from the Father by Christ's redemption. This grace, Augustine notes, leads Christians to an equality with the angels. He grounds his assertion in the depravity of man, saying that since mankind already possesses an inferior nature and their sin plunges them into a greater unworthiness, then God must make man close to an angel.[10]

Although Christians receive greater love from God through the Son's reconciliation, the Son experiences greater love from the Father than members of his body. Augustine states that Christ shares equality with God, which leads God to love Christ as the "Only-begotten Himself, being Lord of all."[11] In this manner, Christ's nature is superior to the angels because he is Lord of all of them. Therefore, God loves Christ more than all other created things.

In short, Augustine establishes his doctrine of divine love from the Gospel of John on the foundation of God's love for Christ. God loves all things; yet, he loves members of Christ more than non-members, and loves Christ more than all of creation. God's love for the members of Christ rests in Christ's reconciliation which removes the hatred of God from sinners

---

[8] Ibid.
[9] Ibid.
[10] Ibid., 6–7.
[11] Ibid., 6.

whom God has loved from the foundation of the world. His love never changes and brings those predestined in Christ to become members of his body. For Augustine, this is incomprehensible love.

De Trinitate

In *De Trinitate*, Augustine seeks to penetrate into the nature of the Trinity and the relationship of the Trinity to mankind's redemption. In order to describe this relationship, Augustine frequently points to the love of God. He presents the detestable state of humanity caused by their sin and reveals how the missional love of God manifests itself.

The Mission of God and the State of Humanity

In books two through four of *De Trinitate*, Augustine represents the manifestations of God in history as missional events. In particular, he expresses the incarnation as a missional activity for the redemption of mankind.[12] The Son's mission transpires when the Father sends the Son into the world to become incarnate. Bradley Green points out that "for Augustine the *purpose* of the incarnation is redemption."[13] Thus, God the Father sent God the Son to take on human flesh for the redemption of mankind, which is to cure and heal them.

This implies Augustine believes something is gravely wrong with humanity. The problem is much worse than any human may think, for they have sinned against God, which has resulted in separation from him. At one point, human beings were able to participate in the divine joy of God; however, they are no longer able so to do. Augustine writes:

> "For God's essence, by which he is, has absolutely nothing changeable about its eternity or its truth or

---

[12] Augustine, *De Trinitate*, ed. John E. Rotelle, trans. Edmund Hill, 2nd ed (New York: New City Press, 2017), 2.7.

[13] Bradley G. Green, *Colin Gunton and the Failure of Augustine: The Theology of Colin Gunton in Light of Augustine* (Cambridge: James Clark, 2012), 112, emphasis in original.

> its will; there truth is eternal and love is eternal; there love is true and eternity true; there eternity is lovely and truth is lovely too. But we were exiled from this unchanging joy, yet not so broken and cut off from it that we stopped seeking eternity, truth, and happiness even in this changeable time-bound situation of ours."[14]

The divine is full of eternal love and delight, in which human beings can no longer participate because they are exiled from so doing. The *telos* of mankind is to "participate in the Word", but man cannot achieve this because he is "incapable of such participation and quite unfit for it, so unclean were we through sin."[15] Sin effectually cuts off mankind from participating in God as well as making humanity unfit to find their way back to God.

An important doctrine underlies Augustine's thoughts of humanity's separation from God, given the language of "unfit" and "incapable": namely, original sin. Basically, he believes that any offspring of Adam and Eve would contract original sin.[16] The effect of contracting original sin places every man under the wrath of God. Augustine writes, "In fact, every human being is born with this wrath."[17] Thus, all people suffer from sin and cannot escape it.

Therefore, Augustine concludes that sin enslaves humanity. Not only do human beings suffer from a similar sin of Adam, they cannot not sin. He states, "When sin is committed by free choice, sin is the victor and free choice also is lost."[18] Now, sin reigns victoriously in mankind, which cripples free choice. Sin becomes the master of the human mind, leaving humanity in a wretched state.

Lastly, the effects of sin's enslavement leave humanity dead

---

[14] Augustine, *De Trinitate* 4.1–2.
[15] Ibid, 4.4.
[16] Angelo Di Berardino, ed. *Patrology*, Vol. 4, *The Golden Age of Latin Patristic Literature From the Council of Nicea to the Council of Chalcedon*, trans. by Placid Solari (Maryland: Christian Classics, 1986), 436–37.
[17] Augustine, *The Augustine Catechism: The Enchiridion on Faith Hope and Charity*, ed. Boniface Ramsey, trans. Bruce Harbert (New York: New City Press, 2015), 26.
[18] Ibid., 30.

in both body and soul. Sin kills the soul, while sin's punishment kills the body.[19] The soul becomes ungodly and impure due to sin. While sin causes impurity in the soul, it results in the body's perishability, which "ends in the soul's departure from the body."[20] The soul and body, which were at one time conjoined to an everlasting immortality and participation in God, now separates upon the death of the person.

God's Love Demonstrated

Although Augustine believes mankind is helpless in rescuing itself from its depravity, he believes God has provided redemption for mankind, which is a manifestation of God's divine love. Despite redemption having its source in God's love, humanity's depraved state could bring them to despair any hope of reaching God or to believe God redeems them because they are somehow worthy. Thus, God needs to redeem mankind in a way that communicates to humanity that redemption is possible by divine aid and what sort of people they are that he redeems.[21] For Augustine, God provides redemption through the Son's incarnation and subsequent death on the cross.

In this manner, humanity can forgo despair in their incapability of reaching up to God, for God reaches down in the humility of weakness to save sinners. But also, it shows them their depraved state. Matthew Levering comments, "To appreciate the mission of the Son, we must come to recognize our weakness."[22] In short, God provides a way for sinners to see their own unworthiness by becoming incarnate and dying on the cross.

Therefore, in the cross God demonstrates his love for humanity. The power of his love is shown, not by brute strength, but "in the weakness of humility."[23] God showed humanity its

---

[19] Augustine, *De Trinitate* 4.5.
[20] Ibid.
[21] Ibid., 4.2.
[22] Matthew Levering, "On the Trinity," in *The Theology of Augustine: An Introductory Guide to His Most Important Works*, 151–86 (Grand Rapids, MI: Baker Academic, 2013), 157.
[23] Augustine, *De Trinitate* 4.2.

weakness by taking on the weakness of man in the incarnation, thus demonstrating God's love. Augustine does not philosophize the love of God in the same way as the scholastics. Instead of using reason to explain divine love, Augustine directs his mind to a particular point in human history: that is, the incarnation.

It is important to realize that Augustine believes human beings know God's love by the demonstration of the crucified Christ in history to which the Scriptures testify. For he quotes Romans 5:8, "But God shows his love or us in that while we were still sinners, Christ died for us." Augustine labors to explain the love of God through the revelation of God in history. For example, he says, "God became man for us as an example of humility and to demonstrate God's love for us."[24] Here, he describes the mission of God as a sacrament. Whereas today's usage of the word "sacrament" reflects an ecclesiastical rite, Augustine views a sacrament as an historical event revealed in the Scriptures that expresses spiritual realities. Thus, he declares the Son's mission to die as a sacrament.

Conclusion: Augustine's Doctrine of Divine Love

Augustine clearly reveals his view of divine love through these two works. Yet, Augustine displays his view of divine love in different ways. In his exposition of John, Augustine demonstrates God's love through a discussion of divine love's metaphysics and the inequality of God's love among creation. But in *De Trinitate*, Augustine grounds God's love in the mission of the Son.

Through these works, three elements can be found in Thomas and Luther's work. First, Augustine's idea of God loving all things because he originally created them as good found in "Tractate on John 110" is picked up by Thomas when he discusses whether God loves all things.[25] Second, Thomas adopts Augustine's concept of inequality in God's love with respect to his creation.[26] Third, Luther follows Augustine's emphasis of divine love manifesting itself in the mission of

---

[24] Ibid., 8.7.
[25] Ibid., 1.20.2.
[26] Ibid., 1.20.3.

the Son. Luther develops his own thought by placing the love of God in the cross of Jesus Christ.[27]

A THOMISTIC CONCEPTION OF GOD'S LOVE

In the previous chapter, Augustine's theology of divine love was examined in order to understand various aspects of both Thomas and Luther's thought. Augustine speaks of God's love in his "Tractate on John 110" in a systematic manner which provides background into Thomas's own formulation of the doctrine of divine love. He incorporates Augustine's doctrine of God's love for all creation and inequality of love among creation into his own summary of God's love.

Thomas Aquinas, in his *Summa Theologica*, attempts to cover various aspects of theology and provide a structured summary composed of questions, objections, answers, and replies to objections. The concept of love appears frequently throughout his work, finding its place in the discussion of God, of man, and of the virtues, which entails the longest discourse among the theological virtues. He considers God's love to rest in the divine will to will good, with its highest form found in friendship. He also concludes with (along with Augustine) an unequal love of God with respect to *beings* in creation. But first, a preliminary discussion of love in general must take place in order to understand the differences between God's love and all other types of love.

Foundations of Love

The love of God in Thomas's thought begins with love in the basic sense. For Thomas, love is the basis of all reality. Each *being* of creation has a *telos*. The orientation toward each *being's* end is love.[28] Thus, every movement and action of

---

[27] Martin Luther, "Heidelberg Disputation, 1518," in *Luther's Works*, vol. 31, *Career of the Reformer I*, ed. Harold J. Grimm (Philadelphia: Fortress Press, 1957), 57. From this point forward, *Luther's Works* will be abbreviated LW.
[28] Tuomo Mannermaa, *Two Kinds of Love: Martin Luther's Religious World*, ed. and trans. Kirsi I. Stjerna (Minneapolis: Fortress Press, 2010), 11.

a creature moves toward its end. Thomas states, "Every agent acts for an end...Now the end is the good desired and loved by each one."[29] Basically, he means that each agent acts toward the good which it desires (or is proper to it).

Tuomo Mannermaa provides a helpful illustration of a seed growing into a tree to demonstrate this concept of love. Within each seed lies the goal of becoming a full-grown tree. As the seed orients toward becoming a full-grown tree, the seed loves the good inherent to it.[30] Thomas conceives of this as a self-love, which finds its roots in the works of Pseudo-Dionysius, whom he quotes defending this general sense of love.[31] Dionysius's formula of love consists of a unifying and binding effect.[32] The movement of a creature toward its end results in a unification of the lover and its good.

Returning to the seed analogy: once a seed reaches its goal, it becomes unified with the good of a full-grown tree. This also takes place in relation to others. For a seed to become a tree it must orient itself to other goods so that it might reach its end. A seed's substantial form develops nonsubstantial forms, such as roots, branches, and leaves. In order for the tree to grow, its branches and leaves must turn toward light, and its roots to water. In effect, this orientation toward their inherent good comprises love because it helps them reach the final good of a full-grown tree. In this manner, the lover (the branches and roots) and the beloved (light and water) unite with each other.[33] This conforms to Thomas and Pseudo-Dionysius's idea of self-love.[34]

Although the love within vegetation does not exactly match the different variations of love within humanity's capacities, it accurately reflects the essential nature of love within Thomistic thought. This love first and foremost orients toward the good proper to each *being* and loves others through its orientation.

---

[29] *ST*, 1-2.28.6.
[30] Mannermaa, *Two Kinds of Love*, 11.
[31] *ST*, 1-2.28.6.
[32] Pseudo-Dionysius, "The Divine Names," in *Pseudo-Dionysius: The Complete Works*, trans. Colm Luibheid (New York: Paulist Press, 1987), 83; see also Norman Kretzmann, *The Metaphysics of Theism: Aquinas's Natural Theology In Summa Contra Gentiles I* (Oxford: Clarendon Press, 1997), 243.
[33] Mannermaa, *Two Kinds of Love*, 11–12.
[34] *ST* 1-2.28.1; see also Pseudo-Dionysius, "The Divine Names" 83.

Thomas cites Augustine as an authority that every *being* only loves the Good, which, for Thomas, corresponds to every *being* orienting to the good.[35] Consider a new born baby whose good consists of becoming an adult. Every act with an aim toward becoming an adult constitutes love; it can extend to others, for example, through the necessary care of a mother as she aids the child in becoming an adult. By this, a unification takes place between the mother and the child. This self-love characterizes Thomas's basic notion of reality.

Goodness and Will

Nuances exist between greater and lesser *beings* regarding love. The love found within inanimate objects does not exactly correspond to love in animals, nor to human love, nor to divine love. Yet, even divine love displays this basic concept of love found in all *beings* to an extent. When Aquinas addresses the subject of divine love, he first attempts to show that it exists in God. In Thomas's philosophy, divine love is evident in two ways: one by the concept of goodness,[36] and the other by the existence of the will.[37] Thomas's connection between love and goodness follows from the basic understanding of love explained in the previous section.

Goodness and Love

Given that every *being* has an orientation toward the good inherent to it, Thomas also affirms that the *telos* of everything is toward the form of goodness. Thomas states, "Since goodness is that which all things desire, and since this has the aspect of an end, it is clear that goodness implies the aspect of an end."[38] This means that goodness contains the *telos* that all things aspire to reach. For example, even though a new born

---

[35] *ST* 1-2.27.1; see also Augustine, *De Trinitate* 8.4.
[36] Divine love is evident in God in Thomas's thought by logically following the concept of Goodness. Thomas does not explicitly use Goodness as a means to prove the existence of love in God, but his idea of Goodness necessitates love in God.
[37] *ST* 1.20.1.
[38] *ST* 1.5.4.

baby may have the inherent good of becoming an adult, it also has the desire for *the* Good. Thus, goodness has the nature of what Thomas calls a *final cause*.[39]

The language of *final cause* follows from Aristotelian philosophy. Aristotle considered the final cause to be the Unmoved Mover (God). The final cause moves everything, for it is the end of all things.[40] Thus, the final cause attracts everything to itself. Aristotle likens this to love, just as Thomas does.[41] Thomas follows Aristotle by equating God with the Good. He asserts, "God is the supreme good."[42] When Thomas describes God as the supreme Good, he proclaims that Goodness is the essence of God.

This reasoning stems from the doctrine of divine simplicity. For Thomas, divine simplicity asserts that God's essence is always actual and without potentiality, as well as whatever can be said of God's attributes also corresponds to the nature of his essence.[43] Every *being* (whether an animate or inanimate object) wishes to unite with the Good and lack any defect; but in order to achieve this, it must become totally actual and lack all potentiality. In Thomas's view, total actuality is goodness.[44] Thus, goodness applies to the whole *being* of God. In this way, God is the Good.

Yet, how is love in God evident from the concept of goodness? He returns to the basic principle of love: namely, the orientation of everything to the Good. Even every act of God orients toward Goodness, and since God's essence is Goodness then God necessarily loves himself.[45] Therefore, even this basic notion of self-love exists in God as well.

---

[39] Ibid.
[40] R. J. Hankinson, "Philosophy of Science," in *The Cambridge Companion to Aristotle*, ed. Jonathan Barnes (Cambridge: Cambridge University Press, 1995), 121.
[41] James Fieser and Samuel Enoch Stumpf. *Philosophy: A Historical Survey with Essential Readings*, 9th ed. (New York, NY: McGraw-Hill Education, 2015), 85.
[42] *ST* 1.6.2.
[43] Eleonore Stump, *Aquinas* (London: Routledge, 2008), 97.
[44] Ibid.
[45] Although the idea of orientation toward the Good is fundamentally similar with God as everything else that exists, this does not imply God has potentiality. God does not orient toward the Good so that he may achieve his final end as a seed grows into a full-grown tree. God orients toward goodness because his essence is goodness. All actions must orient toward the Good, and this results in a self-love with God.

Will and Love

Another way that Thomas proves the existence of love in God comes through God's will. After affirming will exists in God, Thomas writes, "We must needs assert that in God there is love: because love is the first movement of the will."[46] Here, Thomas connects love and will. He continues by stating that the acts of the will regard either good or evil. However, evil resides as an indirect and secondary object of the will, whereas good remains the primary object. Love regards goodness and follows from the first act of the will.[47] Therefore, since will exists in God, so does love.

Thomas raises an objection which stems from Pseudo-Dionysius's formula of unifying love and divine simplicity. Fundamentally, unitive love cannot exist in God because God is simple. A unifying force seems to imply bodily composition, which negates simplicity. Yet, Thomas attributes a unifying love even to God by using the concept of God's will. He declares that the good he wills for himself is that he wills himself; and this does not necessitate composition. God also wills good to others and regards the good done to them as good done to himself.[48] Thus, unifying love also exists in God.

Passions and Divine Love

Another characteristic of Thomas's doctrine of divine love to explore regards whether God is passible or impassible. Impassibility means that God has no *passions*.[49] Following an Aristotelian account of anatomy, Thomas breaks the soul down into two parts. One part is the intellectual side of the soul, while the other is the sensational part of the soul. In each part, an appetite exists. Passions (i.e. love, sorrow, anger, joy, etc.) reside in the sensitive appetite, not the intellectual appetite.

---

[46] *ST* 1.20.1.
[47] Ibid.
[48] Ibid.
[49] Brian Leftow, "God's Impassibility, Immutability, and Eternality," in *The Oxford Handbook of Aquinas,* ed. Brian Davies and Eleonore Stump (Oxford: Oxford University Press, 2012), 173.

The intellectual appetite refers to the will, where choices are made. "Passions are *potencies*" or capacities. Passions denote passive potencies which entails that the bearer experiences a change.[50] For, example this happens when a person experiences sadness, for sadness causes the possessor to be affected from one state (happy) to another (sad).

Thomas considers it absurd to attribute passions to God. Passibility suggests that something outside of God affects his *being* from one state to another. This entails a change in God's *being*. Yet, Thomas proposes that God does not change.[51] Indeed, God is pure actuality; this means God has no potential to change and has actualized all perfections in himself. Furthermore, passive capacities lie in the sensitive appetite. Thus, if passions exist in God, then this implies God possesses a body, which Thomas denies.[52] Therefore, Thomas rejects any notion of passions existing in God.

So, what about the love that exists in God? Rather attributing an emotional love to God, Thomas equates love with will, since the first movement of the will always regards love. Thomas locates the will in the intellectual appetite. Whereas in humans, the will runs through the sensitive appetite, in God, there is no sensitive appetite.[53] Thus, love never moves through a sensitive appetite in God. Thomas claims that love is a passion insofar as it describes an act of the intellectual appetite, and in this manner, love exists in God.[54]

Therefore, Thomas can say that no passions exist in God. Love abides in the intellectual appetite which lacks any capability of change in God. In the occasions of Scripture where biblical writers credit an affectionate love to God, Thomas attributes this to metaphor.[55] Principally, the writers describe the character and actions of God in a manner which can grasp as much as possible the nature of an infinite and transcendent love.

---

[50] Peter King, "Aquinas on the Passions," in *Thomas Aquinas: Contemporary Philosophical Perspectives*, ed. Brian Davies (Oxford: Oxford University Press, 2002), 353–54.
[51] *ST* 1.9.1.
[52] Ibid., 1.3.1.
[53] Ibid., 1.20.1.
[54] Ibid.
[55] Brian Davies, *The Thought of Thomas Aquinas* (Oxford: Clarendon Press, 1993), 150.

God's Differentiated Love

Now comes the issue as to whether God loves anything but himself, following from the previous discussion of God's self-love. In addition to God loving things outside of himself, Thomas also tackles the issue of God's differentiated love among creation. He devotes two articles to explaining his logic of God's differing love. Since, fundamentally, love unites the lover to the beloved—which places the lover outside of himself and into the beloved—then it appears God cannot love other things because God cannot "pass" into another being.[56] Thomas first battles this objection and others to establish that God loves *beings* outside of himself.

Whether God Loves All Things

Thomas declares that God loves all things outside of himself. Thomas attempts this by a logical argument flowing from the will of God. First, he claims that all things are good, insofar as they exist.[57] For Thomas, the Shakespearean question "To be or not to be?" is always a resounding "to be." For having *being* or existence is good. This follows from the assertion that the will of God causes all things to exist. If existence is good and God wills things to exist, then God wills some good to everything that exists.[58] On account of Thomas equating love with will, he proclaims, "Hence, since to love anything is nothing else than to will good to that thing, it is manifest that God loves everything that exists."[59] This logically follows from everything Thomas asserts thus far. If God creates things and preserves them by his will, then he gives good to them because existence is good; thus, God must love all things that exist.

However, Thomas desires not to confuse the love of God with respect to creation with human love. He avers that humans do not create goodness in an object. Rather, a person's will "is moved by it as by its object."[60] This means that Goodness

---

[56] *ST* 1.20.2.
[57] Ibid.
[58] Ibid.
[59] Ibid.
[60] Ibid.

attracts the will of man. God, however, does not discover things to love, as if they have their own existence or goodness apart from him.[61] Instead, God creates goodness in an object by giving it existence. Therefore, although both human and divine love have traits in common, human love lacks the ability to create goodness in an object.

Thomas deals with four objections, two of which are noteworthy for elaboration. The first objection regards whether God loves things outside of himself since love unites the lover and the beloved. Thomas answers, "A lover is placed outside himself, and made to pass in the object of his love, inasmuch as he wills good to the beloved."[62] In the unification of love, a real, physical union does not take place. Nor does some mystical unification exist between the *beings* of the lover and the beloved. A unification exists inasmuch as one wishes good to the other. Hence, God does not pass into another *being* other than by wishing good to that object.

Second, Thomas supplies another objection to his argument which claims God cannot love all things because the Scriptures claim he hates sinners. He handles this objection by professing both (1) God's hatred for sinners and (2) love for them to be true. In one manner, God loves sinners insofar as they have existing natures.[63] Again, Thomas applies his basic notion of God's love to wicked persons. Even wicked persons are good inasmuch as their nature exists. Therefore, God loves them. This does not mean Thomas believes God loves their acts. Otherwise, God loves evil.

Whereas God loves sinners in one way, he hates them in another. Sinners, by virtue of sinfulness, lack existence. In fact, Thomas claims they fall short of existence. They cannot attribute this shortcoming to God, for he initially caused them to have existence.[64] For Thomas, sin is a privation of goodness or *being*.[65] Therefore, a sinner lacks existence because of the privation of his *being*. Thomas follows Augustine's line of reasoning, since Augustine roots God's love for sinners in the

---

[61] Davies, *The Thought*, 151.
[62] *ST*, 1.20.2.
[63] Ibid.
[64] Ibid.
[65] Ibid., 1.49.1 and 1-2.82.1.

fact they have existing natures and roots God's hatred in the instance of sinners falling short of what God creates them to be.

Whether God Loves All Things Equally

Next, Thomas moves to discuss whether God loves all things equally. He proposes several formidable objections arguing for the equality of God's love among all creation. Nonetheless, Thomas concludes that God does not love all things equally and loves more that which is better. Here, he cites Augustine's "Tractate on John 110" as authoritative proof of God's differentiated love among creation.[66] He begins by describing two ways something may be loved more, or less. First, a lover may love something more by the will's intensity.[67] The act of the will can love something more, or less, intensely. Thomas denies this explanation with respect to God because God's will is unified and simple, never lacking or gaining intensity.[68]

Despite God's will remaining the same, Thomas asserts another way God can love things unequally. "In another way on the part of the good itself that a person wills for the beloved."[69] Basically, Thomas states an unequal love exists when a greater good is willed for one beloved and not another. God loves some things more than others by willing a greater good to some things and not others. Thomas does not qualify the goodness God may bestow on a thing; yet, it is certainly the case that in all instances of speaking of the Good, at the very least he means a thing orienting to its proper end.

Logically following comes the assertion that God always loves things that have greater goodness. Thomas writes, "Now the better a thing is, the more like it is to God. Therefore the better things are more loved by God."[70] Thomas defines a "better thing" as something which is closer to God in terms of *likeness*. Having already shown that God loves one thing more than another by willing it a greater good, Thomas says that since

---

[66] Ibid., 1.20.3.
[67] Ibid.
[68] Ibid.
[69] Ibid.
[70] Ibid., 1.20.4.

God's will causes goodness in things, and things have greater goodness because of God's will, then God loves the better things.

Thomas's assertion does not insinuate God loves something more because of its *own* goodness, as if something attains goodness apart from the will of God. Rather, God grants goodness to an object through his creation and preservation. For a thing to become godlier depends on the will of God. Jesus Christ serves as an example of God loving a better thing. Thomas utters that God loves Christ more than all of creation because God willed a greater good for him by giving him the name above every name.[71] This logic extends to individuals in the created universe as well, although Thomas declines to answer whether God loved Peter or John more, stating the presumptuousness of the objection.[72] In short, Thomas follows Augustine in declaring that God loves some more than others, most notably the Only-begotten Son.

The Highest Form of Love

Thus far, Thomas's basic view of love, connection of love and will in God, doctrine of impassibility, and differentiation of God's love have all been examined. Lastly, it is time to discuss Thomas's highest form of love between God and creation: friendship between God and man. Friendship finds its place in Thomas's thought through the theological virtue of charity. Thomas adopts the model of friendship-love from "the Philosopher," Aristotle. He then begins to describe each element of friendship-love and how it corresponds to God and man.

Thomas draws from Aristotle's *Nicomachean Ethics* the concept of friendship-love. He gives three criteria for friendship: (1) good will to another (for his or her own sake), (2) mutual love, and (3) communication.[73] Thomas states not every love has the character of friendship, for it may not meet this criterion. These three principles of friendship-love set it apart from Thomas's basic idea of love. For example, friendship cannot

---

[71] Ibid.
[72] Ibid.
[73] Ibid., 2-2.23.1; see also Joseph Wawrykow, "The Theological Virtues," in *The Oxford Handbook of Aquinas*, ed. Brian Davies and Eleonore Stump (Oxford: Oxford University Press, 2012), 296.

exist between man and food. Man does not wish good upon food for food's own sake. Instead, he wishes it good as for himself.

Yet, good will toward another man for his own sake does not constitute friendship-love either. Thomas believes friendship must have mutual love.[74] This greatly limits the extensiveness of friendship-love. For friendship cannot exist with an enemy. Thus, God's friendship with man extends only to members of Christ because he cannot extend it to an enemy. Joseph Wawrykow notes that God gives friendship-love to those who possess charity. God's love infuses charity into the soul, which gives man the ability to love God in return through divine grace.[75] Basically, not only does God now will good (love) to a human being, but that human being also wills good to God.

Thirdly, Thomas affirms that mutual love must exhibit some type of communication. Since God communicates his happiness to believers, Thomas considers the relationship between God and man to meet the criteria needed for friendship-love. He cites John 15:15, which states, "No longer do I call you servants ... but I have called you friends," as proof that charity equals friendship.[76] Thus, Thomas declares both from Scripture and the Philosopher that charity must be friendship.

Conclusion of Thomas's Summary of Divine Love

Classical theism dictates the direction of Thomas's view of divine love. Thomas follows Aristotle in his formation of the philosophical nature of God, leading him to assert that the love of God consists of willing good to another. This stems from his foundational notion of an object orienting toward the good proper to it. Furthermore, the highest form of love, namely, friendship-love, follows this pattern as it does not constitute just benevolence to another object, but a mutual love. God and man share this love as God communicates his happiness to his beloved and mutual love takes place. Thomas sees friendship-love taking center stage as the chief way to describe the relationship between God and man.

The next chapter will examine Martin Luther's theology

---

[74] Ibid.
[75] Wawrykow, "The Theological Virtues," 296.
[76] *ST* 2-2.23.1.

of love, with special attention to his *Heidelberg Disputation*. Luther's work provides a different perspective than Thomas's medieval philosophy. As Luther turns away from scholasticism, he propounds a doctrine of love rooted in the revealed Son of God. Basically, he follows the Augustinian emphasis of love found in *De Trinitate*.

MARTIN LUTHER AND THE THEOLOGY OF THE CROSS

Thus far, the doctrine of divine love has been examined in Augustine and Thomas's work. Augustine and Thomas both argue that God loves all of creation insofar as he created everything. In addition, both attributed inequality to God's love with reference to different *beings* in creation. Thomas asserts that love is nothing more than the divine will of goodness to things and claims that the highest form of this love is found in friendship between God and man. Now, a discussion of Luther's thought is in view, which contains a few similarities but many differences regarding the Thomistic view of God's love.

Martin Luther unveils himself as a theologian of love above all else. Recent Finish scholarship claims the center of Luther's theology is not justification by faith, but love.[77] The heart of Luther's theology lies in the *Heidelberg Disputation*. Here, Luther defends twenty-eight theses, drawing distinctions between a theologian of glory and a theologian of the cross, as well as human love and divine love. Of all Luther's theses, thesis 28 is crucial for understanding Luther's entire concept of divine love and the "theology of the cross," and is perhaps the most important piece of the reformation and Luther's evangelical work.[78] He follows a different conception of God's love than Medieval theologians, and follows the Augustinian approach in *De Trinitate* to demonstrate the love of God.

---

[77] See Mannermaa, *Two Kinds of Love*.
[78] Ronald K. Rittgers, "Martin Luther as a Theologian of Love" (lecture, Union University, Jackson, TN, March 15, 2018).

Departure from Medieval Philosophy

The foundations of philosophy in the Middle Ages largely centers on Aristotelian philosophy.[79] Thomas's *Summa Theologica* is the crowning achievement of Christianizing Aristotelian philosophy. Yet, shortly before Luther's time, schools of thought develop which begin to break the Medieval tradition of harmonizing Christianity with Aristotelian philosophy. For example, William of Ockham sought to eliminate the synchronization of Christianity and pagan philosophy. Luther grows up in the Ockhamist tradition and develops several issues of his own with classical theism espoused in the Aristotelian tradition.[80]

Luther maintains orthodoxy in his diversion from Medieval thought and has more similarities with Thomas Aquinas in his doctrine of divine love than meets the eye; however, Luther also maintains real differences with his sharpest disagreement lying in the difference between human and divine love. For Luther, Aquinas equates the two, which leads to a "theology of glory." This leaves no hope for salvation of wicked persons.

A critical caveat follows in interpreting Luther. Luther's emphasis is speaking pastorally rather than in strict philosophical categories which leads him to differ with Aquinas in the essential nature of God's love. In fact, at times, Luther appears to think irrationally and throw philosophical sense to the wayside. Yet, Luther must be engaged on his own terms in a pastoral manner, and to say that Luther disbelieves in philosophical contribution to theology is an injustice.[81]

Human Love and Divine Love

Luther's distinction between human and divine love originates in Thesis 28 of the *Heidelberg Disputation*. He states, "The love of God does not find, but creates, that which is pleasing to it. The love of man comes into being through that which is

---

[79] Mark C. Mattes, *Martin Luther's Theology of Beauty: A Reappraisal* (Grand Rapids, MI: Baker Academic, 2017), 18–19.
[80] Ibid., 21-23; see also Alister E. McGrath, *Luther's Theology of the Cross* (Oxford: Blackwell Publishers, 1990), 36.
[81] Ibid., 15.

pleasing to it."[82] Luther's second claim refers to human love, which can be found permeating Thomas's thought. Elementally, this refers to Thomas's concept of orientation to the Good. As man orients himself to the Good, he, in effect, loves the Good. This designates a self-love toward each man's own *being*. All other loves (including love for God and neighbor) spring forth from man's desire to orient toward goodness. Luther asserts that all philosophers, including himself, agree with this natural definition of human love.[83]

The problem for Luther rests in equating human love with divine love and the deficiency of self-love to be a Christian ethic.[84] In Thomas's thought, human love is directed toward "what is." Its orientation always aims at what exists and what consists of goodness. It can never seek "what is not," which Luther characterizes as that which does not exist or that which is evil, lowly, and needy.[85] Luther derives this idea from 1 Cor. 1:18-31 when Paul speaks of God bringing the things that are not to tear down the things that exist. In Luther's thinking, this leaves no room for humans to love one another in a Christian ethic, for it leaves no room to love sinners who are weak, needy, and evil. On account of this, Luther ascribes Thomas's view as "erroneous."[86]

Luther perceives Thomas to apply the same self-love to God. Since Thomas believes that God is *being* itself and the supreme good, then God's first object of love is himself, for God's orientation aims toward the Good along with all other creatures. Mannermaa explains, "Within the Holy Trinity, the inner love of the Holy Trinity loves another in the most perfect way when loving itself."[87] Thus, the Trinity first and foremost love its own members.

Yet, Luther's first statement in Thesis 28 describes the opposite. The love of God always creates good in its object of love; God does not seek his own good. Luther explains his reasoning:

---

[82] *Heidelberg Disputation*, LW 31:57.
[83] Ibid.; see also Mannermaa, *Two Kinds of Love*, 18.
[84] Mannermaa, *Two Kinds of Love*, 18.
[85] Ibid., 1–3
[86] Ibid., 10.
[87] Ibid., 18.

> The love of God which lives in man loves sinners, evil persons, fools, and weaklings, in order to make them righteous, good, wise, and strong. Rather than seeking its own good, the love of God flows forth and bestows good. Therefore sinners are attractive because they are loved; they are not loved because they are attractive.[88]

The fullness of God's love focuses on "what is not" rather than "what is." He conceives of the divine love as selfless, for sinners are not attractive and lack goodness to give God. God does not love sinners so that he may gain good from them as a tree loves water or sunlight.[89] Nothing good draws God's attention. Rather, whatever God loves is loved because God makes it good.

Tuomo Mannermaa notes a major consequence of Thomas's philosophy which connects with Luther's criticism of Thomas. As already stated above, Thomas's view makes God's love a self-oriented friendship-love. God can never love that which is evil because his love always aims toward the highest good. Since God's essence equals goodness, then he loves himself more than all creation. Following this, God directs his love depending on a *being's* goodness or lack thereof. God's love is in proportion to the degree of goodness found in each *being*. Therefore, God does not love creation equally.[90] This is precisely the conclusion Thomas draws.

In Luther's view, God equally directs his love to "what is not."[91] When Thomas speaks of a human's orientation to the Good, Luther interprets this as a "work (*ergon*)."[92] Fundamentally, this means self-love is a self-actualizing love, done by the lover himself. Thus, Luther cannot conceive of God loving an object on account of its own actualized goodness. In Luther's theology, this is akin to self-righteousness.

Luther rejects any notion of attaining self-righteousness or justification by good works through an Aristotelian ethic. Man can only attain goodness or perform good works after

---

[88] *Heidelberg Disputation*, LW 31:57.
[89] Mannermaa, *Two Kinds of Love*, 2.
[90] Ibid., 19.
[91] Ibid., 3.
[92] Ibid., 12.

justification.⁹³ For Luther, man is sinful, and his will opposes the Good. Man does not have free choice, but sin holds him captive to enslavement.⁹⁴ Therefore, God's love must be distributed equally because no one possesses goodness. If God directs his love toward what is good, then only God himself can be the object of his love.

For Luther, the absurdity of Thomas's doctrine leads God to only hate sinners. Rather, "God saves no one but sinners, God instructs no one but the foolish and stupid, God enriches none but paupers, and God makes alive only the dead."⁹⁵ Luther's doctrine of divine love aims at that which lacks goodness, that is, sinners. Whereas classical theism focuses on the Good, Luther emphasizes the wicked. This causes Luther to separate himself from classical theism and the Aristotelian tradition. In his disputation, Luther expounds several theses distinguishing what he calls a "theologian of glory" from the a "theologian of the cross." At the heart of these distinctions lies Luther's contention with the classical definition of God's love.

Two Theologies: The Glory and The Cross

The distinction Luther makes between human love and divine love corresponds to what he calls a "theology of glory" and a "theology of the cross." He explains these conceptions in Theses 19, 20, and 21 of his *Heidelberg Disputation*. In thesis 19, he describes a theologian of glory, uttering, "That person does not deserve to be called a theologian who looks upon the invisible things of God as though they were clearly perceptible in those things which have actually happened."⁹⁶ Here, Luther demonstrates his frustration with classical philosophy in general. It seeks to inquire of the "invisible things" of God as if they are transparent in creation. These things include divine attributes, such as goodness, love, wisdom, and justice.⁹⁷

Fundamentally, Luther casts theologians of glory as

---

⁹³ Alister E. McGrath, *Luther's Theology of the Cross* (Oxford: Blackwell Publishers, 1990), 139.
⁹⁴ *The Bondage of the Will*, LW 33:67.
⁹⁵ *Lecture on Romans*, LW 25:418.
⁹⁶ *Heidelberg Disputation*, LW 31:52.
⁹⁷ Ibid.

presumptuous metaphysicians. They handle the doctrine of God by attempting to perceive into the nature of God through created things. Naturally, this implies the human intellect's ability to see through an object to its form.[98] Thus, Luther severs the ability of the intellect to understand the nature of God's invisible attributes through history or creation. Applying this to Luther's critique of Thomas, Thomas incorrectly assumes the human intellect can behold the invisible nature of God's love. For Luther, it is mere speculation to speak of the essence of God's love without God manifesting that love visibly to the world.

In contrast, thesis 20 proclaims how a true theology functions. It states, "He deserves to be called a theologian, however, who comprehends the visible and manifest things of God seen through suffering and the cross."[99] This distinction effectively splits the Thomistic method and Lutheran method of describing God's love. Luther claims a true theologian does not look through creation to understand the nature of God; instead, a true theologian attends to where God manifests himself, in suffering on the cross.

For Luther, the love of God which pursues "what is not" is visible in Christ's death and suffering. He says concerning the theologian of glory, "it does him no good to recognize God in his glory and majesty, unless he recognizes him in the humility and shame of the cross."[100] Whereas the theologian of glory speaks of God's transcendence, the theologian of the cross speaks of his humility and weakness. Luther follows the Augustinian position outlined in *De Trinitate*. Augustine perceives God to display his love chiefly in the death of Christ.[101]

Luther stresses the difference between these positions by emphasizing the peculiarity of God dying on a cross. Most would not investigate the slums in order to find God the Son. Yet, Luther presents a God who finds his sinful creation there.[102] God reveals himself in the cross, which is contrary to human

---

[98] Gerhard O. Forde, *On Being a Theologian of the Cross: Reflections on Luther's Heidelberg Disputation, 1518* (Grand Rapids, MI: Eerdmans., 1997), 72.
[99] *Heidelberg Disputation*, LW 31:52.
[100] Ibid., 52-53.
[101] Augustine, *De Trinitate* 4.2.
[102] Robert Kolb, "Luther on the Theology of the Cross," in *The Pastoral Luther*, ed. Timothy J. Wengert (Grand Rapids, MI: Eerdmans., 2009), 33.

understanding. Luther's view leads him to a concept called *Deus absconditus*, the hiddenness of God in the cross.[103] Thus, the greatest manifestation of divine love is found in the place where people least expect it, hidden away in foolishness.

For Luther, because God's love functions contrary to human understanding, all the actions of God are hidden as well. For example, divinity hides in weakness, righteousness in injustice, and life in death. God's love always aims downward toward evil and nothingness. Thus, his actions manifest in ways which also seem evil. When God's love saves sinners, they see not a God of glory, but a God found in humility. So, God's actions intend to bring the sinner to recognize his own unworthiness and weakness because God brings him to where he resides, not in heaven or glory, but in suffering and poverty.[104]

Through the effects of God's love, God takes sinners to "hell" and brings them back again. Luther believes that as God's love drives human beings to recognize their own nothingness (hell), he brings them back as strong and wise in Christ. They must first become weak in order to be strong, and foolish in order to be wise.[105] This describes the process of God creating what is lovable in sinners. He brings them to nothingness in order to create goodness in them. Elementally, God replaces one form of man with another, an evil form with a good form.

Love Unifies by Faith

Earlier, this paper described the unifying concept of God's love in Thomas Aquinas's thought. Thomas saw the unification of lover and beloved exhibited in the orientation of one thing to its proper end. As an object orients toward its end, it passes into its object of love. Therefore, as a man turns to God, his proper end, a unification in love takes place as the lover becomes more like his beloved. Luther also holds to an idea of unifying love between God and man; although he explains this concept in a different manner than Thomas.

Luther describes unifying love by explaining how Christ identifies with humanity. Since God directs his love to creatures

---

[103] McGrath, *Luther's Theology*, 164.
[104] Mannermaa, *Two Kinds of Love*, 32–33.
[105] Ibid., 32.

who are weak, foolish, and evil, he places himself among them so that he may unify with them. As Christ dives into the wretchedness of humanity, he gives himself to lowly man. This divine giving includes an exchange of attributes. For instance, the omnipotent God unites with weak man, which unites strength and weakness, and as the righteous God becomes sin, he unites righteousness and sinfulness.[106] A real, unification takes place between Christ and man through the cross.

Yet, one distinguishing factor of Luther's unifying love involves faith. Luther interprets Thomas's position of unification to hold that unification by love can exist even with humans who unknowingly love God.[107] This appears to imply the absence of faith within the process. Thus, Luther maintains that in order to receive the love of God hidden in the cross, faith is necessary. He states, "Where [theologians of glory] speak of love…we speak of faith…Thus faith is a sort of knowledge or darkness that nothing can see. Yet the Christ of whom faith takes hold is sitting in this darkness as God sat in midst of darkness on Sinai and in the temple."[108] Theologians of glory speak of unification in terms of strictly love, but Luther denotes faith as the means by which the love of God unifies with man.

Only faith can unite man and God in love because the love of God remains hidden in the cross. Therefore, man needs a way to pierce the dark cloud of weakness and humility which surrounds the omnipotent and righteousness God on the cross. If people solely perceive Christ from the outside, they cannot penetrate his lowly state and observe the glorious Son of God. Since human understanding cannot *see* in this manner, it needs something else to enter the darkness of God. Hence, Luther describes faith as "the kind of knowledge that sees nothing."[109] Paradoxically, only a faith which sees nothing perceives the nothingness of Christ on the cross and recognizes the hidden God in suffering.

A splendid summary of Luther's position lies in thesis 21 of the *Heidelberg Disputation*. Luther writes:

---

[106] Ibid., 60.
[107] Ibid., 20.
[108] *Lectures on Galatians*, LW 26:129; see also Mannermaa, *Two Kinds of Love*, 61–63.
[109] Mannermaa, *Two Kinds of Love*, 61.

A theologian of glory calls evil good and good evil. A theologian of the cross calls the thing what it actually is. This is clear: He who does not know Christ does not know God hidden in suffering. Therefore, he prefers works to suffering, glory to the cross, strength to weakness, wisdom to folly, and, in general, good to evil.[110]

Faith brings a theologian to speak truly of the cross, while a theologian of glory prefers to call the suffering of God on the cross an evil and misunderstands the love of God. Faith, then, serves as the foundation of unifying love between man and God. Without it, sinners can never recognize their own unworthiness through seeing the unworthiness of Christ crucified.

So, the highest form of God's love, which unifies God and man, is a giving of himself to sinners through the hiddenness of the cross. Then, man receives God's love by faith. Basically, this is a willful act on God's end, which leads to the unification of godliness and sinfulness. Love, then, does not constitute sappy emotions, but the death of God. Only faith can grasp this reality because of its absurdity from reason's point of view.

Conclusion of Luther's Cross-Centered Divine Love

Luther's entire theological framework rests on divine love. He emphasizes Augustine's main aspect of divine love (God displaying his love on the cross) found in *De Trinitate* but not others. He is one type of Augustinian while Thomas displays characteristics of another type. Just as Augustine asserts the clearest picture of God's love lies in the cross,[111] Luther holds the love of God is manifest in no other place than the cross, although it is hidden by weakness. God does not love the Good, nor himself, but rather what is evil and lowly. Thus, self-love does not characterize God's love. Instead, a selfless love found in giving himself and his attributes to sinners lies at the heart of God. A sinner accepts the love of God through faith, for the love of God upsets human understanding, Human love

---

[110] *Heidelberg Disputation*, LW 31:53.
[111] Augustine, *De Trinitate* 4.2.

and divine love could be no farther apart than a theologian of glory and a theologian of the cross.

Chapter four puts forth an evaluation of Thomas and Luther's positions. First, the foundational aspect of love is examined in both thinkers. This section deals with important aspects of Thomas's metaphysic and Luther's theology that accurately represents the nature of God's love. The purpose of evaluating their thoughts is an attempt to combine them to form a wholistic picture of God's love. Second, the idea of differentiated love is examined in both thinkers. Third, an examination of Thomas's concept of friendship follows for the purpose of showing how Luther's concept of divine love provides a better representation of the highest manifestation of God's love.

AN EVALUATION OF THOMAS AND LUTHER

Sections one, two, and three work to explain the positions of Augustine, Thomas Aquinas, and Martin Luther. Thus far, this paper, concerning Thomas's philosophy, found that: (1) Love, at the foundational level, is an orientation to the Good; (2) Thomas follows the philosophical Augustinian emphasis of God's love found in his "Tractate on John 110;" (3) he declares that love is God's will; (4) Thomas does not attribute passions to the nature of God's love, which leads him to divine impassibility; (5) God loves all creation but unequally; and (6) God displays his highest form of love through friendship.

Concerning Luther, though, this paper found that: (1) Luther believes God directs his love to "what is not," thus creating that which is pleasing to him; (2) Luther follows a different Augustinian emphasis found in *De Trinitate* (3) divine love and human love are radically different (i.e. God's love is not a self-love); (4) God shows his love through the suffering and death of Christ on the cross; and (5) faith receives the love of God and unifies God and man.

In this section, Thomas and Luther's view of divine love will be evaluated. Firstly, the idea of foundational love will be evaluated in Thomas and Luther, then, secondly, the inequality of God's love, and, thirdly, the idea of God's highest form of love. This section also intends to show how Thomas and Luther's position can be combined to form a full picture of God's love. Each thinker will be incorporated into the picture by evaluating them on their own terms.

Foundation of Love in Thomas and Luther

With regard to philosophical presuppositions, not every aspect of Aristotelian philosophy Thomas uses necessitates error. For example, while Aristotelian philosophy contains errors,[112] Pseudo-Dionysius's formula of everything acting for an end holds true. From simple observation, everything in its beginning contains a potentiality to become that for which it was designed. The examples of a seed and newborn baby point to the accuracy of this Aristotelian contention. Concerning man, Ecclesiastes 3:11 declares that God has put eternity into the heart of man. Therefore, the final end of man, or his highest desire, is found in God. Augustine remarks, "Thou madest for Thyself, and our heart is restless, until it repose in Thee."[113] Man finds rest for his soul in God, the final cause of all things. In addition, Augustine agrees that every person loves the Good;[114] this entails, following classical theism, that every *being* orients to the Good. This gives ground for Thomas to rightly argue that, foundationally, love is an orientation to the Good.

Thomas's correlation of love and will holds together his entire framework of unifying love. Since love consists of the first movement of the will, then any creature's orientation or will to the Good constitutes love, including God. Thus, love is the driving force and basis of all reality. If God truly is the supreme Good and the final cause of all things, then God's *being* is essentially the basis of reality. In short, this logic is crucial for affirming the biblical concept that God is love.

Thomas's contention of divine simplicity greatly aids him in maintaining this position. An attribute of God does not

---

[112] See *Heidelberg Disputation*, LW 31:42 for Luther's thirty-sixth thesis which states Aristotle wrongly finds error with Plato, and Plato's ideas are greater that Aristotle's.

[113] Augustine, *The Confessions of St. Augustine* (New Jersey: Barbour and Co., 1984), 5.

[114] Augustine, *De Trinitate* 8.4.

merely constitute a "part" of God; rather, love and all the other attributes of God are one in the essence of God. So, to state that love exists in God equals the claim that love is the essence of God. In this manner, Thomas binds his framework together, making God's love the basic nature of reality. His philosophy holds coherently and rightly affirms such a basic concept of life.

Thomas's declaration that love equals will has great importance for the doctrine of God's love; for without it, impassibility and the immutability of God is lost. For the past two hundred years, process theology has deserted the immutability and impassibility of God. This has led to unconventional claims about the doctrine of God, such as God possessing the potential to be affected by *beings* outside of himself, which clearly deny scriptural affirmations of God's immutability (Mal 3:6; Num. 23:19; and Heb. 6:17).

As immutability falls away, so does impassibility. Since the Romantic movement, passions appear to reign supreme concerning the nature of love. From movies and television shows to poetry and novels, the emphasis of passion characterizes love. In order for love to exist, a deep-rooted affection and desire for the beloved is required. Yet, when passions are applied to God, God exhibits a potentiality that leads him to be affected by outside forces. If potentiality exists in God, then full actuality is lost, thus causing God to lack perfection.

Therefore, these aspects of Thomas's metaphysics are important for accurately representing the nature of God's love as will. Both Thomas and Luther agree with each other that love, at its basic level, equals will. Luther's theology of the cross finds God's love manifested through action or will by the death of Christ. Although Luther concedes to Thomas that love functions in this manner with respect to will and that human love naturally consists of orientation toward the Good, Luther suggests that God does not love in the same way that humans love.

Remember, Luther denies that God loves the Good. God's love does not orient toward goodness, but evil. Thus, as humans love by orienting toward the Good, God loves by loving the wicked. Luther holds that God cannot love the Good because it insinuates he cannot love wicked, depraved sinners. The foundation of Luther's theology, thesis 28 of the *Heidelberg Disputation*, states, "The love of God does not find, but creates, that which is pleasing to it."[115] Yet, Luther misunderstands the metaphysics of Thomas in several ways.

Luther's Misunderstanding of Thomas

First, it appears that Luther assumes that in classical metaphysics God discovers an object outside of himself to love and this object attracts God in the same manner as God (Goodness) attracts man. Luther's claim implies that only his view describes God as creating the Good that he loves, since he says that Aristotle's philosophy is "contrary to theology."[116] However, this is not the case, for Thomas explicitly differentiates the two basic loves between God and man. Thomas writes, "It is manifest that God loves everything that exists. Yet not as we love. Because since our will is not the cause of the goodness of things, but is moved by its object, our love ... is not the cause of its goodness ... the love of God infuses and creates goodness."[117] For Thomas, the love and will of God causes goodness in an object. However, with man's love, an object's goodness moves or attracts it.

Thus, God does not stumble upon something to love: he creates that which he loves by giving it goodness. Insofar as a thing exists, it possesses goodness. Since all things exist by the will of God, then God necessarily gives goodness to the things he creates and preserves. As he wills goodness to an object, he also loves that object, which means that God loves everything that exists inasmuch as it possesses some goodness. Nothing exists outside of God that causes God to be attracted to it. So, surprisingly, whereas Luther does not agree with Thomas, Thomas agrees with Luther's thesis. Although, Luther seems to not grasp Thomas's position, both Thomas and Luther affirm that the love of God creates that which is pleasing to it.

Second, Luther fundamentally misunderstands Thomas's anthropology and his description of how God loves sinners.

---

[115] *Heidelberg Disputation*, LW 31:57.
[116] Ibid.
[117] *ST* 1.20.2.

Basically, Luther's claims against Thomas's philosophy suggests that since God loves the Good, he cannot love sinners who lack goodness. Thus, Thomas's view has no room for the love of wicked persons. This appears to be a logical entailment of Luther's position since he states that the love of man (which, for Thomas, contains similar overtones in God because he loves the Good) avoids sinners.[118] Yet, Thomas asserts God certainly loves sinners. A sinner possesses an existing nature, which metaphysically speaking, is good. Because God loves everything good, he loves a sinner insofar as he has an existing nature.[119] Thus, it possible for God to both despise a sinner inasmuch as he sins and love him inasmuch as he has an existing nature.

In addition, Thomas's position does not necessitate that lowly, needy, stupid, foolish, and weak people lack goodness that disqualifies them from God's love, even though Luther suggests this. Sure, lowly and needy people lack things typically associated with greatness or goodness, such as wealth, power, or influence. Yet, this does not mean they lack goodness. In Thomas's system, a poor person may have the same goodness as a rich person, for the goodness of a *being* is in proportion to its orientation to the Good. For example, as a poor man increases in godliness, he increases in likeness to God. The more a thing is like to God, the more God loves it.[120]

Thus, a poor man and a rich man may possess similar likeness to God as they orient toward their proper end. Also, a *being's* goodness depends not on itself, but on God who wills it good. Therefore, Thomas makes room for the love of God to include the poor as well as rich. Although certain physical and mental deficiencies and degrees of sinfulness all play a factor in keeping some persons from the same perfection as others, this does not keep the love of God away from such people. No matter how sinful they act, or how great their deficiencies appear, God loves them insofar as they possess existing natures.

Third, Luther fails to understand the importance of attributing the basic notion of love to God as well. Thomas claims that not only does human love orient to the Good, but the love of God

---

[118] *Heidelberg Disputation*, LW 31:57.
[119] *ST* 1.20.2.
[120] Ibid., 1.20.4.

does so as well. Given Luther's claims, he appears to assert that God does not truly love goodness if it is always directed downwards toward evil.[121] If God's love, at a basic level, does not include a love for himself, then he cannot be considered the Good at all. Since love equals will and will always moves first to the Good, then God first and foremost loves himself because his essence is goodness.[122] Luther may not know that his position leads to a denial of God's goodness once logically drawn out. Yet, this is certainly what his position entails.

Positive Aspects of Luther's Theology

Luther's position, in a strict philosophical sense, appears to avoid rational consistency. His philosophy contains untraditional metaphysical contentions. However, this is exactly what Luther wants. He does not speak in strict, philosophical categories. Again, his points are pastoral. Now, this does not mean Luther should be exempt from proposing philosophical truths, but it should urge readers of Luther to esteem his practical and personal concerns regarding God's love.

Thus, it is admirable for Luther to provide a theology which tries to make sense of Paul's words in 1 Corinthians 1:27-28, which says, "God chose...even things that are not, to bring to nothing things that are." Even though it contains serious metaphysical problems, there is great value in Luther's position from the human and biblical perspective. According to human understanding, it appears Christ hides in the shadows of the cross as Luther says. Thomas's adoption of Greek philosophy causes some issues metaphysically, for it seems foolish for God, who is full of goodness and perfection, to take on flesh, which is full of weakness and deficiency. Thus, Luther's emphasis on God saving wicked sinners by becoming like them and lack of concern for himself holds merit.

Luther's contention about God's hiddenness in the cross finds a place in the gospels. In the gospel narratives, the Israelites did not recognize Jesus Christ to be divine as he hung on the cross. In fact, the Son of God looked weaker than anyone present. Yet,

---

[121] *Heidelberg Disputation*, LW 31:57.
[122] *ST* 1.6.2.

in the midst of Christ's weakness and humility lies his divinity. Luther's theological analysis seems to grasp this reality.

Luther's anthropology greatly affects how he perceives the cross of Christ. His claim that God loves "what is not" assumes that sinful human beings lack any goodness in their *being*. Luther would agree with Thomas that sinners lack existence. But he goes farther than Thomas. His position also insinuates that a sinner's existing nature is evil or lost, for a sinner must lack existence and possess an evil nature if he truly considers a sinner to be nothing. Therefore, Luther concludes that God must love nothingness or evil since he came to die for it.

Both Thomas and Luther are correct with respect to anthropology to an extent. Metaphysically, sinners lack existence, as Thomas says, because sin is a privation of *being* or existence. The more a man sins, the less goodness he possesses. Yet, Thomas maintains that a sinner still possesses an existing nature that remains good.

Thomas fails to recognize, however, what Luther emphasizes: The Scriptures speak of man having a sinful nature, not a good one. Ephesians 2:3 mentions that man is, by nature, a child of wrath. Yet, Luther perhaps overemphasizes the lostness of man's nature, because it still exists. Fundamentally, man's nature is marred, lacking perfection and containing sinfulness, but not totally lost. Therefore, since man's nature is marred, he does not always exhibit the nature of what God intended to create.

Thinking in terms of the great chain of *being*, a human being who acts in accordance with his nature given by God, rests above inanimate objects, vegetation, and animals. Conversely, when a man sins, he acts more like an animal than a true human being, for he does not attain to his proper end. Elementally, a sinful human being does not always act how a human ought to act. At the same time, though, whether he acts like a human or an animal, his nature still exists.

Thus, sinful human beings both lack existence and possess a marred, sinful human nature that keeps humanity from attaining to their proper end. From the human eye, humanity does not appear to be human as the world is full of evil and wickedness. It appears Christ dies for sinners who sink down metaphysically lower than animals or to nothingness. Yet, from the metaphysical perspective, God loves a sinner, who has an existing, marred nature.

Looking *At* and Looking *Along*

A helpful way to think about this dichotomy comes from C.S. Lewis and his distinction of looking *at* and looking *along*. Lewis notes there is a distinction between looking at something from the outside and having experiential knowledge of it. He uses an example of a young boy who falls in love. A boy who falls in love with a girl looks *along* the situation as he greatly values time with her. But a scientist can look *at* the situation by examining the chemical reactions that takes place in the young boy's brain.[123]

In this manner, Thomas and Luther's positions can be combined to form what appears to be a paradox with regard to philosophy and Biblcal revelation. By looking *at* the situation from a metaphysical perspective — fundamentally, as a theologian of glory who investigates the transcendence and glory of God according to Luther — Thomas's views of the simple nature of God's love (namely, will toward an object's end) can be accepted with the caveat of modifying his anthropology with respect to sinners' existing nature. It is not wrong to use reason, which is a gift by God, to inquire of God's nature as far as reason and logic permit. God's essence is logic and reason (along with his other attributes). Thus, as creatures created in his image, it is appropriate to use both to theologize about God.

At the same time, looking *along* the situation allows for an incorporation of Luther's concepts. By also noting the deficiencies of human reason, Luther's emphasis on the God revealed on the cross and in Scripture remains just as important. From the human perspective, nothing is attractive about sinners. So, God's descent into the world is truly a remarkable picture of love.

Paul's complex and mysterious statements about God's salvation in 1 Corinthians does not exclude either Thomas

---

[123] C. S. Lewis, "Meditations in a Toolshed," in *God in the Dock*, ed. Walter Hooper (Grand Rapids, MI: Eerdmans, 1970), 212.

or Luther's emphases. Paul makes a pastoral point to the Corinthians to not boast in their excellence. Thus, Paul observes that God often works contrary to human understanding. Metaphysically speaking, Paul does not shun what Thomas later articulates. Rather, Paul moves beyond philosophical categories to demonstrate the abounding love of God.

The Differentiated Love of God

Luther and Thomas disagree regarding whether God loves all things equally. Luther holds that God loves "what is not" equally in his death on the cross.[124] Thomas, however, asserts that God loves the better things.[125] Again, Thomas edges Luther logically and Scripturally on this matter. For Thomas, God's will accounts for why an object exists in the first place. Now, since an object exists, God loves it. Yet, in Thomas's view, God may will a greater good to one object than another. Because he wills one object a greater good than another, he loves more that which has the greater good. God does not love an object based off its *own* goodness apart from himself. He loves one object more than another solely because of his will.

Luther, on the other hand, holds that God gives all creatures equity. Since God's love aims towards "what is not" and all people are sinners (i.e. "what is not"), then God equally loves all creatures because he gives himself on the cross to all. However, Luther would not hold that everyone receives the love of God and unites with him in love because faith is required. And not all people exhibit faith; some reject it. Thus, for those who do accept faith, they receive a greater good from God: namely, unification with him.

Given the West's progressive philosophy of equal opportunity and equal outcome, it seems insensitive and mad to attribute to God a love which does not spread equally among creation. Yet, this philosophical point finds Scriptural warrant. D. A. Carson mentions that Scripture demonstrates several different ways God loves which includes some that correspond to Thomas's

---

[124] Mannermaa, *Two Kinds of Love*, 3.
[125] ST 1.20.4.

reasoning.[126] First, God has a special love for his Son. This point is captured not only by Carson,[127] but also Augustine and Thomas. John 17:23b which states, "loved them even as you loved me," evidences a special love for the Son because, following Augustine's exposition, God loves the body of Christ on the basis of his love for the Son.[128]

Thomas also asserts Christ is loved more than all because God has willed him the greatest good of giving him the name above every name.[129] Thus, Thomas roots God's love for Christ in giving him the greatest good among all creation. His view rests on the biblical notion of Christ's ascension into heaven.

Second, Carson points out that God has a providential love for all creation. In Genesis 1, God creates everything as "good." Thus, since God is a loving God, his creative and preservative acts demonstrate love for creation.[130] Carson puts an argument forth from Genesis 1 that Thomas makes philosophically. Yet, this love for all things is not as great as God's love for the Son.

Third, God shows a general, salvific love for sinful humanity but also a special, selective love for the elect. John 3:16 and 1 John 2:2 exhibit God's love for sinful humanity in general. God calls all men to repentance and does not exclude them on the basis of race, power, or prestige.[131] The call of the cross remains open to *whosoever* believes in Christ.

In addition, the Bible speaks of a selective love for God's elect. Now, it does not matter whether God's elect refers to individuals or the church collectively because in either case God shows a peculiar love for his chosen people. In Deut. 7:6-8, Moses recounts God's election of Israel, stating that Israel was not chosen because of its strength. God chose Israel because he simply loves it. In verse 6, the text says, "The Lord your God has chosen you to be a people for his treasured possession, out

---

[126] D. A. Carson, *The Difficult Doctrine of the Love of God* (Wheaton, IL: Crossway, 2000), 16–21.
[127] Ibid., 16.
[128] Augustine, "Tractate on John 110," 6.
[129] *ST* 1.20.4.
[130] Carson, *The Difficult Doctrine*, 16–17.
[131] Ibid., 17.

of all the peoples who are on the face of the earth." Notice, God chose Israel and *not* other nations.[132] God acts lovingly to the people of God in a way that he does not for others.

Augustine also draws this concept from John 17:23b as well. In his exposition, as he says that God loves all people simply because he created them, he also states that God loves the members of Christ's body more. Since God loves his Only-begotten Son more than all creation, he must also love the members of his Son more than the universe.[133] Thus, the magnitude with which God loves his elect, follows from the greatness of God's love for the Son.

Therefore, the idea of God distributing his love unequally holds philosophically and scripturally. Luther's efforts, though noble, fail to incorporate the overwhelming amount of biblical passages detailing God's special love for the elect. Also, being a member of the body of Christ suggests that a greater likeness to Christ exists than with a non-believer. Since God loves that which is more like to him, then it follows God loves members of Christ more. This satisfies the Thomistic method of attributing differentiated love in God.

The Highest Form of Love

Lastly, another important concept between Luther and Thomas regards what the highest form of love in God looks like. For Thomas, the highest form of love constitutes friendship. Mutual well-wishing between lover and beloved through some type of communication characterizes the love of God for his elect. God wishes his elect good, followed by an act of goodness from the elect to God. This well-wishing takes place through the communication of God's happiness to the elect.[134]

Luther, on the other hand, considers God's love to be a selfless giving of himself on the cross to sinners, which creates a new form of goodness in them.[135] This type of love rests in the will of God but consists of more than mere willing good to another. For Luther, God has nothing to gain through the

---

[132] Ibid., 18.
[133] Augustine, "Tractate on John 110," 6.
[134] *ST* 2-2.23.1.
[135] Mannermaa, *Two Kinds of Love*, 2; see also *The Heidelberg Disputation*, LW 31:57.

cross. He freely gives goodness to sinners who receive his love and unite to him by faith.

Concerning what constitutes the highest form of God's love, Luther maintains a more consistent biblical picture of God's love. As a matter of the basic definition of love, Thomas's concept of self-love accurately depicts reality, even when found in God. But self-love fails to demonstrate the highest manifestation of God's love for humanity.

Thomas's idea of friendship as the highest form of love between God and man attempts to move past self-love and depict a more selfless love of God. Yet, his definition of friendship prevents him from fully attributing a selfless love to God. For Thomas's second principle of friendship, namely, mutual benevolence, necessitates that the beloved gives good back to the lover. Thus, a lover never truly loves selflessly because friendship always concerns itself with receiving love back from the beloved. Philosophically, it fails to provide a framework for a lover to love an object for its own sake and expect nothing in return.

The Bible does not speak about friendship-love as the highest form either. Lewis points out that the Bible rarely speaks of friendship as the nature of God's loving relationship with people.[136] Instead, the Bible speaks of God's love in Luther's terms, by the death of Christ on the cross for sinners. 1 John 3:16 says, "By this we know love, that he laid down his life for us." 1 John 4:9 follows suit as well, "In this the love of God was made manifest among us, that God sent his only Son into the world, so that we might live through him." Romans 5:8 also speaks of God demonstrating his love by the death of Christ.

Thus, the New Testament is explicit about what reveals the love of God most clearly: that is, the cross. In the cross, God gives himself to those who would believe for no cost. Although man can certainly sacrifice his mind and body for the Lord, thus signaling a good willed to God, God owns everything, including the minds and bodies of human beings. So, even if man decides to sacrifice these things for the Lord, he is not giving God something he does not already own.

God truly gains nothing in return for sending Christ to

---

[136] C. S. Lewis, *The Four Loves* (New York: HarperCollins, 1960), 100.

die for sinners. It is a totally self-less act on God's end. This corresponds to what Lewis would call "Divine Gift-love." Divine Gift-love simply loves for the beloved's sake in a disinterested manner.[137] Through death, God and man unite by faith, which creates a new form. What once was a marred nature that sunk to the level of an animal is now a new nature in Christ attaining to the end designed by God.

CONCLUDING THOUGHTS ON THOMAS AND LUTHER

Both Thomas and Luther have interesting positions regarding God's love for humanity. Thomas's position posits an essential element to God's love: namely, will. Without Thomas defining love as will, his metaphysical system fails and leads to great problems regarding immutability and impassibility. However, Thomas avoids this and puts forward a metaphysic which modern-day theologians and metaphysicians ought to reconsider. In fact, much of the mess in theological and philosophical circles exists because of a deviation from classical theism.

His basic notion of love wonderfully captures a crucial biblical element: that human beings are made for an end, and their *telos* lies in God. As members of Christ, the orientation toward godliness constitutes a love for God. In addition, it serves to describe the perfect love of the Trinity which is a love for itself. The Trinity's own delight allows God to love long before anything was created. God has forever loved himself and does not need anything outside of itself to love.

Luther's theology *seems* to deviate from reason, philosophically speaking. However, it has several biblical positives. Luther concerns himself with displaying the love of God in the clearest way: through the cross. He finds the greatest manifestation of God's love in Christ becoming man in order to save humanity through his death. 1 John speaks of God revealing his love in

---

[137] Ibid., 164.

this way numerous times; other biblical passages use this language as well.

However, Luther exhibits metaphysical problems in his theology on account of his departure from classical theism. Most importantly, he fundamentally misunderstands Thomas in various places. Had Luther read Thomas correctly, perhaps he would have agreed on more metaphysical points. His flaws do not outweigh the positives from this thinking, however. Luther must be interpreted on his own terms in a pastoral manner.

A combination of both theologies helps capture the different facets of God's love. By looking *along* the love of God, that is, from the human and experiential perspective, God appears to do the unthinkable: he becomes man to save sinners. The depth of this love, in its highest form, is beyond human reason to contemplate. Thomas's notion of friendship-love does not lead to the full character of God revealed in Scripture. It merely describes the philosophical nature of God and leaves the idea of God's love as a distant, less personal love. Thus, God's descent to love "what is not" is true from the human perspective; for God comes to love the unlovable. He gives himself to "nothing."

Also, by looking at the love of God from a metaphysical standpoint, logic and reason can be used to probe into the transcendent God as much as humanly possible. Thomas's metaphysics works perfectly for this endeavor. The theoretical aspect of theology is no less important than the practical. For both aid in accurately contemplating God's love. However, if the theoretical is emphasized more at the expense of the practical, then the force of God's good news of sinners' salvation is diminished. On the flip side, if the practical is overemphasized, then metaphysical problems arise. Neither theologian is the unsung hero of championing an accurate view of divine love. A balance must be struck between the two in order to truthfully proclaim the love of God.

SCHOOL OF THEOLOGY & MISSIONS FACULTY

Ray Van Neste, Ph.D., University of Aberdeen, Dean, School of Theology & Missions, Professor of Biblical Studies

Jacob W. Shatzer, Ph.D., Marquette University, Associate Dean, School of Theology & Missions, Associate Professor of Theological Studies

Frank Anderson, Ph.D., Mid-America Baptist Theological Seminary, Stephen Olford Chair of Expository Preaching & Associate Professor of Ministry and Missions, Director, Center for Racial Reconciliation

Hayward Armstrong, Ph.D., New Orleans Baptist Theological Seminary, Professor of Missions and Director for MCS
Randall Bush, D.Phil., University of Oxford, University Professor of Philosophy

Todd Brady, D. Min., Southern Baptist Theological Seminary, Assistant Professor of Ministry, Vice President for University Ministries

Randall Bush, D.Phil., University of Oxford, University Professor of Philosophy

Mark Dubis, Ph.D., Union Theological Seminary, Professor of Biblical Studies

Brad Green, Ph.D., Baylor University, Professor of Theological Studies

Paul Jackson, Ph.D., Southwestern Baptist Theological Seminary, Professor of Biblical Studies

C. Ben Mitchell, Ph.D., University of Tennessee, Graves Professor of Moral Philosophy and Special Assistant to the President

Kelvin Moore, Ph.D., New Orleans Baptist Theological Seminary, University Professor of Biblical Studies

Harry Lee Poe, Ph.D., Southern Baptist Theological Seminary, Charles Colson University Professor of Faith & Culture

www.ingramcontent.com/pod-product-compliance
Lightning Source LLC
Chambersburg PA
CBHW030851170426
43193CB00009BA/568